PLURALISM IN THE SOVIET UNION

Pluralism in the Soviet Union offers an illuminating and original discussion of a popular but controversial approach to the study of the Soviet Union. There is much debate in this volume. Each of the contributors takes a distinctive stand on the usefulness of the concept "pluralism," broadly defined, for the understanding of Soviet politics and society.

The book begins with a study by Susan Gross Solomon of the history of the concept of "pluralism" in Western political science. She finds that there has been no prototypical usage of the term within the discipline and suggests that Sovietologists need not be concerned, therefore, about whether the use of "pluralism" in their field extends the concept beyond its accepted meaning in American studies. Jerry F. Hough laments the fetish of Sovietologists with model-building, which in his view deflects attention from the critical task of empirical research. But if there must be models, "pluralism" still has some advantages over its now-fashionable competitor "corporatism." Archie Brown adds a new dimension to the discussion by contrasting Western and Soviet usages of the concept "pluralism." He shows that while Western scholars pay attention to the influence on government of societal groups, some of their Soviet counterparts focus on the relative autonomy of the state from society. Włodzimierz Brus examines the implications for Soviet politics of the growing marketization of the economy in the USSR. Unlike proponents of convergence Brus does not expect that political pluralism will evolve directly from the new economic relations. In the concluding chapter Frederick C. Barghoorn performs a test for the litmus of pluralism in any society by examining the Soviet regime's treatment of dissent. He provides fascinating new evidence about the ways in which the regime's relationship with the dissidents constrains not just the dissidents but the regime itself.

This volume of essays is a tribute to H. Gordon Skilling – distinguished pioneer in the field of Soviet and East European studies. The contributors are drawn from three countries, and appropriately so. For Skilling was born in Canada, did his graduate work in England, taught in the United States, and then returned to his native Canada, there to found and direct for its first decade the well-known Centre for Russian and East European Studies at the University of Toronto.

Gordon Skilling   Photograph by Rudolf L. Tőkés

Pluralism in the Soviet Union

Essays in Honour of H. Gordon Skilling

Edited by
Susan Gross Solomon

St. Martin's Press   New York

Library of Congress Cataloging in Publication Data

Main entry under title:

Pluralism in the Soviet Union.

"Major publications of H. Gordon Skilling": p.
Includes index.
Contents: "Pluralism" in political science / Susan
Gross Solomon — Pluralism, corporatism, and the Soviet
Union / Jerry F. Hough — Pluralism, power, and the
Soviet political system / Archie Brown — [etc.]
1. Pluralism (Social sciences)—Soviet Union—
Addresses, essays, lectures. 2. Soviet Union—
Politics and government—1953-   —Addresses, essays,
lectures. 3. Corporate state—Soviet Union—Addresses,
essays, lectures. 4. Dissenters—Soviet Union—
Addresses, essays, lectures. 5. Skilling, H. Gordon
(Harold Gordon), 1912-   . I. Solomon, Susan Gross.
II. Skilling, H. Gordon (Harold Gordon), 1912-
JN6581.P58   1983   320.947   82-24117
ISBN 0-312-61769-0

Contents

Notes on the Contributors

John N. Hazard is Nash Professor of Law Emeritus at Columbia University, New York.

Susan Gross Solomon is Associate Professor of Political Science, at the University of Toronto.

Jerry F. Hough is Professor of Political Science at Duke University, North Carolina.

Archie Brown is a Fellow of St Antony's College, Oxford, and Lecturer in Soviet Institutions at the University of Oxford.

Wlodzimierz Brus is a Fellow of Wolfson College, Oxford, and Lecturer in Modern Russian and East European Studies at the University of Oxford.

Frederick C. Barghoorn is Professor Emeritus of Political Science at Yale University.

Acknowledgements

In the course of preparing this Festschrift, I have benefited immeasurably from the support of individuals and institutions. First and foremost, Professor Gleb Zekulin, Director of the Centre for Russian and East European Studies of the University of Toronto, was a constant source of encouragement from the inception of this project to its completion. My colleagues Timothy J. Colton, Richard B. Day, Franklyn J. Griffiths, Donald V. Schwartz and Peter H. Solomon, Jr, offered sage counsel on a wide range of matters. Archie Brown of Oxford University took more than a contributor's interest in this venture. I have no doubt that these individuals gave of their time the more graciously because the volume was in honour of H. Gordon Skilling. The same was surely true of the contributors. Each and every one responded with warmth to the invitation to be part of the volume and endured with unfailing good humour the queries and red pencillings of the editor.

Generous financial assistance for this volume was provided by the Centre for Russian and East European Studies and the Office of Research Administration, both of the University of Toronto.

Edith S. Klein was an invaluable assistant. She did research, editing and correspondence with a rare intelligence. On numerous occasions, she served as sounding board. Only she knows how much I depended on her.

Gloria Rowe typed the final manuscript with speed and accuracy. The assistance of Jana Oldfield of the Centre for Russian and East European Studies was also much appreciated.

Finally, a special word of thanks to my children, Rafi and Rachel, who took pleasure in the involvement of their mother in this project.

S.G.S.
Toronto, May 1982

Foreword

Few scholars seeking understanding of Soviet and Eastern European politics have sampled as many countries or inquired as deeply into the social structures of polities as H. Gordon Skilling. Born a Canadian and educated at the University of Toronto in the early 1930s and immediately afterwards, in England, first as a Rhodes Scholar at Christ Church, Oxford, and then at the University of London, he seems to have absorbed something of the famed English sense of scholarly balance in probing to the bottom of things without passion. It has never been his practice to crusade in the popular mode of the day, nor has he permitted his work to be swayed by the winds of the time.

Skilling has demonstrated the courage necessary to strike out in new directions, to explore the possibility that popular North American analyses of communist-oriented systems have been misdirected, and to develop something novel as an approach. In no area has this inquisitive bent been so marked as in his call to a re-evaluation of the wellsprings of Soviet politics and the impact of these politics upon the USSR's neighbours. This volume is testimony to his adventure. It has been devised by its distinguished editor to honour Skilling's innovative approach. Friends and colleagues from the international scholarly community have presented essays which reflect the influence of his innovative explorations begun at the outset of the 1960s.

Skilling's presence has been characterized by modesty. He carries his torch high, but without fanfare, presenting in his lectures often quite novel ideas with a quietness of voice and understatement that seem to conceal from his listeners the full impact of his ideas until they appear in print. Some scholars of prominence have been stimulated to combat his ideas with vigour, marshalling what they conceive to be the relevant facts differently from Skilling. Such a conflict of views was most evident after Skilling attacked the thesis so popular in the 1950s that the Soviet system of government could be best analysed as totalitarian, guided by one man with a few comrades-in-arms oblivious to popular pressures.

In an innovative study, Skilling suggested that the 'group theory' could be used to examine Soviet politics, even though that theory was not totally compatible with the monopoly party system in the USSR. For the post-Stalin phase of Soviet history, Skilling found public manifestations of the influence of special interests in policy formulation and interpreted these as clear proof of the correctness of his approach. And he raised the possibility that even Stalin had been unable to rule a polity in disregard of the interests of all save himself and his immediate coterie. Even as he put forward his novel view, Skilling made clear his reservations in using group theory. He declared unequivocally, 'To avoid misunderstanding, it should be stated at once that this is not an attempt arbitrarily to apply to the Soviet system interest group theories which have been developed in the West in the past sixty years.' And a few pages later in his introduction to *Interest Groups in Soviet Politics* he added, 'The application of the group concept to political behaviour in the USSR, it should be stressed, does not necessarily involve an interpretation solely in terms of interest groups and group conflict.'

Not all scholars agreed with even this careful formulation. Skilling's willingness to listen to the arguments of his critics rather than to enter into polemics with them is characteristic of his nature. Thus he was content to work on his innovative study of Soviet interest groups with a colleague who questioned his position, proposing another term to explain Skilling's findings.

Skilling did not approach the study of the USSR from the West, vaulting over Central Europe as so many other scholars have done. He came to the study of Soviet politics across the bridge of Central Europe. His articles in the early 1950s concerned Czechoslovakia. Undoubtedly his interest was fired by his study in England with the legendary R. W. Seton-Watson, from whom he learned to admire the Czechs and Slovaks for their struggle against the forces of the Habsburg Empire, and for their continuing struggle to survive as an independent entity in Central Europe between the two great wars. If Skilling were asked today to identify his great love, I suspect the answer would still be Czechoslovakia. His many scholarly works, and most especially his *magnum opus, Czechoslovakia's Interrupted Revolution*, testify to that.

Skilling's concern with the Soviet political model seems to have been stimulated by his concern with the reception of it by the communists of Central Europe when Soviet pressures opened the way for them to establish power in their homelands. Because of this concern, Skilling made himself one of the pioneer specialists in comparative communism. In his treatment of the variations on the Soviet model emerging in Central Europe, Skilling was always sensitive to the different political cultures which characterized those nations. For example, he sought to identify the efforts of the Czechs and Slovaks during the 'spring' in 1967–8 with their distinctive past. That provided a basis for their desire to 'humanize' communism, to restore what they believed to be its promise of a 'human face'. He saw the Czech and Slovak communists as no traitors to the cause to which they had devoted their lives, in spite of Soviet charges that they were trying to restore the hated capitalist system. He saw them as honest men and women, wedded to the dreams of their youth and intent upon purging the Soviet model of excrescences accumulated in the USSR during the Stalin period. Discontented with the bureaucratism, the centralization and the resulting dehumanization of what had become the Stalinist model, they seemed to Skilling to have sought a variant suited to their culture. Their concern was to re-establish the balance between community and individual which they thought the essence of humanist Marxism. Their method was to introduce a measure of decentralization of decision-making to bring the governing process closer to the factories, offices and farms.

With his understanding of the goals of the 'Prague Spring', Skilling saw the intervention of the Soviet politicians into the Czechoslovak communist party's decision-making process in 1968 as a tragedy, reinforced by what amounted to an occupation, albeit masked by some Czech and Slovak communists. Skilling's *magnum opus* paints the picture of the Dubček period in the restrained, non-polemical style of the unimpassioned scholar. It is both a history and a political analysis beginning with the First Czechoslovak Republic and taking the reader through the events of 1968.

Skilling asks his readers at the end to consider whether Dubček's period may not stand in history with the Paris Commune of 1871, as an inspiration for those in search of new ways to solve the problems of mankind. He expresses the confidence 'that

Czechs and Slovaks will again, as in the past, seek a new solution
for the ever present problems of survival and progress'.

Skilling's associations in North America have not been limited
to Canada and the distinguished Centre for Russian and East
European Studies at the University of Toronto which he founded
in 1963 and continued to direct until 1975. He has had much to
do with scholarship and the nurturing of scholars in the United
States. For eighteen years he taught in the United States, first at
the University of Wisconsin, then at Dartmouth College, and for
one year as a Visiting Professor at the Russian Institute of
Columbia University in New York. This latter experience, which
followed an earlier year as a Senior Fellow of the Institute, may
have influenced him in the choice of a model for the Centre
which he created in the University of Toronto.

When the founding of that Centre was being discussed, he
suggested to the President of the University of Toronto that
faculty members from both Columbia and Harvard Universities
be invited to consult on appropriate models for such an area
study centre. The result is unique, for Skilling was no more ready
to accept a model made elsewhere for an area centre than he was
to accept the Soviet model for Czechoslovakia. He knew that
different cultures require different institutions and his Centre was
suited to Canada. It is also without doubt one of the most noted
area institutes in the Western world. And it is his monument.

Most recently Skilling has thrown the weight of his authority
behind the international protection of human rights. His
experience with Central European Marxists and political reformists seems to have given him a sense of mission, although
always expressed in the calm and understated phrases that have
become his trademark. The vehicle for his concern with human
rights has been the review conference to assess the practice of
states in implementing the Act of Helsinki.

Not finding the doors of the review conference in Madrid in
1980–1 open to scholars, he sought for himself the status of a
news correspondent. In his early days he had reported both for
the British and Canadian Broadcasting Services, and this experience opened the way for accreditation as a correspondent of
one of the great Canadian dailies. His reports from Madrid and to
colleagues on his return showed him to be the balanced searcher
after facts that he had always been. With his deep understanding
of politics and his keen perception of motives he missed no

element of Eastern or Western politicking to achieve respective goals. He saw and appreciated also the absurdities that inevitably accompany the bureaucratic process of contemporary conferences. To Skilling with his sophisticated understanding of international manoeuvring by governments the reports by diplomats at a conference must be related to the tides of history as it unfolds under the pressures from various quarters and in accordance with varying and opposing concepts of power and acceptable limitations upon that power. It is tempting to suppose that Skilling's thinking on political processes as an interplay of interests within the communist-dominated world has aided him in reporting on the interplay of interests within the international community as well.

In this volume of essays internationally known scholars hail their friend and colleague in a form that is commensurate with his academic achievements and interests. As one who has known and worked with Gordon Skilling for more than thirty years, I consider it my good fortune to have been invited by the editor to share in this tribute of respect and affection.

JOHN N. HAZARD

1 Introduction

SUSAN GROSS SOLOMON

To present a Festschrift to a scholar with as wide-ranging interests as H. Gordon Skilling is no simple matter. Professor Skilling's writings and speeches over the past thirty-five years cover an amazing gamut of subjects: the distribution of power in the USSR, the governmental structure of East European nations, the Czech 'Spring' of 1968, opposition and dissent in contemporary Czechoslovakia, human rights in Eastern Europe. To produce a volume of essays which would enshrine Skilling's idea of scholarship is no easier a task. As his long-time friend and colleague John Hazard puts it so eloquently in the Foreword to this volume, Skilling is a man with passionate intellectual commitments who listens to, indeed seeks out, contrary opinions. He does not do so in order to engage in polemics, but because his own understanding is always fired by a soundly argued view which is opposed to his own.

If one stands back from Skilling's work, certain patterns emerge very strongly. His major writing, it seems to me, has been animated by the concept of 'pluralism' – not in the narrow sense in which the concept has appeared in American political science (how vigorously Gordon Skilling has resisted any suggestion to this effect!) – but in the broader sense used by the philosophers William James, John Dewey and G.E. Moore in the late nineteenth and early twentieth century to convey their belief that the world was not monistic, but was shot through with diversity, flux and contest. It was Skilling's acknowledgement of the pervasiveness of diversity and contest in all polities that led him to question what most other Western experts on the Soviet Union were taking for granted – namely that the Soviet political system was a monism. It is Skilling's appreciation of the positive value of diversity and challenge which has marked his approach to

1

intellectual life. Not for him, then, a Festschrift in which contributors tested the utility of a concept he had introduced or replicated a case study he had conducted. For Gordon Skilling, it seemed appropriate to produce a volume of essays each of which would take a controversial point of view, a position against the prevailing intellectual fashion.

In the opening essay, the editor takes a fresh look at the controversy over the application of 'pluralism' to the analysis of Soviet politics. Examining the history of 'pluralism' in the discipline of political science, she finds that there is no 'classic' usage of the term, that the concept has appeared differently in each field within the discipline. It therefore makes no sense to argue over whether the introduction of 'pluralism' into Soviet studies has stretched the concept beyond its breaking point. The concept *is* being used and one can only ask whether the usage has been satisfactory: has the application of 'pluralism' met the expectations of those Sovietologists who propounded it? Has the application led to new ways of seeing the political world?

In 'Pluralism, Corporatism and the Soviet Union', Jerry Hough compares the relative merits for the analysis of Soviet politics of the 'corporatist' model which is gaining some currency among Sovietologists today and the 'institutional pluralist' model which he himself introduced into Soviet studies a decade ago. Having made the comparison, Hough transcends the two models to formulate the hard question to which both point: what is the relationship between inputs and outputs in a political system and how is this relation affected by institutional arrangements? But Hough's major interest here is not models; indeed, against the prevailing fashion, he decries the emphasis on labels and classifications and calls for empirical research to answer the questions.

In his chapter, 'Pluralism, Power and the Soviet Political System: A Comparative Perspective', Archie Brown sets Western and Soviet analyses of political power side by side. The juxtaposition brings to light some intriguing a-synchronisms. Unlike Western theorists of 'pluralism' who begin with the assumption of the autonomy of society from government, Western specialists on the Soviet Union pay little attention to the issue of autonomy; instead, they emphasize the variety of influences on the government of outside bodies or the existence of a variety of points of view within government. Soviet scholars writing on the state *do* discuss autonomy, but it is the relative autonomy of the state from society which occupies their attention. Brown's close analysis of Soviet discussions of the state provides compelling evidence of the degree of diversity within the scholarly community in the USSR and thus his work cautions against blanket assumptions of intellectual control, even on a subject as central as the Soviet state.

In his contribution, 'Political Pluralism and Markets in Communist Systems', Włodzimierz Brus addresses a critical question which has had a long history in the study of Soviet politics and East–West relations: will the marketization of economic relations in the USSR lead to political pluralism there? In the face of much conventional wisdom on the subject, Brus submits that developments in the economic sphere will not in and of themselves affect the political sphere. His conclusions suggest that political pluralism is a vulnerable plant which, if it is to exist, must be nurtured for its own sake.

In the final essay, Frederick C. Barghoorn examines the relationship between dissenters and the regime in the USSR. In contrast to much contemporary literature on dissent, Barghoorn focuses on the way in which this relationship constrains not only the dissidents, but the regime. He brings evidence of a nascent understanding between the democratic movement and one of the key social groups – the workers. Should this understanding continue to grow, the regime might find it harder than before to maintain the firm 'in-group'/'out-group' distinction which has lain at the base of its treatment of dissent thus far. Yet Barghoorn is far from optimistic about the fate of dissent in the Soviet Union and issues a clarion call for its nurturing and support in the West.

2 'Pluralism' in Political Science: The Odyssey of a Concept

SUSAN GROSS SOLOMON

I. INTRODUCTION

For over a decade now, the field of Soviet studies has been riven
by a debate over the appropriateness of applying the term
'pluralism' to the study of Soviet politics. At one time or another,
most of the leading scholars in the field have been drawn into the
discussion and yet the debate is no closer to being resolved today
than it was when it first erupted. What, if anything, can be
usefully added at this point? To rehearse the issues in the dispute
would be superfluous for, reminiscent of the life-histories of other
controversies in the social sciences, there have of late appeared
review articles which summarize the positions of the leading
participants in the dispute.[1] To bring empirical evidence in
support of one or the other position in the debate seems similarly
fruitless, for there are no agreed-upon criteria of pluralism. To
add yet another definition of pluralism to a scientific disagreement
already bedevilled by lack of terminological clarity would surely
be to confuse rather than to edify. Therefore instead of entering
the lists, I propose to stand back and analyse the controversy over
pluralism as a manifestation both of the thorny problem of
concept formation in Soviet studies and of the strengths and
weaknesses of pluralism as a conceptual tool in political analysis.

The debate over pluralism in Soviet studies is remarkable,
among other things, for the lack of consensus on every point.
Those who study Soviet politics cannot agree on the evidence of

4

their eyes: are there groups (opinion groups, skill groups, occupational groups) which genuinely reflect interests in the USSR? Scholars also diverge over how to interpret what they observe: do the identifiable groups play a meaningful role in the Soviet political process? And finally, Sovietologists disagree over what conceptual name to give to what they interpret: does the nature and activity of Soviet groups justify the label 'pluralist'?

Underlying the overt (and heated) disagreements are two assumptions shared by almost all the participants in the debate. First, there is the assumption that the *locus classicus* of the concept of pluralism was the field of American studies in the 1950s. The pervasiveness of this assumption may be judged from the fact that in measuring and evaluating Soviet reality both opponents and proponents of the use of pluralism in Soviet studies took as their yardstick the concept of pluralism current in the study of American politics.[2] To be fair, in their choice of baseline the Sovietologists showed themselves most orthodox: the notion that the American usage of pluralism was in some sense classic dominated the profession of political science as a whole. And second, Sovietologists have assumed that the basic enterprise of comparative politics is the application of an old or known concept to a new instance such that the range of instances covered by the concept is broadened but the concept itself is not altered. That students of Soviet politics viewed the comparative analysis of political systems in this way is clear from the fact that the debate over the applicability of pluralism in Soviet studies invariably turned on the question of whether the new instance (Soviet politics) was stretching the concept of pluralism beyond its breaking point.[3]

I want to argue that both these assumptions are without basis and that their refutation would have salutary effects on the field of Soviet studies. With respect to the first assumption, conventional wisdom notwithstanding, the concept of pluralism has a long lineage in political science. The concept can be traced back to 1915 when it exercised considerable authority in the field of political theory in Britain. Its next major appearance was in America at mid-century where it informed the study of American politics. In the mid-1960s, as it began to decline in influence in American studies, 'pluralism' surfaced in the field of Soviet studies. Of necessity, the retrieval of this lineage puts the use of pluralism in Soviet studies in a new perspective. Pluralism in Soviet studies becomes not the first deviation from the classical usage, but the latest in a series of applications of the same term. Now the questions become: what commonalities are carried forward from usage to usage? What are the significant variations from application to application? Further, once we discard the notion that the American usage of pluralism was in some sense classic, the ideological stakes in the debate are reduced. Sovietologists applying the term pluralism to the USSR can no longer be accused of devaluing the American experience; opponents of the new usage can no longer be caricatured as dogmatic exponents of the superiority of the United States. That is, the debate now turns not on the speaker's position on American society but on the nature of Soviet politics.

Second, despite the popular view, the subsumption of new instances or examples under old conceptual rubrics in a way which leaves the old concept intact is but part of the enterprise of comparative politics, indeed of political analysis in general. As Donald Schon has argued, concepts also develop in a second way – by extension. An old concept is carried forward as a metaphor to a new site. Once displaced, the old concept goes through a process (often lengthy) of elaboration and correction out of which a new concept emerges. The new concept bears but a family resemblance to the old.[4]

In my view, Schon's notion of concept of extension describes most aptly the odyssey of pluralism in political science. But note: the relevant extension occurred not in the mid-1960s when the term surfaced in Soviet studies, but in 1915 when pluralism first appeared in British political theory! For, in the late nineteenth and early twentieth century in both England and America, the concept of pluralism occupied a very important place in the field of metaphysics where it served as a powerful counterweight to Hegelian monism.[5] By the 1920s, the concept was appearing in a number of fields – aesthetics, ethics, sociology as well as political science.[6] We suggest that by the end of the first decade of the twentieth century, pluralism had achieved broad currency in intellectual parlance; it had become a metaphor for flux, diversity and contest. As a metaphor it was displaced into a number of fields in each of which there subsequently occurred a process of elaboration and correction. Some might object that such important displacement could not have occurred without fanfare, without notice. In fact, the very currency of the notion pluralism made it unlikely that the extension of the concept into new fields would be perceived as displacement. That is, we have here a prime example of what Schon has termed 'masked' displacement, a process which takes place imperceptibly when the concept being displaced is an integral part of common vocabulary.[7]

The application of Schon's notion of concept extension to the development of 'pluralism' in political science inevitably alters the way in which we approach the question of 'pluralism' in Soviet studies. Because we envisage the period 1915 to the present as a protracted period of elaboration and correction of pluralism within our discipline, we *expect* variation in the use of the concept from field to field. Our interest centres on the intellectual and professional variables which shaped the various usages. In this essay, three such variables will receive special attention: the profile of the sub-discipline in which pluralism was elaborated (its explanatory goals, dominant methodologies, research priorities); the status and ambitions of the leading spokesmen for the concept; and the character of the monism or unity against which pluralism was ranged. Further, we will no longer be riveted on the question of whether this new case (Soviet politics) will stretch the concept of pluralism too far. Extension *has* taken place and we want only to know whether it has been successful. Has the extension of the concept fulfilled the aspirations of its proponents? Has it led to new ways of seeing the political world?

The essay will proceed chronologically. It will begin with an examination of the concept of pluralism in the field of political theory in Britain in the second decade of this century. It will then move to an analysis of what is popularly regarded as the heyday of pluralism – its commanding position in the study of American politics in the 1950s. It will end with a study of pluralism as it has been used in Soviet studies since the mid-1960s.

This retrieval of the lineage of pluralism will highlight the changes in the concept. But we are also interested in the question of conservation. For as Donald Schon has argued, the displacement of concepts permits one to deal with the new while retaining as much as possible of the past structuring of the world. What facets of pluralism were conserved for over half a century? How can one explain the commitment of three generations of scholars to the preservation of the concept? What does the future augur for pluralism in political studies?

II. BRITISH POLITICAL PLURALISM, 1915–25

For a brief period in the first quarter of the twentieth century, there flourished in England a well-articulated concept of 'political pluralism'. The exponents of the concept included such leading intellectuals as the historian J.N. Figgis (1866–1919), the legal historian F. W. Maitland (1850–1906), the political theorists A. D. Lindsay (1879–1952) and Harold Laski (1893–1950), and the theoretician and later historian of guild socialism, G.D.H. Cole (1889–1959). The English political pluralists were highly individualistic thinkers. They were too eclectic in their approaches to be considered a 'school'. At best, they may be treated as representatives of an intellectual movement. The hallmark of that movement was its antipathy both to the existence in fact and to the pre-eminence in political theory of the monist (read 'absolutist') state.

The leading fashion among commentators on British political pluralism has been to explain the movement as a direct reaction to the glorification of the state by the prominent, Oxford-based political idealists. F. H. Bradley, T. H. Green and Bernard Bosanquet. According to such accounts, the development of the notion of pluralism in politics was provoked by the idealist championing of the expanded role of the state and depiction of the state as having a moral character.[8] This reading of the history of political ideas is certainly plausible, but it gives no play to the wider intellectual context within which the concept of political pluralism unfolded. Specifically, between 1870 and 1925, philosophic teaching in British universities (especially Oxford) was dominated by the idealist monism of Hegel's metaphysics. Around the turn of the century in both England and America, that monism was called into question by philosophers who identified themselves as 'pluralists' (William James and John Dewey in America; G.E. Moore and Bertrand Russell in England, to name but a few). Taking strong issue with Hegelian thought, the pluralist philosophers emphasized flux and diversity in the world and insisted on seeing things 'in their disorderly struggle and in their free harmony'.[9]

Apart from nomenclature, was there any link between the 'pluralism' of the philosophers and that of the political theorists? A few studies of British political pluralism, read carefully, give support to the idea of a real linkage between the two movements. The connection is clearest in the case of Harold Laski, for Laski himself acknowledged his debt to the philosopher William James.[10] But one historian has gone beyond the single instance of Laski to discuss the 'philosophic background' of the group as a whole. 'It cannot be denied', he wrote, 'that although Mr. Laski is the only writer who explicitly acknowledges indebtedness to William James, there exists a genuine sympathy in spirit between James and the pluralists in general.'[11]

To be sure, once resituated in the discipline of political science, pluralism bore but a family resemblance to its earlier incarnation in philosophy. What was preserved was the protest against the absolute, the all-inclusive. But now that protest was directed not against the notion of Absolute Being, but against the notion of the absolutist state.[12]

In British political studies, the concept of pluralism enjoyed high visibility. Part of the reason was disciplinary location: pluralism made its first appearance in the field of political theory which, in the first quarter of the twentieth century, was the oldest and most developed field of political studies in Britain.[13] But the high visibility of pluralism may also in part be traced to the use to which the concept was put. Its exponents touted pluralism as an alternative to the reigning philosophy of the state – monism.

The British political pluralists made their case against the monist state with three interrelated arguments.[14] In no case was the pluralist point novel. Indeed, as we shall see, the pluralists invariably joined existing currents of thought. The originality of the political pluralists lay in their so combining these currents as to create an estimable challenge to the accepted theory of the state.

The first argument made by the political pluralists was that the traditional view of the state as legal, political and moral sovereign was false. This attack was the linchpin of the pluralist case against monism, for it was upon the traditional notion of sovereignty that the idealist theory of the state implicitly rested. Although their target was clearly the political idealists, in making their case against the accepted view of sovereignty, the political pluralists took as their stalking horse John Austin (and the line of analytic jurists who followed him in England).[15] Writing in 1861, Austin had defined sovereignty as follows: 'If a determinate human superior, not in the habit of obedience to a like superior, receive habitual obedience from the bulk of a given society, that determinate superior is sovereign in that society.'[16] Austin's definition implied that in every independent political community one can locate a definite sovereign whose function is to establish the law and whose position is above the law. As one commentator has pointed out, the Austinian doctrine of sovereignty is best understood not as a normative or descriptive statement, but as an ideal type.[17] Yet that doctrine of sovereignty occasioned much criticism as a description of power and rights in actual states. From the late nineteenth century on, Austin and his British followers were attacked on the grounds that sovereignty *is* in fact not unlimited, that sovereignty *is* not in fact the source of law, that sovereignty *is* not the exclusive possession of the state.[18] It was on this last point that the political pluralists took up the cudgels. They contended that it made no sense to stop at the identification of a formally competent authority in the nation, for this was to ignore relevant political and moral facts. There is never a single source of authority in a society; there are always plural social forces each of which is legitimate and should therefore have rights *vis-à-vis* the state.[19]

Second, the pluralists insisted that non-political groups and associations are not dependent upon the state for their existence; they are prior to the state and hence should have legitimate claims upon it. For much of the nineteenth century, it should be remembered, groups and associations were treated as having fictive personalities, personalities accorded them as a concession by the state. By the beginning of the twentieth century, the assault on the fictive theory of group personality was gathering force, fuelled in the main by corporate case law which was widely read as attributing to corporations real personality.[20] The British political pluralists became part of the wave of criticism of the fictive theory of group personality. While they were not of one mind as to whether groups could be said to have real personality,[21] they were united in the belief that groups and associations were social facts which legal theory was ignoring at its peril. Law, they pointed out, could only function as an effective instrument of social control if such facts were acknowledged.[22]

Third, the pluralists attacked the concentration of power in the absolutist state as an impediment to liberty. In their view, liberty – the *summum bonum* – would be best preserved through the dispersion of power to groups and associations. The pluralists admitted that by dispersing power, one limited the ability to do good. But very much in the tradition of Whig thinkers who distrusted power, Laski and his group argued that the purpose of power was not to do good, but to prevent the worst.[23]

The pluralists' argument had certain characteristic features which deserve mention. First, there was a pervasive blending of normative and descriptive discourse. For example, one reads in the pluralist writings that no organization (such as the state) can be absorptive of all the interests of citizens and that no organization ought to be all-absorptive. As early as 1903, G.E. Moore had written of the logical pitfalls of proceeding from 'is' to 'ought' (the 'naturalistic fallacy'),[24] but the British political pluralists had a studied disinterest in ethical theory. Curiously, it was the American political scientists, influenced by Max Weber, who would take the British pluralists to task on this point.

Second, the 'pluralism' of the British thinkers was premised on the traditional dichotomy of the public and private spheres cast in a new light. By the final third of the nineteenth century, it was widely agreed that the liberalism of the Utilitarian school with its image of the individual pitted against the state had been outmoded, rendered obsolete by the increased activity of the state in such areas as education and social welfare. The pluralists recognized the inapplicability of the old dualism.[25] In place of the liberal 'individual', they substituted the group. Thus, in an altered form which testified to the influence of the new discipline of sociology,[26] the old public–private dichotomy was preserved.

Third, those who made the case against the monist state failed to raise the crucial question of the appropriate sphere of state activity. There was some discussion among the pluralists of the nature of the state. Laski and Maitland argued that the state was to be treated as an association with the same status as other associations in the society, while Figgis and Lindsay contended that the state must have some superior status.[27] But what was to be the *role* of the state *vis-à-vis* society? One commentator has depicted the American pluralists of the 1950s as believing that society was essentially self-regulating.[28] How much more true this is of the British pluralists in the first quarter of the twentieth century! With the monist state as their target, their interest extended only to the securing of the autonomy and rights of non-political groups and associations; they never considered that such groups, once accorded autonomy, might operate at cross purposes and that the state might have to act as arbiter. Still less did they reflect that the state might play a constructive role in policy formulation.

Its flaws notwithstanding, British political pluralism endured until the second half of the 1920s. During its lifetime, it commanded a good deal of attention – attention disproportionate to its actual contribution to political thought, one commentator has argued.[29]

How can one assess the success of the displacement of pluralism in British political theory? Any evaluation must begin with the goals of the leading exponents of the concept. Their subject matter, theory of politics, lay at the heart of political studies yet, for the most part, the British political theorists had only secondary interest in the development of theory and even less concern with the delineation of the subject matter of political science itself.[30] Their main purposes were practical – namely to make the case for the legitimacy of non-political groups and associations and to propose a structure of government which would accord those groups and associations power and autonomy. This preference for practical over theoretical goals is not as surprising as it may seem at first glance. For, as a prominent historian of political theory has observed, political theorists as a rule have been less concerned with persuading their colleagues and building disciplines than they have been with changing the political world.[31]

Considering its prominence in the decade 1915–25, the concept of political pluralism had a rather incongruous end; in the second half of the 1920s, it simply slipped into desuetude. To a great extent, the fate of the concept can be explained by the original goals of its proponents. The practical goals of the pluralists revolved around political decentralization and distribution of power. With the concern over the rise of fascism and communism at the end of the 1920s, those goals came to be seen as threats to order.[32] Nor could the concept be rescued by scholarly activity; because the pluralists had only secondarily been interested in theory-building, when the practical goals of pluralism became suspect, the intellectual excitement generated by the concept dissipated.[33]

Curiously, British political pluralism received the most systematic attention in America where Harold Laski imported and popularized the notion. In light of the subsequent appearance of 'pluralism' in North America, the reactions of American political scientists to the writings of Laski and his compatriots are of more than passing interest. If one reads some of the histories of intellectual thought written in America in the 1930s and 1940s, one gets the impression that British political pluralism was given both extensive play and credence in American scholarly circles in the 1920s.[34] A detailed examination of the literature of that period, however, brings home the crucial distinction between notice and approval. Although the British works were well known and many of their virtues acknowledged,[35] more often than not the American response to political pluralism was critical. Some commentators argued that political pluralism implied a denigration of sovereignty which might culminate in a crisis of authority.[36] Others pointed out that the core notions of that 'pluralism' (group, society, state) were ill-defined.[37] Still others inveighed against the blending of normative and empirical discourse in pluralist writing.[38] But, from our point of view, perhaps the most interesting criticism of political pluralism was that it had a deleterious effect on the growth of political science. As one critic put it, with the advent of political pluralism, the notion of sovereignty was rescued from the lawyers only to fall prey to the sociologists. Where was the political element? Where was power?[39]

How should one interpret this last criticism? It is well to remember that in contrast to British political science, which by Laski's own admission was very weakly developed, the 1920s was the formative period in the professionalization of American political science. The American Political Science Association had been in existence for over two decades, the Association's journal had been publishing regularly since 1907, and higher education in political science was spreading rapidly. Equally important, as the profession of political science was emerging, its representatives were looking desperately for theories, hypotheses, methodologies which would serve as their unique brand of esoteric knowledge and thus would justify their differentiation from social science as a whole. In the attempt to forge a discipline, to create a unique identity, the British concept of pluralism was not found serviceable. As we shall see, thirty years later in America another concept of pluralism would again be evaluated in terms of its contribution to the goal of building a discipline of political science.

III. PLURALISM IN THE STUDY OF AMERICAN POLITICS

After a flurry of notice – much of it critical – British political pluralism faded from view in the United States. Reading the American journals in the discipline in the latter half of the 1920s, one looks hard to find a reference to pluralism as it was discussed by Laski and his compatriots. Nearly three decades later, however, the concept of pluralism made a major reappearance in the discipline of political science in the sub-field of American politics. This time the names to conjure with were David Truman, Robert Dahl, Nelson Polsby and Raymond Wolfinger.

How can one characterize pluralism as it appeared in the study of American politics at mid-century? The question is not susceptible of an easy answer for, once introduced, the term was used pervasively in almost all literature dealing with groups in American political life. Who said 'groups' said 'pluralism'. To complicate matters further, pluralism as a term appeared on every level of inquiry into the role of groups in American politics. At its most felicitous, the term was used to designate certain specific hypotheses about the American political process or about the fragmentation of American governmental structure.[40] But the concept was also used more loosely – to refer to broad foci of interest (groups or group life)[41] or to research methodologies (the 'decision-making approach').[42] Even more lamentable, pluralism was sometimes used to denote something as vague as the ethos of American political life.[43] So pervasively was the term pluralism used that commentators felt the need to develop sub-categories of the concept.[44] Indeed, it is no exaggeration to say that in the 1950s, pluralism appeared to be the master concept in the study of American politics. At its height, pluralism was even treated as a theory of politics![45]

The pre-eminent position of pluralism understandably provoked extensive interest in the concept itself. If that interest was widespread, it was also selective; that is it centred on a small net of issues. Great was the concentration of attention on the utility of the concept in inquiry and on its implications for the values of democracy. But there was little examination of the historical antecedents of the American usage of pluralism or of the dynamics of the development of the concept. In this case, absence of inquiry did not mean absence of opinion. Quite the contrary. There were two articles of faith about American pluralism. First, American pluralism was held to be an indigenous plant whose roots could be traced directly to the writing of Arthur Bentley in 1908.[46] The seminal work of Bentley was 'discovered' by David Truman in 1956;[47] thereafter it became commonplace among writers on American pluralism to acknowledge Bentley as intellectual forefather.[48] Second, American pluralism was believed to be different in kind from British pluralism: the latter was dismissed as 'philosophic' for it dealt with normative issues while the former was hailed as 'scientific' on the ground that it dealt only in the empirical. This distinction can be found not only in the works of such apologists for American pluralism as Earl Latham but also in the writing of Mancur Olson, a scholar highly critical of pluralism in its American variant.[49]

Inquiry casts serious doubt on the widely held belief about the origins of American pluralism. With due respect to David Truman, Arthur Bentley is at best an ancestor *malgré lui*. Recent examination of the total works of Bentley leaves no doubt that Bentley was first and foremost an epistemologist; he used the concept of groups not to develop a group theory of politics, but to illustrate the 'process' epistemology he was recommending for adoption in social science.[50] On the other hand, there *are* some intriguing intellectual filiations between the British political pluralists and the group around Dahl. To take but one, the term 'polyarchy', common coin in our day thanks to Robert Dahl, occurs in 1913 as 'polyarchism' in the writing of Ernest Barker, a fellow traveller of the British pluralists![51] That vestiges of the British literature survived in America ought not to surprise, for between 1917–30 the pages of the American Political Science Review reverberated with discussions pro and con of British political pluralism.

Similarly, sober examination does not support the widely touted 'philosophic/analytic' distinction between British and American pluralism. To be sure, the British pluralists did openly integrate normative and descriptive discourse, whereas their American counterparts publicly disavowed value considerations. But the American scholars were not nearly so free of values as they would contend. As a wide variety of critics has taken pains to point out, the American pluralists examined the 'is' and conflated their findings into the 'ought'.[52]

That is not to say that there was no distinction between the two groups of writers on the question of values. There was a marked contrast in the *way* in which value statements were made by the two groups. That contrast can be explained in great part as a function of the differential legitimacy accorded normative discourse in the two sub-disciplines. The British pluralists were writing on political theory in the first quarter of this century, a time when value statements were seen not only as legitimate, but as intrinsic to the enterprise. Hence those writers were able to make value statements directly. The group around Robert Dahl was writing in the sub-field of American politics at a time when the dominant mode of political inquiry was empirical, the preferred methodology was quantitative, the goal was discipline-building in the positivist mode. With this sub-disciplinary profile, the explicit recourse to values fit ill.[53] As a consequence normative positions were implicit, though no less clear for not having been directly articulated. A second difference between the two groups of pluralists lies in the *character* of the values which each supported. The writings of the British pluralists trumpet the importance of systemic change; the political pluralists argued strenuously for a decentralization of power and for the granting of rights and autonomy to non-political groups and associations. The analyses of the American pluralists pointed to the importance of system maintenance. If the existing distribution of power was desirable (assuming, as the pluralists did, the unlimited right of citizens to form groups and the equal access of groups to governmental structure), then the primary political problem was to preserve the status quo. Critics, of course, were quick to point out that the emphasis on stability made the pluralists 'sophisticated apologists for the existing order'.[54]

The contrast in the nature of the values underlying British and American pluralism may in good part be accounted for by the differences in the counter-instances which animated the two brands of pluralism. The target against which the British pluralists took aim in the first quarter of the twentieth century was internal: the British state which was steadily increasing its functions and its power. As Jerry Hough has correctly pointed out, the American pluralists were products of the New Deal; they were comfortable with the expanding role of their own state.[55] The counter-instance which animated American pluralism was external – the totalitarian state which in its Hitlerite and Stalinist forms was seen as the archetype of a monism noxious to its own population and threatening to foreign nations.[56] The fact that the negative instance which underlay American pluralism flourished outside the country had an important effect on the values to which the concept pointed. For American pluralists, the chief value was the preservation of the status quo in the face of a far less desirable alternative. They accepted the existing state of affairs as the best of all possible worlds and counselled conservation, where their British counterparts had urged deep-seated change.

The emphasis of American pluralism on system-maintenance was enhanced by the fact that the proponents of the concept of pluralism were leaders in their profession, scholars who spoke authoritatively not only on behalf of the study of American politics, but on behalf of the discipline of political science in America.[57] Their British counterparts had been self-styled reformers (if not radicals) pressing for change in the political structure using arguments drawn not from the traditional legal theory of the state but from the new discipline of sociology.

Thus, the sub-discipline of American politics exerted a discernible influence on the concept of pluralism. The explanatory goals and preferred methodologies in the study of American politics, the nature of the monism against which this pluralism was ranged, and the professional standing of the major spokesmen for the concept – all these factors combined to produce a concept whose underlying values differed in important respects from the pluralism of the British writers.

Nor was the variance between American and British pluralism confined to the question of values. The two groups of writers differed in their foci of attention. To be specific, the American pluralists shared with their British ancestors the view that the nation was fundamentally associational in character and that groups had an important role to play in the political process. But the pluralists of the 1950s departed from previous usage by focusing on the governmental structure itself. They saw that structure as fragmented into a myriad of non-hierarchically organized political institutions from which public officials competed with one another in the delineation of public policy. In the view of the American pluralists, the fragmentation of government produced a felt need for compromise and generated a pervasive bargaining culture which put a premium on the politician's talents as entrepreneur.[58]

Striking though these differences in values and focus may appear to be, they existed within a framework of similarities.

To be specific, in both instances, scholars maintained a public–private (state–society) dichotomy. The British pluralists made their argument for the autonomy of groups and associations on the assumption that one could (and must) divide the public from the private realm. The American pluralists focused not on autonomy, but on political participation.[59] Their writings emphasized public sector groups rather than private sector lobbies. *But they never repudiated the notion of a division between private and public realms.* One commentator has suggested that the old dichotomy was retained out of a desire to preserve the innocence of the private realm.[60] Whatever the motive, the retention of the dichotomy meant that the American pluralists, like their British ancestors, did not come to grips with one of the most important by-products of the increasing complexity and scope of government – namely the blurring of the demarcation between state and society.

Second, the Americans like their British counterparts, seem to have assumed that the polity was self-regulating. They believed that the interplay of multiple overlapping groups would ensure that no single group dominated and that all got a fair hearing. Some thought was given to the role of the state as arbitrator between groups, but the state was not envisaged as taking an active role in the delineation of policy. As one scholar has put it pithily, with American pluralism 'the withering away of the State was complete'.[61]

In my view, the similarities between American and British pluralism far outweigh the differences. Therefore I would argue that we are not dealing with two different concepts united only by shared terminology; rather we have here a single intellectual tradition which can boast intriguing, but not definitive, variations.

In its denouement, the American episode in pluralism differed somewhat from the British. Pluralism in Britain fell into quiet desuetude; the American usage of pluralism was subjected to a barrage of criticism and attack. The grounds of the attack were empirical, methodological and normative. Some critics maintained that pluralism was an inaccurate description of American politics (it paid too much attention to interest–group activity, to broad consensus within the polity; it minimized the importance of out-groups and of 'non-decisions').[62] Others argued that the pluralist methodology was defective (its research strategy was self-confirming, its methodological range was too narrow).[63] And still other critics scorned the impact of pluralism on the values of democracy (it had replaced participation with the value of stability; it had read out of court the public interest).[64]

How shall we assess the record of pluralism in the study of American politics? To be sure, the extent and the range of the criticisms suggest that if pluralism was the master concept in American political science, its mastery was uneasy, tenuous. But, it is germane to recall that one of the major goals of the American pluralists was discipline-building – specifically, the construction of an empirically based science of politics. In this project, the concept of pluralism was accorded a key role. It was to provide a framework to integrate a wide variety of studies of American politics and to stimulate research on the salient features of American political process. In fact, at its peak, pluralism did integrate important research and did spawn new inquiries. But, as one commentator suggests, the very success of pluralism in this endeavour created problems for its exponents. For as pluralism began to be touted as the star in the conceptual galaxy of the new science of politics, it created a 'revolution of rising expectations'. It began to be treated as a theory of politics rather than as a concept. Predictably, pluralism did not fulfil expectations on this score, but as a result of the overbilling, it became legitimate to attack pluralism not only for sins of commission, but for sins of omission. One commentator has argued that it was the disappointed hopes for pluralism that ultimately sealed its fate in American political science.[65] In the late 1960s and early 1970s, pluralism declined palpably relative to other frameworks (choice theory, exchange theory, critical social theory, neo-élitist theory, political economy) which attempted to supplant it in the discipline.[66]

Although it has not occupied centre stage for over a decade, the concept of pluralism has far from disappeared from the discipline of political science. It is still reflected in major texts on American politics. And even where it is most roundly attacked, it continues to cast a long shadow. For example, in the 1970s, the concept of 'corporatism' was elaborated in order, as its leading exponent Philippe Schmitter put it, 'to offer an explicit alternative to the paradigm of interest politics which has heretofore completely dominated the discipline of North American political science: pluralism'.[67] The concept of 'corporatism' has a long lineage of its own, dating back at least as far as that of pluralism.[68] But in his initial elaboration of corporatism, Schmitter did not draw on that history; rather he defined corporatism as the inverse of pluralism:

> Corporatism can be defined as a system of interest representation in which the constituent units are organized into a limited number of singular, compulsory, noncompetitive, hierarchically ordered and functionally differentiated categories, recognized or licensed (if not created) by the state and granted a deliberate representational monopoly within their respective categories in exchange for observing certain controls on their selection of leaders and articulation of demands and supports.[69] . . .
>
> Pluralism can be defined as a system of interest representation in which the constituent units are organized into an unspecified number of multiple, voluntary, competitive, non-hierarchically ordered and self-determined (as to type or scope of interest) categories which are not specially licensed, recognized, subsidized, created or otherwise controlled in leadership selection or interest articulation by the state and which do not exercise a monopoly of representational activity within their respective categories.[70]

On all the crucial aspects of the relation of groups to the state, corporatism was presented as the inverse, the negation of pluralism. Supporters of the notion of corporatism have decried this approach by negation; they argue that it has reproduced all the lacunae of pluralism. One of the instances cited in this regard is of particular interest to us. It was alleged by two sympathetic critics that corporatism, like pluralism, conceived of society as a dualism between the state on one side and civil society on the other; no real theory of the state had been elaborated.[71] This criticism was launched in the late 1970s; it is already clear that the effort to elaborate a theory of the state will be high on the agenda of exponents of corporatism in the coming decade. Perhaps more than anything else the pursuit of this objective will require the casting off of the shackles of pluralism.

IV. PLURALISM IN THE STUDY OF SOVIET POLITICS

In the course of its elaboration within the discipline of political science, the concept of pluralism was to undergo yet another major relocation. Just as the concept was experiencing a marked decline in intellectual authority in the study of American politics, it surfaced in the study of Soviet politics. It appeared first in studies of interest groups in the USSR,[72] but soon it animated research on Soviet decision-making,[73] and appeared in characterizations of the Soviet polity as a whole.[74]

The appearance of pluralism in Soviet studies has caused some consternation among commentators. In the first place, how can one justify introducing into the study of Soviet politics a concept which was losing its intellectual authority in the field in which it was allegedly formulated?[75] In the second place, what empirical warrant was there for the application of pluralism to the analysis of Soviet politics? To be sure, by the second half of the 1960s, one could identify the beginnings of a literature on groups in Soviet politics. But before that literature had progressed very far, the discussion shifted from a consideration of the nature and activity of groups in the Soviet political process to a debate over whether the character of those groups justified the designation of the Soviet system as a whole as 'pluralist'.[76]

On a certain level, the riddle posed by the appearance of pluralism in Soviet studies can be explained. If one stands back from the field of Soviet studies and looks at the discipline of political science as a whole, one could very possibly construe the latest appearance of pluralism as the response by Sovietologists to cues given by leading scholars in the field of comparative politics. Some of the most prominent specialists in comparative politics had repeatedly expressed the desire to have their conceptual frameworks applied to non-Western and even 'totalitarian' nations.[77] In the mid-1960s, interest groups (one of the most prominent concepts in comparative politics) were studied in a variety of national settings of which the Soviet Union was but one.[78] Given the pervasive linkage in American studies between interest-group activity and pluralism, it is hardly surprising that the term pluralism would have been applied to interest groups in the Soviet Union.

But this explanation begs the real question. Why did the

concept of pluralism strike resonance *within* the field of Soviet studies? Or put another way, how did the concept of pluralism give effect to some of the leading goals in the field of Soviet studies?

To appreciate the attraction for Sovietologists of the incorporation of the concept pluralism in their research, it is necessary to think back to the field of Soviet studies as it was in the mid-1960s. Like all fields of area studies, Soviet studies had consistently been marked by a tension between the insistence on the uniqueness of Soviet society and the desire to find points of comparison between the Soviet Union and other societies.[79] In the late 1950s and early 1960s, the period during which Soviet studies experienced great expansion both as a teaching and as a research field,[80] the familiar tension was strongly weighted in favour of the goal of comparison. At this point, the goal of comparison expressed itself in the desire of Sovietologists to adopt (and adapt) in their studies of Soviet politics concepts which had been developed in the broader field of comparative politics.[81] This desire is not difficult to understand. In the mid-1950s, the field of comparative politics was reoriented from its traditional concentration on institutions to conceptually oriented research.[82] Today, the heady excitement and unbounded enthusiasm with which the pioneers of the 'new' comparative politics set forth their goals and research strategies seems remote; it has been dimmed by the widespread acknowledgement of the logical and empirical problems that attend – indeed bedevil – cross-cultural research.[83] But to scholars studying Soviet politics in the 1960s, accustomed as they were to doing single-country studies (most often in the institutional mould), the trumpeted accomplishments and grandiose designs of their counterparts in comparative politics must have seemed alluring indeed. That allure was not simply a question of cosmetics. The building of real conceptual bridges between comparative politics and Soviet studies would have accomplished two real objectives. First, it would have demonstrated more forcefully than any argument that the Soviet Union was not an outsider in the family of nations, a pariah.[84] And, in destigmatizing the Soviet system, it would have moved specialists on Soviet politics more squarely into the mainstream of the discipline of political science. In pursuit of these very legitimate objectives, Sovietologists touted the advantages, indeed the indispensability, of a comparative approach to the study of Soviet politics.

During this period, two distinct rubrics for the comparative study of the Soviet Union were advanced: 'comparative communism' and 'industrial society'.[85] Perusal of the literature argues strongly that it was research on East Europe which prompted the first use of the term 'pluralism' in Soviet studies.[86] However the claims for priority be resolved, it is clear that for Sovietologists using the term pluralism, the critical yardstick was not Czechoslovakia or Poland, but the United States. Indeed, all the usages of pluralism in Soviet studies – whatever their lexical form – shared one feature: the reference (explicit or implicit) to American pluralism as the classical formulation of the concept. To illustrate, early on Gordon Skilling described Soviet politics in the post-Stalin period as a 'pluralism of élites'. To clarify this novel term, Skilling referred the reader to 'Robert Dahl's expressive term, a "polyarchical" system', adding the qualifier that the Soviet Union was 'oligarchical rather than democratic in character'.[87] Somewhat later, Jerry Hough introduced the model of 'institutional pluralism'. In arguing for the heuristic value of this model, Hough drew attention to the fact that institutional pluralism contained many features of 'the conventional American model of pluralism'. With this major difference: in the model of institutional pluralism, those who wished to effect change had to work within existing institutions, whereas the American model of pluralism allowed for the formation of new pressure groups or parties which might reflect the citizens' interests more closely than existing institutions.[88] More recently, Darrell Hammer put forward the term 'bureaucratic pluralism' to describe contemporary Soviet politics. In so doing, he qualified immediately, 'The USSR is not a truly pluralistic system. We will not find interest groups, in the usual American sense of the term, in Moscow.'[89]

In the mid-1960s, the field of Soviet studies was witness not only to an escalation of scholarly interest in comparative analysis, but also to a declining attachment to the concept of totalitarianism.[90] The significance for the field of the disaffection with 'totalitarianism' cannot be overestimated. Recall that totalitarianism was not simply one of a number of competing concepts in Soviet studies; it was not even *primus inter pares*; totalitarianism was the concept which animated Soviet studies since the second world war. The commitment by some scholars to set aside or even to modify this concept was tantamount to a decision to reorient the study of Soviet politics.[91]

In the service of both goals, the concept of pluralism seemed remarkably useful. The concept appeared a most effective conceptual bridge between the area study of the Soviet Union and the larger discipline of political science. And pluralism seemed to be a most useful wedge against totalitarianism – the monism which had dominated Soviet studies.

In light of what has been said thus far about the field of Soviet studies, it might be imagined that the proponents of pluralism were drawn from the younger generation of Soviet specialists.[92] This proposition, however attractive from the point of view of sociology of science, simply does not hold up under scrutiny. Some of the leading scholars who used the concept pluralism were senior, while not a few junior Sovietologists remained wedded to the concept of totalitarianism, albeit in one of its revised forms. Thus, the proponents and opponents of the use of pluralism in Soviet studies divide not according to the ascribed characteristic of age, but rather according to intellectual and political outlook – namely according to whether or not they believe that the image of Soviet politics under Stalin was appropriate to the Khrushchev and particularly the post-Khrushchev, period.

How successful has the concept of pluralism been in Soviet studies? In meeting the immediate goals of its proponents, pluralism may be judged only a partial success. There is little question that the goal of integrating Soviet studies and comparative politics has been furthered in the wake of the introduction of pluralism into the study of Soviet politics. Works on pluralism or on interest groups by comparative politics specialists now routinely contain references to research conducted by Sovietologists.[93] On the other hand, the goal of eliminating or even reducing the credibility of totalitarianism (either in pure or in modified form) has not been notably furthered. After a decade and a half of applying pluralism to the study of Soviet politics, any epitaph for totalitarianism would be premature.[94] In part, at least, this is because the concepts of pluralism and totalitarianism do not address the same question. As Benjamin Barber has incisively pointed out, pluralism raises the question of rulership (who rules), whereas totalitarianism, however defined, raises questions about the scope of rulership, or the boundaries between public and private spheres of activity. In and of themselves, the findings on rulership do not preclude a variety of responses to the question of governmental scope.[95]

To turn next to the long-range goal of fostering more revealing and insightful research on Soviet politics: here the introduction of the notion of pluralism into the study of Soviet politics has had a mixed effect. To be sure, today we know more about groups and about decision-making in the Soviet Union than we did a decade ago; and much of that new knowledge has undoubtedly been stimulated by the discussion of pluralism. But the invocation of pluralism has also had some deleterious consequences for Soviet studies. Specifically, it has shaped (some would say misshaped) inquiry into the nature of groups in the Soviet Union. In the mid-1960s, Sovietologists began to identify clusters of actors, opinions, interests in Soviet society. Before there could be sustained examination of the nature of those clusters, the basis of their formation, their activities *vis-à-vis* their members, the way in which and level at which they were co-ordinated, scholarly attention was directed to the participation of groups in decision-making, to the process of bargaining among groups, to the fragmentation of governmental structure – preoccupations characteristic of the concern with pluralism in American studies.[96] In and of itself, this shaping of inquiry on groups in the Soviet Union would not be so serious were it not for the fact that it was accompanied by a very heavy concentration on questions of political process. This has led some critics to talk of the emergence of a 'group theory' of Soviet politics.[97] To the proponents of the notion of groups in Soviet politics, this charge makes no sense, for they have always declared that the notion of groups was merely one of the many relevant to the analysis of Soviet politics, not a prism through which all of Soviet reality was to be studied.[98] But opponents have found it difficult, if not impossible, to take these disclaimers at face value. For ever present in their minds is the American case in which the concept of groups was transmuted into a group theory of politics. In addition, the proclaimed modesty of the proponents of the study of groups in Soviet politics seems suspect because those proponents, like their English rather than their American ancestors, were challenging the reigning orthodoxy in their field.

This leads us to the crucial question: how much *does* the usage of pluralism in Soviet studies actually have in common with previous usages of the concept? Are we dealing with a single tradition, or is the usage of pluralism in Soviet studies so idiosyncratic as to be linked by name only to the British and American chapters?

There are some arresting similarities between the Soviet and the other two usages of pluralism. First, those who use pluralism in the study of Soviet politics share with their colleagues in the other fields an emphasis on flux, diversity and contest. At its base, this emphasis is empirically grounded; political scientists using the term pluralism are referring to something which is observable in the political universe. But, as in the British and American cases, the concept of pluralism in Soviet studies also has a 'normative slope'.[99] To be sure, Sovietologists like their American colleagues have presented the case for pluralism on empirical grounds. 'The Soviet political system includes multiple social forces/groups which have a role to play in politics...'; so would run the argument. But in using 'pluralism', Sovietologists are also making judgements about the factors which are worthy of study and, even more important, they are evaluating the Soviet political system. Specialists on American politics have been notably unwilling to admit that their analyses are 'philosophic', even in part. Need Sovietologists follow this lead? What disadvantages would flow from the acknowledgement by Sovietologists that the term pluralism as they use it bespeaks certain value commitments? Some might argue that such acknowledgement would heat up the debate, for disputants would now disagree not only about the fit between the concept (pluralism) and reality (Soviet politics), but also about conflicting values. Let us be clear about this. The debate among Sovietologists over pluralism has always been overlaid with value disagreements. The acknowledgement of the normative slope of pluralism promises to clarify the area of value disagreement and thus to de-escalate the debate.

Second, in the field of Soviet studies as in the other two fields of political science examined here, the term pluralism has been associated with the public–private dichotomy. That is not to say that those in Soviet studies who use the term pluralism portray the groups they study as units autonomous of the Soviet state. On the contrary, excellent research has been done in Soviet studies integrating actors who would traditionally have been divided into public and private sectors.[100] But apparently, some nagging doubt remains. For critics of the application of pluralism to Soviet politics base their opposition on the fact that Soviet groups lack sufficient autonomy from the state.[101] And in response, defenders of the use of pluralism often add qualifiers (limited/quasi) to pluralism. That is, to many the term pluralism seems indelibly linked to the separability (at least in theory) of public from private spheres.

Yet in one important respect, the latest chapter in the evolution of pluralism differs from the previous two. Unlike their counterparts in British political theory and in American studies, Sovietologists who use the term pluralism (in modified or unmodified forms) have never assumed that the polity was self-regulating, that the spontaneous interplay of groups would ensure that all got a fair hearing. They have always seen the firm hand of the state or Party apparatus in policy formation. But then, those scholars most convinced of the salience of this issue are precisely the ones who will entertain most readily arguments for the supercession of pluralism by corporatism.[102]

This leads to some sobering conclusions about the concept of pluralism itself. It may well be that the concept cannot be severed from the public–private dichotomy, however much proponents of pluralism may recognize that the dichotomy is anachronistic in the current age.[103] It may also be that the concept of pluralism may be particularly unsuited to handle the questions of policy formation in nations where the state has a major role to play. That is, the concept of pluralism may be particularly problematic for the analysis of a certain range of questions in Soviet politics.

Where does this leave us? Several paths seem possible. First, scholars may set aside the concept of pluralism and focus *de novo* on the nexus of state–society relations. Some movement in this direction has already begun. Jerry Hough has drawn our attention to Ernest Griffiths's concept of 'whirlpools' or 'complexes' which bring together actors from public and private spheres.[104] Other scholars have been showing interest in the notion of corporatism in the expectation that that concept will provide a more heuristic framework for the analysis of group–state relations.[105]

Second, scholars may decide to begin their study of state–society relations by focusing on the Soviet state. The study of the state, it should be noted, has become very fashionable in political science, both among neo-Marxists[106] and among liberal political economists.[107]

The risk in the adoption of either strategy is clear. There is more than a passing danger that Sovietologists pursuing either line of inquiry will again fall into the understandable trap of using American or Western European concepts as a baseline against which Soviet reality must be first conceptualized and then measured. In the face of this danger, which has proven very real in the case of pluralism, I would counsel a temporary suspension of the passion for comparison and a new focus on the uniqueness of Soviet politics. To some, this counsel may appear retrograde. Willy-nilly, the stress on uniqueness calls to mind the old preoccupation with totalitarianism. But the insistence on an important degree of uniqueness ought not to be seen as tantamount to an acceptance of the model of totalitarianism. On the contrary; an analysis of Soviet politics which explicitly rejects the dichotomy between state and society and which begins with the affirmation of the uniqueness of the Soviet system may spawn the first viable alternative to totalitarianism.

NOTES AND REFERENCES

1. See 'Symposium on Pluralism in Communist Societies', *Studies in Comparative Communism*, 12 (Spring 1979) 6–39; H. Gordon Skilling, 'Pluralism in Communist Societies: Straw Men and Red Herrings', *Studies in Comparative Communism*, 13 (Spring 1980) 82–8. The first major review article on the debate appeared almost a decade earlier. Bohdan Harasymiw, 'Application of the Concept of Pluralism to the Soviet Political System', *Newsletter on Comparative Studies of Communism*, 5 (November 1971) 40–54.
2. This use of the American concept as reference point was blatant and unabashed. See notes 87, 88, 89 below.
3. The classic statement of this argument is William E. Odom, 'A Dissenting View of the Group Approach to Soviet Politics', *World Politics*, 28 (July 1976) 542–67.
4. Donald A. Schon, *Displacement of Concepts* (London, 1963). The only reference to Schon's work by a Sovietologist I have encountered is Richard D. Little, 'Communist Studies in a Comparative Framework', in Frederic J. Fleron (ed.), *Communist Studies and the Social Sciences* (Chicago, 1969) 94–111. Little touts the advantages of Schon's notion of concept extension, not specifically for the analysis of pluralism but for the comparison of Soviet and Western politics in general.
5. The most complete treatment of the pluralist movement in British and American philosophy is Jean Wahl, *Pluralist Philosophies of England and America* (London, 1925).
6. Ibid., 114.
7. Schon, *Displacement*, 104–5.
8. For representative examples of such commentaries, see Henry Mayer Magid, *English Political Pluralism* (New York, 1941); David Nicholls, *The Pluralist State* (London, 1975).
9. Wahl, *Pluralist Philosophies*, 275.

10. Bernard Zylstra, *From Pluralism to Collectivism: The Development of Harold Laski's Political Thought*, 2nd edn (Assen, The Netherlands, 1970) 45.

11. Kung Chuan Hsiao, *Political Pluralism* (London, 1927) 206.

12. 'What the Absolute is to metaphysics, that is the State to political theory' – Harold Laski, *Studies in the Problem of Sovereignty*, cited by Zylstra, *From Pluralism to Collectivism*, 24.

13. For an insider's assessment of the state of political studies in Britain at this time, see Harold Laski, 'Political Science in Great Britain and France', *American Political Science Review*, 19 (February 1925) 96–9.

14. The three arguments are presented as the 'pillars' of political pluralism in Nicholls, *The Pluralist State*.

15. Austin and the analytic jurists are discussed in F.W. Coker, *Recent Political Thought* (New York, 1934) 501–3, 523–6; F.W. Coker, 'Pluralist Theories and the Attack on State Sovereignty', in Charles E. Merriam and Harry E. Barnes (eds), *Political Theory, Recent Times* (New York, 1935) 80–120.

16. John Austin, *Lectures on Jurisprudence*, cited by Coker, *Recent Political Thought*, 501–2.

17. G. David Garson, *Group Theories of Politics* (Beverly Hills, Calif., 1978) 19–20.

18. Coker, *Recent Political Thought*, 501–3, 523–6; Caleb Perry Patterson, 'Recent Political Theory Developed in Jurisprudence', in Merriam and Barnes (eds), *Political Theory*, 141–8; Coker, 'Pluralist Theories', 80–9.

19. Nicholls, *The Pluralist State*, 36–54. On this point G.D.H. Cole was the exception. He was willing to entertain the notion of the state as sovereign, if that state represented the will of the whole people. Ibid., 44.

20. Ibid., 64ff.

21. Maitland accepted the notion of a group personality, but Laski and Cole ended by rejecting the idea.

22. Nicholls, *The Pluralist State*, ch. 4.

23. Ibid., 29.

24. G.E. Moore, *Principia Ethica* (Cambridge, 1903).

25. Ernest Barker, *Political Thought in England* (London, 1927) 20.

26. The case for the impact of sociology on political theory was most persuasively – and persistently – argued by Harry Elmer Barnes. Barnes wrote articles in a variety of journals on the contributions to political analysis by leading sociologists. For a sample of the argument, see Harry Elmer Barnes, 'Some Contributions of Sociology to Modern Political Theory', in Merriam and Barnes (eds), *Political Theory*, 357–401.

27. Nicholls, *The Pluralist State*, ch. 5.

28. Alfred Stepan, *The State and Society* (Princeton, N.J., 1978) 10.

29. Adam Ulam, *Philosophical Foundations of English Socialism* (Cambridge, 1951) 80–6.

30. The exception that proves the rule was Harold Laski. See Harold Laski, *On the Study of Politics* (London, 1926); Harold Laski, *A Grammar of Politics* (London, 1925).

31. Sheldon Wolin, 'Paradigms and Political Theories', in P. King and B. Parekh (eds), *Politics and Experience: Essays in Honour of Michael Oakeshott* (London, 1968) 125–51.

32. 'We have seen enough of pluralism, of the anarchy of co-ordinated sovereigns recognizing no superior' – Rupert Emerson, *State and Sovereignty in Modern Germany* (New Haven, Conn., 1928) 273.

33. While interest in the problems suggested by the notion of pluralism (sovereignty, constitutional government, federalism) did persist, systematic inquiry into the nature and activity of groups did not continue past the 1920s. When such research did resume again in Britain in the 1950s, it was very much in the American mould. See W.J.M. Mackenzie, 'Pressure Groups: The Conceptual Framework', *Political Studies*, 3 (1955) 247–55; *Political Quarterly*, 29 (1958), special issue devoted to pressure groups in Britain.

34. F.G. Wilson, *The American Political Mind* (New York, 1949); R.G. Gettel *History of American Political Thought* (New York, 1924) 458–72.

35. Ellen Deborah Ellis, 'The Pluralistic State', *American Political Science Review*, 14 (August 1920) 407. George H. Sabine, 'Pluralism: A Point of View', *American Political Science Review*, 17 (February 1923) 34–50.

36. W.Y. Elliott, 'Sovereign State or Sovereign Group', *American Political Science Review*, 19 (August 1925) 475–99; W.Y. Elliott, 'Pragmatic Politics of Mr. H.J. Laski', *American Political Science Review*, 18 (May 1924) 251–75; Coker, 'Pluralist Theories'.

37. M.P. Follett, *The New State* (London, 1918) 258–320.

38. Ellis, 'The Pluralistic State', 400–1.

39. Ellen Deborah Ellis, 'Political Science at the Crossroads', *American Political Science Review*, 21 (November 1927) 773–91.

40. The hypotheses were most clearly articulated by Robert Dahl. Robert Dahl, *A Preface to Democratic Theory* (Chicago, 1956); Robert Dahl, *Who Governs?* (New Haven, Conn., 1961); Robert Dahl, 'A Critique of the Ruling Elite Model', *American Political Science Review*, 52 (June 1958) 463–9.

41. David Ricci, *Community Power and Democratic Theory* (New York, 1971) 125–61.

42. Nelson Polsby, 'How to Study Community Power: The Pluralist Alternative', *Journal of Politics*, 22 (August 1960) 474–84; Nelson Polsby, *Community Power and Political Theory* (New Haven, Conn., 1963); Raymond Wolfinger, 'Non-Decisions and the Study of Local Politics', *American Political Science Review*, 65 (December 1971) 1063–79.

43. Henry Kariel, *The Decline of American Pluralism* (Stanford, Calif., 1964); Theodore Lowi, *The End of Liberalism* (New York, 1969).

44. For example Andrew S. MacFarland classified pluralist writings into two groups: 'power structure pluralism', which aimed at discrediting the ruling élite model in some political arena, and 'group theory pluralism'. Andrew S. MacFarland, *Power and Leadership in Pluralist Systems* (Stanford, Calif., 1969). David Ricci sees essentially the same dichotomy as MacFarland, but he considers 'power structure pluralism' to be a supercession of or advance over 'group theory pluralism'. Ricci, *Community Power*. William E. Connolly draws a different dichotomy: he distinguishes between 'arena' pluralism characterized by the premise that government is the arena where group conflicts are debated and resolved (political scientists more often than not conduct research that falls into this category)

and 'umpire' pluralism in which major social associations operate outside government and government functions as umpire (sociologists more often than not belong in this category). William E. Connolly, 'The Challenge to Pluralist Theory', in William E. Connolly (ed.), *The Bias of Pluralism* (New York, 1971) 3–25.

45. This point is made in Darryl Baskin, *American Pluralist Democracy: A Critique* (New York, 1971). See also Oliver Garceau, 'On the Origins of Interest-Group Theory: A Critique of a Process', *American Political Science Review*, 68 (December 1974) 1505–19; Garson, *Group Theories*, 112; P. Odegard, 'A Group Basis of Politics: A New Name for an Old Myth', *Western Political Quarterly*, 11 (September 1958) 689–702.

46. The *locus classicus* was Arthur F. Bentley, *The Process of Government* (Chicago, 1908).

47. David Truman, *The Governmental Process* (New York, 1953).

48. Two treatments which did not trace pluralism all the way back to Bentley, but nonetheless insisted that it was a native plant were: Samuel P. Huntington, 'Paradigms of American Politics: Beyond the One, the Two and the Many', *Political Science Quarterly*, 89 (March 1974) 1–27; Theodore Lowi, 'American Government, 1933–1963: Fission and Confusion in Theory and Research', *American Political Science Review*, 58 (September 1964) 589–99.

49. Earl Latham, *The Group Basis of Politics* (Ithaca, New York, 1952) 380–3; Mancur Olson, *The Logic of Collective Action* (New York, 1968) 111–31.

50. Paul F. Kress, *Social Science and the Idea of Process* (Urbana, Ill., 1970).

51. In 1913, Ernest Barker described the state as a 'polyarchism'. Ernest Barker, *Church, State, and Study* (London, 1930) 169. The essay was originally delivered as a paper in 1914. This interesting usage was brought to light in Claude Burtenshaw, 'The Political Theory of Pluralist Democracy', *Western Political Quarterly*, 21 (December 1968) 586. Burtenshaw says: 'In adopting the name pluralist, the pluralist democrats undoubtedly made conscious reference to the English pluralists, Neville Figgis, Harold Laski, the Webbs and Ernest Barker'.

52. Lane Davis, 'The Cost of Realism: Contemporary Restatements of Democracy', *Western Political Quarterly*, 17 (March 1964) 37–46; Jack Walker, 'A Critique of the Elitist Theory of Democracy', *American Political Science Review*, 60 (June 1966) 285–95; Christian Bay, 'Politics and Pseudo-politics: A Critical Evaluation of Some Behavioural Literature', *American Political Science Review*, 59 (March 1965) 39–51.

53. Dahl took great pains to deny that there was any intended normative slope in pluralist theory. Robert Dahl, 'Further Reflections on the "Elitist Theory of Democracy"', *American Political Science Review*, 60 (June 1966) 298.

54. Walker, 'A Critique', 298.

55. Jerry F. Hough, 'Pluralism, Corporatism and the Soviet Union', *infra*.

56. The notion that American pluralism had as its counter-instance an external monism flies in the face of conventional wisdom. The majority of works written over the past two decades portray American pluralism as a conceptual device pitted against C. Wright Mills's description of America

governed by a 'power élite'. For example, see Kenneth Prewitt and Allan Stone, *The Ruling Elites* (New York, 1973). To be sure Robert Dahl and his colleagues did use their notion of pluralism to argue against Mills's image of America run by a power élite. But I suggest the reason that the refutation of Mills seemed so urgent was that Mills had refused to distinguish between democracy and totalitarianism as types of mass society. See C.W. Mills, *The Power Elite* (New York, 1956) 310. To this distinction, the majority of American political scientists writing in the immediate post-war period were deeply committed.

57. Robert Dahl was president of the American Political Science Association in 1967; Nelson Polsby was editor-in-chief of the *American Political Science Review* from 1971 to 1978.

58. This characterization of the American pluralists was drawn from Garson, *Group Theories of Politics*. Garson uses this characterization to distinguish between the pluralists around Dahl and earlier American group theorists. It seems to me that the characterization applies much better to the distinction between the group around Dahl and the British political pluralists.

59. Some commentators have regarded *this* difference of focus as the crucial distinction between the two groups. This paper argues that despite the difference of topic there is an underlying consensus on the public–private dichotomy.

60. Benjamin R. Barber, 'Conceptual Foundations of Totalitarianism', in Carl J. Friedrich *et al.* (eds), *Totalitarianism in Perspective: Three Views* (New York, 1969) 34.

61. Stepan, *State and Society*, 14.

62. J. LaPalombara, 'The Utility and Limitations of Interest Group Theory in Non-American Field Situations', *Journal of Politics*, 20 (February 1960) 29–49; Donald Matthews, *U.S. Senators and Their World* (New York, 1960); P. Bachrach and M. Baratz, 'Two Faces of Power', *American Political Science Review*, 56 (December 1962) 947–52; P. Bachrach and M. Baratz, 'Decisions and Non-Decisions: An Analytic Framework', *American Political Science Review*, 57 (September 1963) 632–42.

63. R.E. Dowling, 'Pressure Group Theory: Its Methodological Range', *American Political Science Review*, 54 (December 1960) 944–54; Stanley Rothman, 'Systematic Political Theory: Observations on the Group Approach', *American Political Science Review*, 54 (February 1960) 15–33; Odegard, 'A Group Basis of Politics'.

64. P. Bachrach, *The Theory of Democratic Elitism* (Boston, 1967); Carole Pateman, *Participation and Democratic Theory* (Cambridge, 1970); Henry Kariel, *The Decline of American Pluralism* (Stanford, Calif., 1961); Davis, 'The Cost of Realism'; Walker, 'A Critique'.

65. Garson, *Group Theories*, 112.

66. Ibid., 140–52.

67. Philippe Schmitter, 'Still the Century of Corporatism?', in Philippe Schmitter (ed.), *Trends Towards Corporatist Intermediation* (Beverly Hills, Calif., 1979) 14.

68. Garson, *Group Theories*, 51; Coker, 'Pluralist Theories', 91ff.

69. Schmitter, 'Still the Century of Corporatism?', 13.

70. Ibid., 15.

71. Birgitta Nedelmann and Kurt G. Meier, 'Theories of Corporatism: Static or Dynamic', in Schmitter (ed.), *Trends Towards Corporatist Intermediation*, 96-9.

72. The first major application of the group concept to Soviet politics can be found in H. Gordon Skilling, 'Interest Groups and Communist Politics', *World Politics*, 18 (April 1966) 435-51. Some of the ideas in this article had been formulated by Skilling in a paper of the same title delivered to the Canadian Political Science Association in June of 1965. Less than two years later, in January 1968, a conference on the question of interest groups in Soviet politics was held at the University of Toronto. Within little more than two years there appeared in print a collection of original research papers on the topic: H. Gordon Skilling and Franklyn Griffiths (eds), *Interest Groups in Soviet Politics* (Princeton, N.J., 1971).

73. See Joel J. Schwartz and William R. Keech, 'Group Influence and the Policy Process in the Soviet Union', *American Political Science Review*, 62 (September 1968) 840-51. Philip D. Stewart, 'Soviet Interest Groups and the Policy Process: The Repeal of Production Education', *World Politics*, 22 (October 1969) 29-50.

74. Jerry F. Hough, 'The Soviet System: Petrification or Pluralism', *Problems of Communism* (March-April 1972) 25-45.

75. As one acerbic critic put it: 'The group approach has not reigned unchallenged even as a model appropriate for American politics. It would be ironic if, as the study of Soviet politics is brought out of isolation, it is introduced not to contemporary concepts in comparative politics, but rather to concepts already losing their relevance to much of Western politics' - Odom, 'A Dissenting View'. See also MacFarland, *Power and Leadership*, 58-63; Charles A. Powell, 'Structural-Functionalism and the Study of Comparative Communist Systems: Some Caveats', in Fleron (ed.), *Communist Studies*, 59; Stephen White, 'Communist Systems and the "Iron Law of Pluralism"', *British Journal of Political Science*, 8 (January 1978) 101-7. Of course, the posing of this question reveals the belief that the American or Western usage of pluralism was classic.

76. The term pluralism was invoked by Skilling with substantial reservations (and almost as an afterthought) in his original *World Politics* article of 1966. See note 72, above. The association of the group concept with the notion of pluralism took hold quickly in the field of Soviet studies. See Andrew S. Janos, 'Group Politics in Communist Society: A Second Look at the Pluralist Model', in S.P. Huntington and C.H. Moore (eds), *Authoritarian Politics in Modern Society* (New York, 1970) 437-50.

77. For example, see Gabriel Almond and James S. Coleman, *The Politics of Developing Areas* (Princeton, N.J., 1960) 49. This instance was cited in Skilling, 'Interest Groups', 438, n.19.

78. For a sense of how wide-ranging this research was, see Garson, *Group Theories*, 153-4.

79. This tension is lucidly discussed in Lucian W. Pye, 'The Confrontation between Discipline and Area Studies', in Lucian W. Pye (ed.), *Political Science and Area Studies: Rivals or Partners* (Bloomington, Ind., 1975) 3-22.

34   *Pluralism in the Soviet Union*

80. In establishing the chronology of the field of Soviet studies, two collections are useful: Harold H. Fisher (ed.), *American Research on Russia* (Bloomington, Ind., 1959); Cyril E. Black and John M. Thompson (eds), *American Teaching About Russia* (Bloomington, Ind., 1959).

81. For a representative sample of such arguments, see the 'Symposium on Comparative Politics and Communist Systems', *Slavic Review*, 26 (March 1967) 3–28; H. Gordon Skilling, 'Soviet and Communist Politics: A Comparative Approach', *Journal of Politics*, 22 (May 1960) 300–13; Robert C. Tucker, 'On the Comparative Study of Communism', *World Politics*, 19 (January 1967) 242–57.

82. For discussion of the catalysts to that transformation, see Roy C. Macridis *et al.*, 'Research in Comparative Government', *American Political Science Review*, 47 (September 1953) 641–75; for some of the early enthusiasm which accompanied the transformation, see Joseph LaPalombara, 'Macrotheories and Microapplications in Comparative Politics: A Widening Chasm', *Comparative Politics*, 1 (October 1968) 52–3.

83. Alistair MacIntyre, 'Is a Comparative Science of Politics Possible?', in Alistair MacIntyre, *Against the Self Images of the Age* (London, 1971); Arthur Kalleberg, 'The Logic of Comparison: A Methodological Note on the Comparative Study of Political Systems', *World Politics*, 19 (October 1966) 69–82.

84. Elsewhere, I have discussed the desire for destigmatization as it was reflected in the writings of Western scholars studying Soviet science. Susan Gross Solomon, 'Reflections on Western Studies of Soviet Science', in Linda L. Lubrano and Susan Gross Solomon (eds), *The Social Context of Soviet Science* (Boulder, Colo., 1980) 1–30.

85. The rubric 'comparative communism' was premised on the belief that communist societies contained an identifiable set of features that differentiated them from non-communist societies. This premise was widely discussed in 'Symposium on Comparative Politics and Communist Systems'. The case for the rubric 'industrial society' was based on the premise that the most important characteristics of the Soviet Union were those it shared with other large-scale industrial societies. This line of thinking took its departure from the so-called 'convergence model', but unlike its ancestor, the USA/USSR comparison urged by Sovietologists in the 1960s, stressed differences as well as similarities. The pioneering study in this group was Z. Brzezinski and S. Huntington, *Political Power: USA/USSR* (New York, 1964). For an excellent discussion of the two approaches to comparison, see John Kautsky, 'Comparative Communism Versus Comparative Politics', *Studies in Comparative Communism*, 6 (Spring/Summer 1973) 135–70.

86. The developments in Czechoslovakia and Poland were very much in the mind of Gordon Skilling when he wrote his original article in 1966. At the same time there appeared a second article using the term pluralism with respect to Czechoslovakia. See A.H. Brown, 'Pluralistic Trends in Czechoslovakia', *Soviet Studies*, xvii, no. 4 (April 1966) 453–72.

87. Skilling, 'Interest Groups', 450.

88. Hough, 'The Soviet System: Petrification or Pluralism', 25–45. In this first article, Hough appeared to use American pluralism as a synonym for

'classical pluralism'. In a later work, the two were clearly differentiated. Jerry F. Hough, *The Soviet Union and Social Science Theory* (Cambridge, 1977) 9.

89. Darrell P. Hammer, *USSR: The Politics of Oligarchy* (Hinsdale, Ill. 1974) 223, 224.

90. The increasing interest in comparative analysis and the declining attachment to the totalitarian model were clearly related. But the nature of the relationship is often misperceived by commentators. Some have suggested that the concept of totalitarianism is incompatible with comparative analysis. For example, see P.H. Kneen, 'Group Conflict Approach to the Soviet Union: Theories and Approaches to Soviet Politics ... The Totalitarian Perspective', Discussion Paper No. 7 (Ser. RC/C), Centre for Russian and East European Studies, University of Birmingham (October 1971) 2–3. In fact, there is no *logical* reason why one could not have a comparative politics which used the concept totalitarianism. What is true is that the concept totalitarianism as it was used in Soviet studies from the second world war to the 1960s tended to stress the uniqueness of the Soviet system, the features which differentiated it from 'normal' polities. It was such a stress on singularity that was clearly at odds with a comparative approach.

91. The *locus classicus* of the totalitarian model was a work written by two members of the Harvard faculty. Carl J. Friedrich and Zbigniew Brzezinski, *Totalitarian Dictatorship and Autocracy* (Cambridge, Mass., 1956). The decade of the 1960s was witness to impressive lexical inventiveness on the part of Sovietologists confronting the question of the utility of the totalitarian model for the study of Soviet politics in the post-Stalin period. Terms like the 'administered society', the 'company town', the 'directed society', the 'mono-organizational society' were introduced as replacements for totalitarianism. For reviews of this literature see Barber, 'Conceptual Foundations'; Michael Curtis, 'Retreat from Totalitarianism' in Friedrich *et al.* (eds), *Totalitarianism in Perspective*, 53–122. One scholar has divided Sovietologists into three camps on the issue of revision: those who attempted to sustain the model (Friedrich); those who attempted to sustain, but refine the model (Tucker, Kautsky); those who attempted to displace the model (Meyer, Skilling). See Robert Burrowes, 'Totalitarianism: The Revised Standard Edition', *World Politics*, 21 (January 1969) 272–94.

92. One commentator has suggested that by and large, the younger scholars seem to reject totalitarianism. See Burrowes, 'Totalitarianism', 289.

93. For evidence on this point from a scholar outside Soviet studies see Garson, *Group Theories*, 153–4.

94. The suggestion for an epitaph for totalitarianism was advanced in Kneen, 'Group Conflict Approach'.

95. Barber, 'Conceptual Foundations', 20.

96. Hough admits that, whatever the history of pluralism, it is the American experience with the concept that has been the baseline for inquiry in Soviet studies. Hough, *The Soviet Union and Social Science Theory*, 9.

97. Odom, 'A Dissenting View'; Janos, 'Group Politics', 447–8.

98. Skilling, 'Pluralism in Communist Societies'.

99. The term 'normative slope' was drawn from Charles Taylor, 'Neutrality in

Political Science', in Peter Laslett and Walter G. Runciman (eds), *Politics, Philosophy and Society*, 3rd ser. (Oxford, 1961) 25–58.

100. Franklyn Griffiths, 'Images, Politics and Learning in Soviet Behavior toward the United States', unpublished Ph.D. dissertation, Columbia University, 1972. Thane Gustafson, *Reform in Soviet Politics: Lessons of Brezhnev's Agricultural and Environmental Policies* (Cambridge, 1981); Peter H. Solomon, Jr, *Soviet Criminologists and Criminal Policy: Specialists in Policy-making* (New York and London, 1978).

101. Janos orients much of his critique of the application of pluralism around the absence of autonomy for the relevant groups. See Janos, 'Group Politics in Communist Society'. The point is answered by H. Gordon Skilling, 'Groups in Soviet Politics', in Skilling and Griffiths (eds), *Interest Groups in Soviet Politics*, 44.

102. Valerie Bunce and John M. Echols III, 'Soviet Politics in the Brezhnev Era: "Pluralism" or "Corporatism"?', in Donald Kelley (ed.), *Soviet Politics in the Brezhnev Era* (New York, 1980) 1–26. It is interesting to note that the foremost spokesman for corporatism in the recent period, Philippe Schmitter, termed the Soviet Union a 'monism'. Schmitter, 'Still the Century of Corporatism?', 16.

103. Barber contended that this dichotomy has long ago been recognized as outmoded by political theorists and that it survives only in the two instances of pluralism and totalitarianism. Barber, 'Conceptual Foundations', 33.

104. Hough, *The Soviet Union and Social Science Theory*, 11.

105. For example, see Valerie Bunce, 'The Soviet Union under Brezhnev: The Rise and Fall of Corporatism', Paper delivered to the AAASS conference, Monterey, Calif., 22 September 1981.

106. For example, see Ralph Miliband, *The State in Capitalist Society* (London, 1969); James O'Connor, *The Fiscal Crisis of the State* (New York, 1973); Claus Offe, 'The Theory of the Capitalist State and the Problems of Policy Formation', in L. Lindberg *et al.* (eds), *Stress and Contradiction in Modern Capitalism* (Lexington, Mass., 1975) 125–44; Jurgen Habermas, *Legitimation Crises* (Boston, 1975).

107. Some classic sources include: John Kenneth Galbraith, *The New Industrial State* (Boston, 1967); Charles Lindblom, *Politics and Markets* (New York, 1977); David Cameron, 'The Expansion of Public Economy: A Comparative Analysis', *American Political Science Review*, 72 (December 1978) 1243–61.

3 Pluralism, Corporatism and the Soviet Union

JERRY F. HOUGH

In significant part because of Gordon Skilling's seminal article of 1966,[1] the last fifteen years in Soviet studies have been dominated by the discussion of interest groups and pluralism. Most of the major research of the period – although not nearly so much the generalizations – has focused in one way or another on the input side of the Soviet political system. Even such work as an examination of the social characteristics of Central Committee members or the attempt to infer local influences on decisions through an examination of budgetary data basically fit within this paradigm, for it assumed the possibility of a multiplicity of social influences on policy. The pluralist approach and the conclusions to which it has led have been the subject of severe and continuing criticism, but this too is evidence of the centrality of the work as the focus of attention and debate.

Paradoxically, just as the pluralist tradition began to have a major impact on Soviet studies, it began to be repudiated by a large number of young American political scientists outside the Soviet field. Some of those who attacked it were committed to quasi-Marxism or to participatory democracy, but as the issues of the Vietnam war began to fade, the Left and the Right began coalescing in a criticism of the pluralists' relative lack of attention to the state as an independent and perhaps determining actor. Scholars such as Theodore Lowi levelled their criticism at the pluralists' failure to speak of the possibility – and the need – for a professional state service to protect universal norms and the common good. Others criticized it for insufficient attention to the role that the state actually did play.

One manifestation of the increased interest in the role of the state has been the growing popularity of the concept of 'corporatism' in comparative political science during the 1970s. The term came out of the study of Latin America and southern Europe where it functioned as a description of the type of authoritarian regimes found there, but Latin American specialist Philippe Schmitter, the foremost proponent of corporatism, has argued that the concept is appropriate for the political systems of West Europe as well. It has now been vigorously nominated as a substitute for pluralism as the new key to understanding the Soviet Union.

As is true with nearly all concepts in political science, corporatism has been defined in different ways. Basically, however, it emphasizes the role of the state in promoting and planning for the common good. Unlike the totalitarian model, it focuses on interest representation, but it treats the latter more as a function of the state's legitimization, informational and control needs.

> Corporatism can be defined as a system of interest represen-
> tation in which the constituent units are organized into a
> limited number of singular, compulsory, non-competitive,
> hierarchically ordered and functionally differentiated cat-
> egories recognized and licensed (if not created) by the state and
> granted a deliberate representational monopoly within their
> respective categories in exchange for observing certain controls
> on their selection of leaders and articulation of demands and
> supports.[2]

A recent article which proposes that the corporatist model be applied to the Soviet Union summarizes the differences between it and the pluralist model in the starkest of terms:

> The state takes an active role in the decision-making process. It
> works with groups to make public policy and does not, as in the
> pluralist model, simply act as a passive broker, mediating
> interests; interest groups are not the autonomous, indepen-
> dent actors they are in pluralism. . . .
>   A pluralist policy, of course, has no explicit goals. Instead,
> the presumption is that a pluralist process is the major concern;
> optimal public policy will necessarily follow. By contrast, a
> corporatist system does tend to feature explicit policy goals,

and the system is designed to ensure the fulfillment of these goals. The goals are economic growth, political, economic, and social stability, and the maintenance of the prevailing distribution of political power.... A successful pluralist system does not, indeed, cannot plan. A corporatist system will not accept an absence of planning.

For the most part, only those groups deemed necessary to making the system work are included: thus, functional interest groups – most notably, business and labor – are the centerpiece of a corporatist system. Others – primarily attitudinal groups – are left out. Under classical pluralism, of course, no group is left out except of its own volition.

In pluralist models, the emphasis is on conflict; in corporatism, consensus and cooperation. Groups do not compete with one another through the state to obtain more for themselves. Instead, they are brought together by the state in active cooperation to achieve more for all; harmony is the watchword of a corporatist regime.... Conflict is still present, but held in check by the state's promise that all will get something and few, if any, will lose.

The economic and political role of the masses in a pluralist system is rather limited; they are to provide for themselves economically and periodically make their political demands known by selecting leaders and agitating for their interests through various groups. By contrast, in a corporatist system... the masses are protected by a welfare state in which a minimal standard of living is guaranteed by the government through income policies, transfers and social services.... The political role of the masses – [at least] in a 'liberal' corporatist order – also diverges from that in pluralism. The public is expected not just to vote but also to participate as representatives of group interests in decision-making areas of particular competence and concern.[3]

It does not take a highly sophisticated scholar to recognize that the reality of the Soviet political system corresponds far better to the corporatist model as presented here than to the pluralist model. Surely we must acknowledge that the state in the Soviet Union does engage in planning and does pursue such goals as economic growth and political stability. We surely must abandon any interest group approach which suggests that the Soviet political scene is dominated by autonomous, independent interest groups and that organized attitudinal groups have as big a role in the system as functional economic ones.

And yet nagging questions remain. Can the scholars who in one way or another have used the words 'pluralism' or 'pluralistic' really have thought that planning is not a part of Soviet life and that Soviet interest groups are best characterized as autonomous, independent actors? Perhaps before we move on to a new set of concepts, it is worthwhile to step back and ask ourselves: what issues have been involved in the use of words such as 'interest group' or 'pluralism' in discussions of the Soviet Union? What functions do they serve and what costs and benefits are involved in abandoning them in favour of other concepts such as corporatism?

I

The debates about interest groups and pluralism in the Soviet Union did not, of course, originate within Soviet studies. Scholars such as Skilling were bemoaning the isolation of Soviet studies from the broader social sciences, and they were insisting that we must ask the questions and use the definitions of that broader literature if the Soviet system of the mid-1960s was to be compared both with the Soviet past and with other political systems. They thought that the concepts of pluralism and interest groups would be useful in this context. Similarly, in the ensuing debate those who opposed this approach frequently went back to the general political science literature to support their arguments about the inappropriateness of these concepts[4] or (as in the case of corporatism) to search for alternative concepts.

As we in Communist studies draw upon these debates, however, we should be fully aware that they have very serious flaws in them. Indeed, if the major disputes in political science are examined at some distance and with some detachment, they leave a very peculiar impression. They often are conducted with great heat, but an argument may be denounced both as a fundamental misunderstanding of reality and as a belabouring of the obvious. Without exception, all scholars claim that their own position has been misrepresented – that, indeed, they are being accused of advancing views that neither they nor any semi-literate high-school graduate could conceivably hold. Instead of making progress, conceptual discussions usually degenerate into repetitiveness, and, as a result, come to be distinguished by their air of exhaustion after a short burst of initial enthusiasm. They then fade away without resolution, to be replaced by a debate about some new concept. The cycle then repeats itself.

But why is this the case? Why do theoretical discussions in political science often seem so sterile? The basic answer, it seems to me, is that there is far more fundamental agreement among the participants in the debates than is usually admitted.

Consider, for example, the following eleven propositions – nine of them about political systems in general, two of them about the Soviet Union. While some might prefer a different formulation of one or another of them, almost every political scientist would surely agree with all of them – in fact, would simply take them for granted as conventional wisdom.

1. Regardless of the claims of the ideology, no society can possibly be united in its political attitudes, let alone in its preferences on immediate policy questions.
2. If a political system has any complexity whatsoever, the leader, no matter how dictatorial, cannot decide every individual question himself.
3. Modern government makes a greater effort to regulate the economy, and consequently it has more impact on people's lives, than governments in pre-industrial society (at least if we speak of governments which control a larger territory than a village or small tribal unit).
4. If government has the ability to affect people's lives in meaningful ways, there will be people who will in one way or another try to influence the decisions of government. On *a priori* grounds, it would seem that the more complex the government and its task, the more the leaders would require information from outside their own ranks. The more the outsiders provide information, the greater the opportunity they have to try to influence the outcome.
5. No political system can survive for long unless it rests on some social forces. It cannot do so unless it takes some interests of some significant societal groups at least partially into account as it makes policy.
6. Except in very rare cases (a revolutionary situation or an event like the Great Purge), the owners or administrators of the means of production are likely on the average to receive more

of society's goods than rank-and-file workers or peasants. Directly or indirectly, they are likely on the average to have more influence on governmental decisions.

7. Government makes a difference. If government always acted as an automatic register of group pressures, then a change in leader or regime could not matter, and sometimes it clearly does.

8. The values of the top leader can make a difference. This is especially true in countries where a revolution has swept away old institutional leaders or where (as in much of Africa) the formal institutions are little-developed.

9. The employees of the bureaucracy are not simply neutral executive agents of the political leaders. They often do represent the interests of those their programmes benefit, but their decisions and policy positions are also affected by their own self-interest and by their own values.

10. Policy-making in the Soviet Union is much more centralized than in the United States, but, in practice, Brezhnev did not have as much personal impact on the majority of decisions as did Stalin or even Khrushchev.

11. The Soviet government is much more repressive of individual freedom – especially political freedom – than the American, but the Brezhnev regime was not as repressive as the Stalin regime was.

No attempt at comprehensiveness has been made in the compiling of this list of statements. Rather, it is a minimum listing of some generally accepted truths. Its purpose has simply been to remind the reader that, since all scholars take all of them for granted, obviously no model should be interpreted as denying any of them. Yet clearly what occurs in practice is that various model-builders tend to emphasize a number of these propositions at the expense of others and that the critics then accuse them of being ignorant of the neglected propositions. The critics then build models centred on the latter, and they in turn are criticized for ignorance of the obvious. And 99 per cent of this takes place unconsciously, without the model-makers being aware of it.

David Easton's categories are very useful in illuminating what happens. Easton distinguishes between outputs (decisions taken by government) and inputs, the latter themselves being divided between demands and supports. Between the inputs and the out-

puts is the black box of the decision-makers. Although these categories are extremely simplified, they do begin to suggest the
complexity of political systems. If political science models or the
propositions just mentioned are examined closely, it often turns
out that they overwhelmingly focus on one or another of the
Easton categories.

In Soviet studies, the totalitarian model or the successor-
directed society models deal almost exclusively with the output
side of politics – with decisions taken by leaders and imposed on
society. They say almost nothing about inputs or even the black
box, except that (at least by implication) there are no inputs and
that the dictator decides everything on the basis of his own values.
Similarly, George Breslauer's 'welfare-state authoritarianism'
focuses only on governmental outputs.[5] On the other hand, my
model of 'institutional pluralism', or other models within the
interest-group approach, deal primarily with the input side: the
relationship of the political authorities to demands and the
supports generated in the process.[6]

The problem, however, goes deeper than scholars talking past
each other. Obviously political scientists are not just interested in
inputs or outputs. They are interested in the relationships
between them. For example, do different institutional arrangements affect the relationship between inputs and outputs? There
is a very real sense in which this relationship between inputs and
outputs (usually phrased as the question of power) is the crucial
question in political science.

But if our models tend to focus on only one side of the political
process, how do we answer the questions that we agree are the
most important? Usually through unspoken assumptions and conceptual confusion. Most of the key concepts of political science
have several different meanings, and we slip back and forth between them. All the problems with the concept of democracy –
the possibility of dictatorship of the majority and the need for
constitutional restraints on the majority and its representatives –
have been discussed for centuries, but in everyday language
'democracy' can mean either rule by the majority or full protection of individual freedom from majority action. 'Dictatorship'
can mean rule by one man, and it can mean a regime that is
repressive in its action.[7] (A phrase like 'party dictatorship' or
'military dictatorship' does not necessarily imply a single leader.)

Not by coincidence, one of the definitions of a confused con-

cept tends to deal with the input side of the political process and
the other with the output side, and the two tend to merge in our
minds. A democracy is not only a system with freedom of making
demands and of choosing between leadership candidates, but also
a system whose outputs are what society wants and which rests on
consent. A dictatorship is government dominated by one man,
which suppresses demands and dictates policies unwanted by
society and whose support is maintained by force. All this would
be fine if there were, in fact, necessary relationships (or non-
relationships) between inputs and outputs in different forms of
government, but, alas, these relationships have not been demonstrated and they clearly do not exist in all circumstances.[8] (One
can cite cases – for example, the American South a century ago –
when the majority was demanding severe repression of a
minority.)

It has been an awareness of the difficulties of these everyday
words that has led political scientists to abandon them, but the
problems that created the difficulties still remain. The new concepts that are advanced usually become popular precisely to the
extent that they 'resolve' difficulties and retain credibility
through ambivalence.

II

The concepts of pluralism and corporatism are perfect examples
of the tendency to ambiguity. Pluralism was originally developed
in Great Britain as an attack upon the notion of a sovereign state
which had a special role in defining and promoting the national
good. The pluralists proclaimed the legitimacy of the group as
autonomous from the state. They saw the best defence of freedom
to be a diffusion of power to a plurality of groups, with the state
occupying a mediating role or perhaps simply being one of the
groups. But British pluralism, it should be emphasized, was
developed in a reaction to the increasing power of the state, and
hence it was more a normative concept of what should be rather
than a purported description of reality.

In American political science, however, those who espoused the
term pluralism were usually New Deal liberals who found the
increasing role of the government quite congenial – who, indeed,
were usually calling for an increase in the role of the Presidency
and federal planning. Moreover, as these scholars used it,
pluralism was meant to be a descriptive term. The American

pluralists wanted to describe the United States that they saw and to suggest that it conformed to the values of a constitutional democracy, even if the evidence of apathy, ignorance and irrationality revealed by public opinion polls indicated that it did not correspond to the individualistic, rationalistic model of democracy.

As a result, the state in American pluralism has a very different appearance from that in British pluralism. Mayor Richard Lee, who is the hero of Robert Dahl's *Who Governs?*, plays quite an active role, and this is typical of the American pluralists' attitude to the state:

> The difference between the European and the American conceptions of a pluralist state is . . . that American pluralist theories see the group as exerting an influence in order to persuade the government to perfect some substantive good which will be in the interest of that group. . . . These theories assume that the government will, and ought to, play an active and substantive role in determining the course of events. . . . between these contemporary American theories and the notion of pluralism advocated by Figgis, there is a great gulf fixed.[9]

Indeed, much of the American pluralist literature spoke of a merger of interest groups and the state, of the merger of individual interest groups with individual agencies of the government, or of interest group leaders being members of a common 'leadership echelon', of which governmental officials were also a part. Pluralists spoke of 'whirlpools' or 'triangles' which included the interest group, the relevant Congressional committee, and the relevant governmental department. They emphasized – in fact, called for – direct interest-group participation in the various specialized spheres of administration. In the words of a leading critic, Theodore Lowi, such participation 'became synonymous with self-government, first for reasons of strategy, then by belief that the two were indeed synonymous'.[10] Yet, much of the British imagery of pluralism still remained, and especially in comparative discussions, groups were portrayed as wholly autonomous of government, channels from society to the state.

Corporatism too has no agreed-upon meaning, and it is fraught with as much or more ambiguity than is pluralism. The term was popularized in the twentieth century as a description of right-wing dictatorial regimes (the article on corporatism in *The International Encyclopedia of the Social Sciences* simply says 'See Fascism'),[11] and many political scientists (notably Alfred Stepan) continue to define it in terms of 'political structures consciously imposed by political élites on civil society' – that is, as a deliberate technique of élite control.[12] The most frequently cited article on corporatism (that by Philippe Schmitter) likewise sees corporatism as 'an imperative necessity for [the maintenance of] a stable bourgeois-dominant regime', but Schmitter focuses on the type of corporatism that he sees as having gradually evolved in Western Europe in response to the needs of the élite and the system.[13] He distinguishes between 'state corporatism' – the Latin American variety more akin to that later described by Stepan – and 'societal corporatist systems', but his generalizations deal almost exclusively with the latter.[14]

The concept of corporatism is also quite ambiguous in its normative overtones. It was meant to be very positive when it was used in fascist Italy (it emphasized state promotion of the common good), but scholars very critical of fascism picked it up and used it as a term of criticism. Schmitter himself asserted that 'the most difficult task is to strip the concept of its pejorative tone and implications'.[15] The negative connotations of the term are still widespread, especially in discussions of Latin America, but in discussions of Western Europe the word is now frequently used in a more neutral sense or even in the original positive sense.[16]

With both pluralism and corporatism ambiguous, a comparison of the two is doubly difficult. The situation is further complicated by the fact that the two concepts have a number of similarities, including many of the same weaknesses. In the words of Birgitta Nedelmann and Kurt G. Meier, 'the very fixation of the concept of corporatism with the previously dominant model of pluralism contains a number of pitfalls. By taking over the dimensions of the latter . . . one risks importing the same conceptual and theoretical difficulties already connected with their previous utilization.'[17]

In particular, corporatism, like pluralism, deals almost exclusively with the input side of politics. Schmitter has been very explicit in defining corporatism as 'a system of interest and/or attitude representation', a 'mode of interest intermediation'.[18] Like pluralism, corporatism centres on the tricky concept of 'group', and, by focusing on state-sanctioned associations, it runs an even greater danger than the pluralists of reifying groups. By concentrating on groups that are successful and by treating as unimportant those that are not legitimated by the government, it has a tendency to intensify a problem already present to some extent in the debate about pluralism: a blurring of the distinction between interest articulation or participation on the one hand and influence or power on the other.

To the extent that the corporatist model takes the form emphasized by Stepan rather than Schmitter and emphasizes 'the state' as an independent entity divorced from social forces, it begins to encounter the very real problems with the concept of the state that led to the rejection of old-time jurisprudence and the development of political science nearly a century ago. It ignores the question that has been at the heart of political science – what influences the attitudes and the actions of the state and what is the relationship of this to other variables such as institutional structure, political stability, and so forth? Indeed, it ignores the obvious fact that the state is itself segmented (for example, note the differences of perspective among the Departments of Agriculture, Commerce and Labor in the United States) and that this segmentation needs to be at least partially understood in terms of different societal interests.

To the extent that the corporatist model is used in its Western European variant, the question that becomes empirically difficult is how to decide whether a country corresponds to the American conception of pluralism or to 'societal corporatism'. After all, Robert Dahl's analysis of New Haven did emphasize the key role of Mayor Lee; it emphasized specialized, segmental decision-making ('minorities rule'); and it was savaged by critics for allegedly underestimating the intensity of conflict in America and for developing an ideology of social harmony. The corporatists sometimes now criticize the pluralists for neglecting phenomena that in the recent past they were accused of overemphasizing.

In Western Europe or the United States, one sees the whole range of associations suggested by any classic pluralist model, not to speak of unorganized interests. One sees some associations more closely linked with government than others, but there are undoubtedly more associations independent of the state than not. The labelling of West Europe or the United States as 'corporatist' must rest on the judgement that associations linked with the state are the more important and influential ones.

Such a judgement, it should be emphasized, is a value one. It usually implies, for example, that economic-planning decisions are more important than value conflicts in which autonomous groups may be more important. It surely implies that groups involved in ongoing decision-making are more important than those who first raise an issue. (The typical pattern is for major changes to be first raised by non-Establishment groups, and then either for the issue to be taken over by other groups or for the non-Establishment groups to change their character as bureaucracies arise to administer the programme or law they succeed in having enacted.)

In addition, the observation of a linkage between associations and the state does not in itself say anything about the nature of that linkage. Is the linkage a sign that the pluralist image is correct, that there is no state but a series of governmental institutions that really are group representatives? Or does it mean that there has been state co-optation and management of group representation? Does the correspondence between a governmental decision and a group proposal show the power of the group, or may it simply be a coincidence (or evidence of governmental shaping of the group proposal), with the power really in the hands of the government?

In the real world, any government – even Stalin's – must be taking decisions that – by coincidence or not – correspond to some combination of leadership, bureaucratic and societal influences. The kinds of judgements that lead to calling the pattern of 'important' interest representation in one system pluralist and that in another corporatist are extremely subtle and difficult ones. This is especially so if, as Schmitter argues, corporatism and pluralism 'often . . . produce generally similar outcomes'.[19] It will require a herculean effort to avoid the danger that Schmitter himself pointed out: that we will consider interest representation which we like 'pluralist' and that which we dislike 'corporatist'.[20]

The problem of distinguishing between pluralism and corporatism in the Soviet setting is particularly great. Whatever the faults of those discussing pluralism in the Soviet Union, they never made the mistake of thinking that they were talking about voluntary associations elected by their members. Instead, they were talking about 'interests' represented by or embodied in governmental agencies and of a 'group struggle' that had to take place within a tightly structured and restrictive framework.[21] One may not like the concept of institutional pluralism for one reason or another, but its author can read the description of the Soviet Union as a corporatist system with a sense of complete familiarity – and, indeed, even with the sense that he is reading an analysis of the Brezhnev era that he had a major role in developing.

III

What, then, are we to say about the use of the pluralist and corporatist models in discussing the Soviet Union? The first correct conclusion, no doubt, is that neither should be used. A man who bowed to editorial pressure to coin 'institutional pluralism' is hardly in a position to cast a stone, but at least he can speak with experience. As one surveys the history of Soviet studies, the striking thing is how obsessed we have been with 'models'. But our models have really been labels, a shorthand phrase for an extended definition. Every change of leader or prediction of future evolution has been encapsulated in a model – or rather in a variety of competing models. The atypicality of this procedure is highlighted by a comparison with scholarship on the American political system, where such a practice is almost totally absent.

If the purpose of models on the Soviet Union is to develop a label in order to 'provide a better description of that system',[22] very serious problems arise. In the first place, models must use words, and words – especially words in the political sphere – inevitably have a variety of meanings in everyday or scholarly discourse. Regardless of how precisely a scholar tries to define his or her terms, he or she will surely be damned (or occasionally praised) for implications that flow from other definitions. This extends to normative implications. The author of the model of institutional pluralism argued – and very explicitly so – that in the Brezhnev era Soviet health policy was largely being made by the doctors, transportation policy by the railroads, and defence policy by the military and the defence industry, and that the Soviet Union was paying a heavy price for this interest-group domination of policy. Perhaps if the phrase 'selfish interest group' had been used in the analysis, the meaning would have been clearer, but the use of the word 'pluralism', even if highly qualified, seemed unavoidably to convey the impression that the Soviet system was being praised. The resulting emotional reaction prevented any serious consideration of the analytical and theoretical points being made.

Even aside from the problems resulting from confusion and ambiguity, a second and even more basic problem arises with our type of models. In the real world, no country can ever correspond completely to any model (or ideal-type, to use the more correct term). As a consequence, we inevitably will be driven to such imprecise statements as 'the Soviet Union is a mixture of corporatist types'.[23] Moreover, the label serves little purpose unless it is implicitly comparative – unless it distinguishes the country from other types of systems. It may be that 'labels facilitate comparisons across different political-economic systems',[24] but the comparison is one between ideal-types – that is between simplifications rather than of concrete political phenomena.

The kind of models or ideal-types that we use can serve a number of functions. Clearly the process of labelling may make an ideological normative point. It can provide a catch-word that serves to gather attention and focus debate (and, since it inevitably will be understood in different ways, provide the occasion for endless articles that permit scholars to publish rather than perish). However, the most useful formulation in terms of advancing understanding is to highlight phenomena and relationships that were poorly understood in the past, to raise questions that lead to new and productive research.

From this perspective, incompleteness of a model is not necessarily harmful. A model or concept that *de facto* deals only with the input or output side of politics, that highlights unexpected similarities or differences between political systems, may be enormously useful in stimulating research and analysis that would not otherwise be undertaken. Moreover, the usefulness of a model can depend on the framework in which it arises. A confused or ambiguous concept or model which corresponds to the conventional wisdom and which only obscures problems may be useful for ideological purposes, but it is worthless from a scientific point of view. The very same ambiguous model which illuminates neglected phenomena or relationships or raises unexpected questions may be extremely valuable.

It is, however, crucial that scholars be aware of what is happening. Concepts or models whose incompleteness is extremely useful for heuristic scholarly purposes can become treated, to some extent by their author but even more by critics, as complete summaries of the political system. If our purpose is a real advancing of knowledge, it is important to try to understand the insight embodied in a model or concept – the point that was trying to be made – rather than simply engage in destructive polemics.

The effort to apply interest group and pluralist concepts to the Soviet Union should be understood in these terms (and the scholars associated with this effort were extremely insistent at the time of the limits on their aims). The specialists on the Soviet Union who began to use the term pluralism or pluralistic came out of the American political science tradition, and they naturally employed these concepts in the American sense. They were trying to describe the functioning of the Soviet system rather than to prescribe for it. The parallels with pluralism which they saw were certainly not with the British 'stateless' pluralism, but with the pluralism of American political science in which the government played an important role, in which different parts of the government come to represent or even merge with the interest groups with which they deal.

Of course, the specialists who used the term pluralism to refer to the Soviet Union were a diverse group, and they varied in what they drew from the Western literature. At one extreme, some scholars did no more than insist that Soviet society had pluralistic elements. Reacting either against Hannah Arendt's conception of an atomized society or the earlier Soviet propaganda image of a monolithic society and Party, these scholars simply argued that Soviet society has many groups with different views and interests.

A second group of scholars gave their definition of pluralism a political connotation as well, but they spoke primarily about the pluralism of political inputs. This was particularly true of those speaking explicitly about interest groups. In positing a 'pluralism of élites', Gordon Skilling, for example, placed his greatest emphasis on the argument 'that a number of political groups exist and possess some means of giving expression to their interests and to conflicting views on public policy'. This analysis certainly included ample room for societal influence on policy, but the limits on group influence were also stressed, and Skilling saw 'imperfect monism' as one proper description of the system.[25]

To a considerable extent, the central aim of these scholars was to call attention to the existence of interest articulation in the Soviet Union, of the input side of politics. In Skilling's words, 'the

model of communist politics implicit in most Western analysis
seemed, strangely enough, to be exclusively concerned with
"outputs," i.e., the imposition of binding decisions, and to be
entirely lacking in the "input" regarded by Easton as an essential
element of every political system.'[26] The purpose of this criticism
was to suggest a series of research questions, a whole direction of
scholarly work that had been largely neglected, and Skilling
himself commissioned such research for a conference on interest
groups, which became the basis for his famous book.

The model of institutional pluralism, with which I have been
associated, went well beyond the arguments of the second group
of scholars working with the concept of pluralism. This model
took for granted pluralism both in society and in political inputs.
Much of the concrete research of its author since 1965 has been
and continues to be on the nature of inputs and of the policy
process in the Soviet system, but the model had a more ambitious
purpose than to legitimate the study of inputs. That had already
been done in Skilling's advocacy of the interest group approach.

The model of institutional pluralism was meant to highlight an
important change that its author saw occurring in the Soviet
system after the removal of Khrushchev. In the Khrushchev era,
the policy outcomes had been affected in significant part by the
arbitrary intervention of the leader, but in the Brezhnev period
they seemed to be largely determined by specialized policy complexes that bore some resemblance to the triangle of executive
department, congressional committee and interest group found
in the pluralist model. That is there seemed to be occurring a
devolution of *de facto* power from the leader or leaders col-
lectively (although not, of course, of the final power to decide) to
a type of differentiated 'leadership echelon' that cut across the
line between state and interest group. (The Ministry of Health is
both a 'state' institution and the representative of the medical
establishment in the broader political process.) Without
leadership dictation by a Stalin or Khrushchev, a bigger role in
the policy process was characterized more than before by bargaining in a framework of limited demands, by incrementalism in the
pace of policy change and budgetary allocations, and by
'minorities rule' (to use Dahl's term).[27]

From a tactical point of view, it clearly would have been wiser
to label the new developments of the Brezhnev period with a
normatively negative phrase such as 'bureaucratic domination'

rather than one containing the normatively positive word 'pluralism', however qualified. Yet the intention was not to suggest any identity between the Soviet and Western political systems, but to raise a theoretical point. In practice, the American pluralists had emphasized those aspects of the American political process which were part of what C.P. Snow called 'closed politics': bargaining, élite representation of mass interests, power to the interested participants, 'responsible' demands, incrementalism, and so forth. The highly visible 'open politics' of the system – demonstrations, confrontation, even to some extent elections – were treated as more peripheral in their impact upon the final policy outcome. 'Institutional pluralism' was meant to point out that many of the features of 'closed politics' which political scientists had been emphasizing in their discussions of the West could have close parallels in political systems with very different 'open politics' and institutional arrangements. The purpose was to stimulate thought and research about the determinants of 'responsiveness' and about the relative impact of open politics and closed politics in determining 'who gets what' in Western societies.

All models, all research strategies, all theoretical questions seem to have a natural life span whether the questions they raise are answered or not. There is no question but that the thrust of Gordon Skilling's appeal has been successful. We are much more aware of the input side of Soviet politics than we were when he wrote his article, and we know much more about it. It shows no disrespect to the pluralist movement in Soviet studies to ask whether it may have exhausted its major impetus, whether we should move on to new concepts (perhaps corporatism) which can move us ahead more rapidly.

Even aside from the fact that the amount of research on the input side of Soviet politics has increased dramatically in the last fifteen years, the various types of models of pluralism clearly do have limitations when used to illuminate the West or the Soviet system. One obvious problem is the difficulty in disentangling the normative and descriptive aspects of the concept of pluralism. Often one cannot tell whether a critic of a pluralist analysis of the West is complaining about the analysis as a description or about the suggestion – real or imagined – that the real is ideal. Unquestionably there is something in the original that has provoked this response. As the experience of the model of institutional pluralism illustrates, the normative aspects of the debate about pluralism in America seem inexorably to intrude into discussions of pluralistic elements in the Soviet system.

Second, although the classic pluralist model suggests that the free competition of groups promotes social justice and harmony, its very nature directs the attention of the scholar to areas in which people have differences rather than those in which they have common goals. It focuses on the politics by which conflict is resolved or mediated rather than the politics in which conflict is absent or by which it is muted. This tendency in pluralism leads it to the neglect of the covert exercise of élite power for which it was criticized in the mid-1960s, but it also leads it to downplay the phenomena highlighted by Talcott Parsons's definition of power: the community coming together to achieve common goals that are otherwise unachievable.

Third, pluralism focuses almost exclusively on the input side of the political process. Even if it were asserting (which it definitely does not) that policy is the automatic resultant of a parallelogram of social forces, that would not change the fact that governmental decisions – however determined – are restrictive of various kinds of individual freedom and are backed by the threat and sometimes the imposition of punishment. Democratic ideology has historically tried to obscure this fact in its discussion of 'consent of the governed', but, as President Reagan has made abundantly clear in his long campaign against government interference in people's lives, the problem will not go away.

The relative neglect of the output side of the political process creates a real problem in any comprehensive comparison of political systems. The major differences between the Soviet Union and the United States today are not nearly so great in the degree of influence of establishment interest groups or even the broad mass of the population on substantive, within-system policy as they are in the scope of governmental action and its restrictive character. The thoroughgoing nationalization of the economy enormously increases the number of questions decided in the political sphere. Moreover, if one distinguishes between 'democracy' (popular influence on policy) and 'liberalism' (degree of individual freedom) in the way that C.B. Macpherson does,[28] there is no question but that the Soviet Union has been and remains a very illiberal state.

IV

The question is: does corporatism as an organizing concept help us to solve these problems in the pluralist approach? Does it lead to new discoveries and does it further understanding?

In some respects the corporatist model clearly does represent an advance over the pure pluralist model. It does get away from any suggestion of totally autonomous groups or of equality of opportunity for all groups. Its emphasis on the activist role of governmental agencies and officials is a useful reminder of a fact well-known to pluralists, but played down in their imagery. It does emphasize an important aspect of modern government – the attempt to manage the economy in order to produce sustained economic growth. (Of course, national leaders who are subject to constant cross-pressures on how to achieve this general goal might find the pluralist emphasis on a multiplicity of self-interests more relevant than the corporatist emphasis on common goals.)

In other respects, however, corporatism is a less satisfactory advance on American pluralism. In general terms, the major defect of corporatism from this point of view is that it shares with pluralism a focus on the input side of the political system and even on groups. Consequently it tends to stimulate many of the same research questions and to draw attention away from similar ones. In particular, it does not call attention to two major questions on which more comparative analysis is needed: (1) the degree and nature of restrictions on individual freedom (that is, freedom beyond that to make political inputs), and (2) the impact of the mechanisms by which those in the black box are chosen (that is, the old question of the impact of elections). In this sense Breslauer's 'welfare-state authoritarianism' is more useful if it is more than a label, if it leads to serious thought about the differences in governmental and non-governmental restrictions of freedom in different political systems and about the causes of welfare-state measures in a system without elections. (However, since it focuses on the output side, it is a more useful supplement to input-oriented models such as pluralism or corporatism rather than a substitute for them.)

Indeed, even on the input side of politics, the more interesting questions are raised not by another concept which focuses on groups, but by work which calls attention to the role of scholarly specialists who purport to analyse objectively rather than to speak as the representative of some group.[29] Often the focus is on the advisory role of specialists in the near or medium term, but the least well-explored question in political science – and, therefore, perhaps the most important – is the gradual impact of new ideas (for example the rise of monetarism and supply side economics in the United States in the 1970s) and those who generate and promote them.

In terms of Soviet studies, the significance of the corporatist model depends to a very large degree upon the variant that is used. The concept has the potential of being enormously useful in advancing understanding about Western Europe (or the United States), for it highlights phenomena that are not emphasized by conventional concepts. If the concept of corporatism becomes firmly accepted as appropriate for Western systems, it certainly should be used for the Soviet Union as well. It would serve much the same function in Soviet studies as pluralism without confusing matters with its emotional overtones. By treating the Soviet political system as having important parallels with the West European ones (of course, without being identical), it would lead to many of the same research questions, including (in my opinion) the most important: what difference does it make in terms of outcomes if a corporatist system permits the existence of non-corporatist associations (as in Western Europe) or essentially bans them (as in the Soviet Union)?

If, on the other hand, the Stepan variant of corporatism is used in Soviet studies, the consequences are very different. We will have returned a long way to the old directed society model, with a strong tendency for people to substitute the reified 'state' for the reified 'party'. State corporatism does at least admit of the input side of politics, which is an advance on the old totalitarian and directed society models, but my suspicion is that this will fade from view in our descriptions of the 'corporatist' Soviet Union. The comparative textbooks will compare Soviet corporatism with Western pluralism, Soviet 'groups' nearly totally manipulated by the all-powerful state with 'autonomous' groups in the West. We will be able to retain all the old black-and-white stereotypes, with all the desired ideological overtones.

Whichever variant of the corporatist model is used, a weary and sinking feeling sets in as one thinks of the differences in the definitions and normative overtones. If we adopt corporatism as a model for the Soviet system, we surely are in for yet another round of straw men, of definitions that float back and forth, of criticisms based on the wrong definitions, and so forth.

Surely it would be far more useful if we focused less on labels and on classifications than on questions. Most of our generalizations about the relationships of inputs, institutions and outputs really rest on ideological assumptions rather than on solid scholarly research. The concrete work in which, for instance, Valerie Bunce has been engaged furnishes an excellent illustration of the type of question and research project that should be at the heart of comparative political science.[30] Concepts like pluralism or corporatism can be enormously useful in pointing to questions that should be raised, but the main work of political science should be to try to answer such questions.

To the extent that labels become inevitable, there is much to be said for using the old familiar ones: 'Western democracy', 'Communist regime', 'Soviet system', and so on. Everybody knows that they are general and imprecise, and, as a consequence, they do not really get in the way of understanding in the way that terms like pluralism and corporatism can. They do not draw us into the endless search for better systems of classification – a search that has consumed enormous energy but that has had very limited payoff, that has led to the very flawed types of debate discussed in this article.

Whatever labels are used for the Soviet Union, the absolutely crucial point to understand is that in any meaningful sense there *is* some societal autonomy in the Soviet Union. The American military is a hierarchy, strictly subordinated to the President. All officers are in the *nomenklatura* of the President to the extent that the President must sign all their commissions. The American military does function fairly pliably in the output sphere, but it certainly seems wrong to deny it all autonomy in the input sphere. Officers and offices have ideas, they try to push them, and sometimes (in fact, often) they have influence.

The same is true of Soviet officials, even if they are in the *nomenklatura* of the Party. Fifty per cent of all college men are Party members, and they are forced to participate in committee work as a condition of membership. As burdensome as committee work always is, it sometimes brings influence to the participants. Moreover, the way in which decisions are drafted at all levels – in committees on which representatives of other interested ministries and other hierarchies are given seats – takes for granted that ministries will have different points of view and will fight for them.

In addition to participating in closed committee sessions, large numbers of Soviet citizens also participate in politically relevant debates in the published media. Americans are aware that there have been economic debates on Libermanism, and they would not be surprised if they were told that there are free-swinging debates on how to handle the new problems of automobile parking, on how to maintain academic standards in high school as the country adopts universal secondary education, or on the extent to which pensions should be reduced if old people have outside earnings. However, these debates also extend to the most fundamental ideological and political questions. Scholars debate whether the Marxist scheme of historical evolution (slave-holding to feudal to capitalist) is right, whether Third World countries usually have dominant classes, whether revolutions are probable in the Third World other than pre-industrial countries such as Ethiopia and Afghanistan, whether the American hostility towards the Soviet Union is unchangeable.[31]

If we do not want to label this type of political activity as a limited form of pluralism, that causes no insuperable problem, although it seems to me we forego a quite useful heuristic tool by failing to do so. What *is* important is that we understand the reality that the label tried to convey – and this is important for reasons far beyond the development of political science. Whatever evolution in views of the Soviet Union has occurred within political science, the old dogmatic views have a deep hold in large and influential portions of the American population. In the United States, we need to understand the debates and politics that are occurring within the Soviet Union, we need to understand the Soviet options, we need to know how the debates are evolving, we need to try to understand how the ideology is shifting. Fifteen years of work on the input side of Soviet politics has made far too little impact on old images of an all-powerful state, directing society and pursuing foreign policy on the basis of a long-established master plan, and it seems to me that the broader audience is one that we should keep in mind as well as the professional one as we decide what is important to study and understand.

NOTES AND REFERENCES

1. H. Gordon Skilling, 'Interest Groups and Communist Politics', *World Politics*, 18 (April 1966) 435–51.
2. Philippe Schmitter, 'Still the Century of Corporatism?', *Review of Politics*, 36 (January 1974) 93–4.
3. Valerie Bunce and John M. Echols III, 'Soviet Politics in the Brezhnev Era: "Pluralism" or "Corporatism"?', in Donald R. Kelley (ed.), *Soviet Politics in the Brezhnev Era* (New York, 1980) 4–7.
4. See, for example, William Odom, 'A Dissenting View on the Group Approach to Soviet Politics', *World Politics*, 29 (July 1976) 542–67.
5. George W. Breslauer, 'On the Adaptability of Soviet Welfare-State Authoritarianism', in Karl Ryavec (ed.), *The Communist Party and Soviet Society* (Amherst, Mass., 1978) 3–25.
6. See Jerry F. Hough, *The Soviet Union and Social Science Theory* (Cambridge, Mass., 1977) 10–11, 22–4, 69–79; and Jerry F. Hough and Merle Fainsod, *How the Soviet Union is Governed* (Cambridge, Mass., 1979) 547–8.
7. As Harold S. Quigley pointed out long ago, 'dictatorship may be viewed either as the rule of an individual exercising absolute rule or as a condition of absolute rule, however produced.' 'Dictatorship in the Far East' in Guy Stanton Ford (ed.), *Dictatorship in the Modern World* (London, 1935) 154.
8. See the discussion in Hough, *The Soviet Union and Social Science Theory*, 173–89.
9. David Nicholls, *The Pluralist System* (New York, 1975) 118.
10. Theodore J. Lowi, *The End of Liberalism* (New York, 1969) 75. Lowi basically accepts the pluralist image of how the American system works, but sharply criticizes the argument that this system is good.
11. *The International Encyclopedia of the Social Sciences* (New York, 1964) 3, 404.
12. Alfred Stepan *The State and Society: Peru in Comparative Perspective* (Princeton, N.J., 1978) 46–113. The quotation is from 47.
13. Schmitter, 'Still the Century of Corporatism?', 107.
14. Corporatism has also been used to refer not to institutional arrangements but to a society with segmented groups; however, this third definition has not gained enough currency to cause great confusion. Ronald Rogowski and Lois Wasserspring, *Does Political Development Exist? Corporatism in Old and New Societies* (Beverly Hills, Calif., 1971).
15. Schmitter, 'Still the Century of Corporatism?', 86.
16. See Leo Panitch, 'The Development of Corporatism in Liberal Democracies', *Comparative Political Studies*, X (April 1977) 61–90.
17. Birgitta Nedelmann and Kurt G. Meier, 'Theories of Contemporary Corporatism: Static or Dynamic?', *Comparative Political Studies*, X (April 1977) 39–60.
18. Schmitter, 'Still the Century of Corporatism?', 86; Philippe C. Schmitter, 'Modes of Interest Intermediation and Models of Societal Change in Western Europe', *Comparative Political Studies*, X (April 1977) 7–38.
19. Schmitter, 'Still the Century of Corporatism?', 102.
20. Ibid., 86.

21. Jerry F. Hough, 'The Party Apparatchiki', in H. Gordon Skilling and Franklyn Griffiths (eds), *Interest Groups in Soviet Politics* (Princeton, N.J., 1971) 87–92.
22. Bunce and Echols, 'Soviet Politics in the Brezhnev Era', 2.
23. Ibid., 19.
24. Ibid., 2.
25. H. Gordon Skilling, 'Interest Groups and Communist Politics: An Introduction', 17, and H. Gordon Skilling, 'Groups in Soviet Politics: Some Hypotheses', 45, in Skilling and Griffiths (eds), *Interest Groups in Soviet Politics*.
26. Skilling, 'Interest Groups and Communist Politics', 8.
27. Robert A. Dahl, *Who Governs?* (New Haven, Conn., 1961).
28. C.B. Macpherson, *The Real World of Democracy* (Toronto, 1965).
29. This point is raised in the Soviet context by Peter H. Solomon Jr, *Soviet Criminologists and Criminal Policy: Specialists in Policy Making* (New York, 1978).
30. See, for example, Valerie Bunce, *Do New Leaders Make a Difference? Executive Succession and Public Policy under Capitalism* (Princeton, N. J., 1981).
31. This subject is being explored in a book the author is writing for the Brookings Institution. For preliminary results of this work, see Jerry F. Hough, 'Evolution in the Soviet World View', *World Politics*, 32 (July 1980) 509–30; and Jerry F. Hough, 'The Evolving Soviet Debate on Latin America', *Latin American Research Review*, 16, no. 1 (1981) 124–43.

4 Pluralism, Power and the Soviet Political System: A Comparative Perspective*

ARCHIE BROWN

Debate among Western scholars on how power is distributed within the Soviet Union has been vigorous ever since the idea that totalitarianism was the key to understanding the Soviet system came under serious attack in the 1960s. In the Soviet Union itself the same decade saw the opening shots fired in a campaign to have power relations within the Soviet and other political systems discussed more realistically and less propagandistically than hitherto in the context of the development of a discipline of political science.[1] It is only in recent years, however, that something like a debate on the nature of political power has got underway in specialized Soviet journals and small-circulation books. This paper will juxtapose these writings of Soviet scholars with the writings of Western political scientists on the nature of power relations within the Soviet system, partly because of the intrinsic interest of both bodies of writing and partly to see what relevance, if any, the Soviet discussions have to Western arguments concerning the nature of the Soviet system. Some attention is paid to theoretical accounts of the relationship between state and society, a common theme in the two bodies of work.

* I should like to record my gratitude to Robert A. Dahl, Michael Lessnoff, David Nicholls, T.H. Rigby and Gordon Wightman who read a previous draft of this essay and commented helpfully upon it.

The first of the two main sections into which the essay is divided considers briefly certain problems involved in conceptualizing Soviet politics and goes on to offer a critique of three of the major ways in which the Soviet system has been viewed by Western scholars – as totalitarian, pluralist and corporatist. The second section looks, first, at the hitherto little-known Soviet discussion of the relationship between the concepts of 'political power', 'the state' and 'the political system', and second at theoretical statements recently advanced by Soviet scholars on the delicate issue of state–society relations and the question of the 'relative autonomy' of the state. As part of the analysis of the different conceptualizations of the Soviet system, the essay introduces some recent evidence on power relations within the system and attempts also to put these relations in a comparative perspective.

'Pluralism', which is a major theme of the essay, is discussed more often by Western political scientists with an interest in the Soviet Union than by their Soviet colleagues, though Western pluralist theory (not to mention practice) attracts a fair amount of criticism in works specifically directed against 'bourgeois ideology'. Only infrequently does the concept of pluralism surface in more general Soviet discussions of the theory of the state. In contrast, however, the issue of autonomy – which is of central importance in Western theories of pluralism – is well to the fore in recent Soviet scholarship, though there is a fundamental difference in the focus of attention of Western and Soviet political scientists when they write about this. Those Western political scientists who apply the concept 'pluralism' to the Soviet polity are not generally those who pay most attention to the issue of autonomy. They emphasize rather the variety of influences *on* the government[2] by outside bodies or the variety of points of view and influences *within* government of different organizations and interests. Western *theorists* of pluralism, however, tend to stress (as a central feature of pluralism) the relative autonomy of society generally, and of organizations and groups specifically, *from* control by the government. 'Autonomy from' rather than 'variety of influences on' is a major emphasis also in certain recent Soviet writing on the state – but with an important distinction from the corresponding Western work. When these particular Soviet scholars write of relative autonomy *from* control, it is the 'relative autonomy' of the state from society (not of society from the state) which they choose to stress.

In this last respect, the discussions of the Soviet scholars have more in common with those of Western Marxists (including 'critical' Marxists) than with the writings of non-Marxist political scientists. This is not surprising, for both Soviet and Western Marxists belong to an intellectual tradition in which a socio-economic determinism has been a prominent part and in which, in the words of a Western Marxist who himself stresses the relative autonomy of the state, there remains 'an insistence on the "primacy" of the "economic base" which must not be under-stated'.[3] An apparent independent power on the part of the state presents a greater intellectual challenge to Marxists than to non-Marxist political scientists, since many of the latter have long taken it for granted. The Soviet case itself has, indeed, more than any other, forced this issue on to the agenda of the serious Marxist. The stress upon the relative autonomy of 'the state', or 'the political system', in some Soviet writings is frequently (though seldom overtly) part of their authors' attempts to comprehend Russian and especially Soviet history just as much of the emphasis among Western Marxists over the past two decades on the 'relative autonomy' or 'high degree of autonomy' of 'the state', or 'the superstructure', is a product of their attempt to come to terms with the Soviet experience.[4]

I. SOVIET POWER RELATIONS THROUGH WESTERN EYES

Problems of concept formation

All attempts to find one term, or one concept, that will encapsulate the essential features of power relations within the Soviet – or, indeed, any other – polity are fraught with serious difficulties. The world of real types is a more difficult one to chart than the universe of ideal types. We might call Bulgaria a Communist Party state of the Soviet type, but attempts to characterize the Soviet Union have to be more inventive if they are not to lapse into absurd tautology. In fact, the whole thrust of the endeavour to find a model or conceptualization that will fit the Soviet Union – if such an endeavour has any point to it at all – is to place the study of Soviet politics within a comparative perspective and to facilitate generalizations about particular types of political systems, in the process clarifying what is distinctive about the

Soviet system and what features it holds in common with other
polities.

The major ways in which the Soviet Union has been characterized by Western political scientists – as totalitarian, as pluralist
and as corporatist (the most recently advanced characterization)
– draw upon concepts that have been elaborated in the course of
study of systems quite different from the Soviet one (as in the case
of pluralism or corporatism) or that have been developed by
studying the Soviet Union in association with a significantly
different system (notably Nazi Germany in the case of totalitarianism). The scope of these concepts varies. The terms totalitarianism and corporatism are generally regarded by those who
use them to interpret the Soviet system as conveying the essence of
the system, as providing the best single key to an understanding of
it. The variations on the pluralist theme – 'institutional
pluralism', 'bureaucratic pluralism', 'centralized pluralism' and
'institutionalized pluralism' – are used by some scholars to
characterize the Soviet system as a whole and by others merely to
describe one important feature of Soviet life.[5]

I shall consider each of these concepts in the order in which
they entered the political science literature relating to the Soviet
Union, but will pay particular attention to pluralistic and quasi-
pluralistic interpretations of the Soviet political system. Such
attention is justified because these interpretations have represented the most serious challenge to the understanding of the
Soviet Union as totalitarian and may, perhaps, by now be
regarded as the intellectually dominant type of interpretation
among Western specialists. They also incorporate some important insights. Yet, at the same time, the formulation of a number
of valid points in pluralist terms has tended to obfuscate important distinctions between the Soviet political system and certain
Western systems and between developments within the Soviet
Union and developments in several other Communist states.

Of particular relevance to the general problem of conceptualizing Communist politics is Giovanni Sartori's criticism of 'conceptual stretching'.[6] Sartori argues that when concepts that have
been developed in the study of one type of political system in one
part of the world are transferred to the study of another type of
political system in a different part of the world, 'the gains in
extensional coverage tend to be matched by losses in connotative
precision'.[7] He recognizes, however, that the broadening of the

meaning of the concepts already to hand represents not only 'the line of least resistance' but also 'a deliberate attempt to make our conceptualizations value free'.[8]

Indeed, the adoption of concepts and techniques of analysis from mainstream political science – a movement that got seriously under way in the 1960s – was based partly on a desire to get away from a separate vocabulary with strong pejorative connotations ('totalitarianism' being a prime example) on the part of many Sovietologists, not only because they felt that they were thereby removing a political bias which was a legacy of the 'Cold War' but also because they felt that by doing so they were making their work in some sense more 'scientific'. Many of the results of the changes that overtook Soviet studies were beneficial, but the 'conceptual stretching' involved had some serious disadvantages, for, as Sartori puts it severely, 'the lower the discriminating power of a conceptual container, the more the facts are misgathered, i.e. the greater the misinformation'.[9] One danger of conceptual stretching is that very frequently major differences between systems are played down while less important similarities are played up, with the result that the gains in universal inclusiveness are largely illusory.[10] (Against these serious disadvantages, we should not, however, overlook several partly compensating benefits to be derived from scholars changing the focus of their conceptual lenses, even if the focus thereby becomes an excessively broad one. In the process of attempting to justify new ways of conceptualizing and classifying the Soviet system, there is no doubt that Sovietologists have come up with much additional information and some fresh insights).

Totalitarianism

Sartori's strictures about the dangers of stretching concepts are explicitly applied to the concept of pluralism, but the disadvantages of conceptual stretching in Soviet studies are by no means confined to the use of that particular concept. They occur in the use of totalitarianism as well. Indeed, it was Alex Inkeles who pointed to one of the central dilemmas with the latter concept: either we keep revising the 'model' in accordance with changing reality within the Soviet Union, so that the Soviet Union remains by definition 'totalitarian' or we stick with a model (or, more precisely, an ideal type) and try to ascertain how far the Soviet

Union has deviated from that model (or ideal type).[11] Though the former course of action can be followed and the concept refined in such a way that the Soviet Union may still not unreasonably be described as totalitarian, this procedure is more misleading than helpful.

Either way, totalitarian interpretations of the Soviet Union suffer from a number of serious shortcomings. First, they have tended to exaggerate the success of the official political socialization effort *vis-à-vis* Soviet society and have assumed the Communist Party itself to be more monolithically united than in fact it is. Second, they have paid very little attention to the policy process, suggesting, usually implicitly, that all policy emanates from the top party leadership. Third, they have contributed virtually nothing to an understanding of political change within the Soviet Union (or other Communist states) and have obscured sources of change other than change initiated by the top leadership or by violent overthrow of the system.

So, though the notion of totalitarianism draws attention to certain important aspects of the Soviet system, it obfuscates as much as it reveals and is particularly unhelpful if we are interested in studying changes within the society and system. It may, nevertheless, be regarded as surprising that in turning away from the concept of totalitarianism, a number of scholars (including some of the best-informed) should have seized upon its antonym, pluralism (albeit a qualified pluralism) rather than upon one of the other variants of authoritarian politics in their efforts to reconceptualize the Soviet system.[12] (While there are enough different definitions of 'totalitarianism' and 'pluralism' to choose from to make it impossible in every case to see one as the antonym of the other, the classic writings on totalitarianism emphasize total power concentrated in the hands of a single leader – or, in later modifications, in the hands of a small ruling group – whereas most definitions of pluralism have in common that they describe a political system in which power is dispersed. In *this* sense, totalitarianism may be regarded as an extreme sub-type of monism and pluralism as its antonym.)

Pluralism

Though the concept of pluralism came to the analysis of Communist politics later than totalitarianism,[13] it has a longer intellectual history. David Nicholls, who has written a substantial study of the pluralism of Figgis and his English contemporaries,[14] has also conveniently isolated 'three varieties of pluralism'[15] – first, 'English political pluralism', the theory found in the writings of Figgis and Laski and others in the first two decades of this century; second, American political pluralism from Bentley to Dahl; and, third, the pluralism of the 'plural society', that is social and cultural sectionalism, or segmentalism, based upon the existence of different ethnic groups. Nicholls very usefully draws attention to the wide range of connotations that the term 'pluralism' has carried and for his part takes '"pluralist state" to refer to a situation in which there are many politically significant groups with cross-cutting membership, and ... pluralism as a belief that such a state is good'.[16]

Throughout its history pluralism has been used as both description and prescription in the context of a number of Western political systems, and, most frequently, that of the United States. If we are to consider it in its prescriptive sense, the question of whether pluralism has been accepted within the Soviet Union can be disposed of very quickly. No ruling Communist Party has accepted *unequivocally* the *principle* of political pluralism, though some of them have had to accommodate themselves to a measure of *de facto* pluralism. Individual Communist scholars within East European countries have accepted pluralism in principle[17] and various non-ruling Communist parties have pledged their support for it,[18] but not even the leadership of the Yugoslav League of Communists under Tito or his successors, the leadership of the Communist Party of Czechoslovakia under Dubček or the leadership of the Polish United Workers' Party under Kania went quite so far.

A number of Soviet scholars have objected, *inter alia*, to the lack of descriptive specificity of pluralism[19] and there is no doubt that the term is still used in very different ways by different scholars. Thus, the Polish political scientists, Jerzy J. Wiatr and Stanislaw Ehrlich, who have long accepted pluralism both normatively and as a description of political relations in Poland (and 'in other socialist countries'), define pluralism more broadly than does, say, Giovanni Sartori. Ehrlich, in a recent article on the relationship of Marxism and pluralism, stresses that '*pluralism is not a characteristic peculiar to some concrete socio-political system or some form of state*' (Ehrlich's italics). Pluralism is the

'current' which 'opposes the uniformisation of public life not
justified by need', the counterposition to 'all monolithic
tendencies', to 'all attempts to monopolise social initiative'.
Ehrlich concludes that while it would be 'nonsensical' to reduce
Marxism to pluralism, 'negation of the pluralist character of the
social and political structures of all societies (except the totalitarian) must be regarded as an extreme distortion of Marxism.
Pluralism, both descriptive and normative, is inseparable from
Marxism'.[20] Wiatr, in somewhat similar vein, has argued that 'in
analyzing the problems of power in the socialist society, one
should direct attention to the nature of political pluralism
characteristic for this system'. By political pluralism, Wiatr
understands the existence in 'political life of organized forces
legally expressing the interest of differentiated social groups' and
holds that, thus conceived, 'political pluralism is an expression
and consequence of social pluralism, socioeconomic differentiation of the society'.[21]

These uses of pluralism are more precise than some of those
that Sartori had in mind when he wrote: 'There is no end to
pluralism, for we are never told what is non-pluralism.' They
would scarcely, however, meet with his approval, for in attempting to rescue the concept from 'conceptual stretching', Sartori
wishes to equate a 'truly pluralistic society' with one 'qualified by
the Western use of the term' and suggests that 'a pluralistic
society is a society whose structural configuration is shaped by
pluralistic beliefs, namely, that all kinds of autonomous sub-units
should develop at all levels, that interests are recognized in their
legitimate diversity, and that dissent, not unanimity, represents
the basis of civility'.[22]

If Nicholls (in his characterization of a 'pluralist state' cited
earlier), Ehrlich and Wiatr are all inclined to stretch the concept
unduly by playing down or ignoring the element of *autonomy*,
Sartori, by making a 'pluralistic society' one 'whose *structural*
configuration is shaped by pluralistic *beliefs*' (my italics), virtually
forecloses any debate on the question of whether pluralism is to
be found in the Soviet Union or any other Communist state. A
better starting-point is provided by Robert A. Dahl in his most
recent work in which he takes the term 'pluralism' to 'refer to
organizational pluralism, that is to the existence of a plurality of
relatively autonomous (independent) organizations (sub-systems)
within the domain of a state' (Dahl's italics). The crux of the
matter is *relative autonomy*, as Dahl recognizes in his pro-

posal of the following definition: 'An organization is relatively autonomous if it undertakes actions that (*a*) are considered harmful by another organization and which (*b*) no other organization, including the government of the state, can prevent, or could prevent except by incurring costs so high as to exceed the gains to the actor from doing so.'[23]

It is a weakness of 'pluralist' interpretations of Soviet politics that they have little, if anything, to say on the question of autonomy. Such interpretations tend to stress the fact that the Soviet party and state leadership does not make up a unified élite, that it is a body in which there are numerous cleavages based, for example, upon the functional and geographical division of responsibilities among different sectors of the all-Union and republican leaderships. They can rightly point also to a body of evidence that suggests that there is substantial *diffusion of influence* within the Soviet Union.[24] However, to equate pluralism with *any* influence on a party or state leadership from outside the ranks of that leadership would mean that even the Soviet Union under Stalin was a pluralist state – surely a *reductio ad absurdum* of such a concept of pluralism.[25] Constraints of time and knowledge and, to some degree, constraints imposed by certain social groups are present in any political system, though it seems reasonable to suppose that these constraining factors have grown in the Soviet Union during the post-Stalin years as a result of the increased specialization of knowledge and the growth (both numerically and in the acquisition of expertise and skills) of the Soviet intelligentsia and working class.

The question, however, is not so much whether any 'elements of pluralism'[26] can ever be detected within the Soviet Union, as whether the Soviet Union should be interpreted as a 'type of pluralist system'.[27] So far as this latter and larger question is concerned, some lessons can be learned from the debate on community power and on pluralism and élites which has been waged by Western (especially American) political scientists and sociologists over many years.[28] The various criticisms of pluralistic analyses of American or West European political systems apply *a fortiori* to pluralistic analyses of the Soviet political system. The control which Soviet leaders have over the political agenda, their control over the flow of information, their capacity to make potential issues non-issues, while not complete, are beyond the dreams even of a Richard Nixon.

Jerry Hough has been the most persuasive advocate of the view that the Soviet Union should be viewed as a type of pluralist system. He has drawn attention to what he calls 'pluralist aspects of the Soviet political system'[29] and has suggested that 'if the Soviet and Western political systems are each visualized as types of pluralist systems, then we are led to explore the respective impact of those aspects of pluralism which they have in common and those on which they differ'.[30] There are, of course, some features that the Soviet system, Western liberal democratic systems and, for that matter, fascist systems have in common. These include rivalries between branches of the bureaucracy and varying degrees of specialist influence in the policy-making process. The trouble with saying that it is a kind of pluralism which they have in common is that this stretches the concept so far that it becomes virtually meaningless and that it plays down differences which are substantially more important than the similarities between the Soviet system and certain Western systems. At least as worrying is the absence of a comparative Communist perspective and the blurring of important distinctions between different Communist states at different times.

To illustrate this last point, Czechoslovakia in 1968 was a pluralistic socialist state, even if it was still a limited pluralism and not a fully democratic socialism. Trade Unions – from the Metal Workers' Union to the Writers' Union – either changed their leaders or forced their existing leaders to be responsive to the demands of their members. On television, radio and in newspapers questions were asked and issues probed which the party leadership made clear it did not want discussed.[31] Public opinion polls on levels of popular trust in individual party leaders were published in the press.[32] There was open debate within the Communist Party itself and there were horizontal as well as vertical links between party organizations.[33] Completely outside the *nomenklatura* system of appointment or approval of office-holders[34] there emerged autonomous political organizations, prominent among which were KAN (the Club of Committed Non-Party Members) and K231 (the organization of former political prisoners).[35]

As is well known, it was the Soviet-led intervention by half a million foreign troops which put an end to pluralistic socialism in Czechoslovakia and the present political arrangements in that country are closely based upon the Soviet model. If personal political rivalries, competition between different branches of the bureaucracy and consultation with specialists (albeit specialists from whose ranks radical political reformers have been purged) are to be the hallmarks of pluralism, then contemporary Czechoslovakia could also be regarded as a pluralist state and the vehement attacks of their contemporary leaders and ideologists on the notion of pluralism might reasonably by regarded as otiose.[36]

In Poland, in 1980–81, to the Catholic Church, which has long been a powerful autonomous force and alternative focus of loyalty to the party, was added the independent trade union movement, Solidarity, which between the late summer of 1980 and December of 1981 extracted a series of concessions from party and government leaders which they were beyond question reluctant to make. A number of demands that were declared to be non-negotiable turned out to be negotiable, and were conceded by a Polish leadership, faced by the actual pressures of the massively supported Solidarity movement.[37] Viewing this independent trade union movement and the Church alongside the Communist Party (the official name of which, the Polish United Workers' Party, acquired an increasingly ironic ring, since the party was deeply divided and a third of its members, not to speak of a majority of the working class, were members also of Solidarity),[38] it is abundantly clear that Poland during 1980 to 1981 was (even in terms of Dahl's stringent definition) *de facto* pluralist.

It is rarely, of course, pluralism unqualified which Western scholars have claimed exists within the Soviet Union, but an 'institutional pluralism', 'bureaucratic pluralism' or, in Jerry Hough's latest variant, 'institutionalised pluralism'.[39] Gordon Skilling, who has taken trouble to indicate that his view that interest groups are to be found within the Soviet Union does not mean he is suggesting that 'genuine pluralism' is to be found there (or, indeed, in any other Communist state), was perhaps nevertheless, the first person to introduce the word 'pluralism' into discussion of Soviet politics when he proposed the term 'pluralism of élites' as one way of characterizing Communist political systems.[40] It is doubtful, however, whether the term 'pluralism', even thus qualified, should be applied so comprehensively to Communist systems or at all to the Soviet system – not least because it blurs the distinction between, on the one hand, the main characteristics of the Soviet political system and, on the other, the clear manifestations of political pluralism that have been seen at different times in Czechoslovakia and Poland.

This is not, by any means, to reject the study of group interests and of opinion groupings (terminology which I prefer to 'interest groups' in this context) within Soviet politics, an area pioneered by Skilling,[41] and the study of institutional interests and relationships, to which Hough has made such a notable contribution.[42] If scholars are more aware than they used to be that within the Soviet Union institutional rivalries are tacitly accepted, that certain party and state institutions may have common interests which differ from those of other party and state institutions, that departmentalism and localism exist, that there is covert competition for political office which takes the form of what some Czech reformists called 'cabinet politics', that federation provides an institutional base for a limited amount of ethnic diversity and promotion of 'national interests', that there is specialist influence on policy-making, that there are opinion groupings within the party, within the intelligentsia and (no doubt) within the wider society, then this body of work has been of value. It has served as a general corrective to the totalitarian model and it has led researchers to uncover concrete details of political life that did not attract much attention among proponents of the totalitarian model of the USSR. But for all that, this does not constitute pluralism.

Apart from the more general objection (already outlined) to the use of 'pluralism' in the context of the Soviet political system, '*institutional* pluralism' and '*bureaucratic* pluralism'[43] suffer from severe limitations as categories of comparative analysis. First, there is the universality in advanced industrial societies of competition for scarce resources, the existence of competition in this and other respects between different branches of the executive, a rather general tendency towards the 'narrow departmentalism' so often castigated in the Soviet press. While it is useful to be aware of those features that the Soviet Union has in common with other polities, it does not take us very far. Secondly, not only is 'institutional pluralism' not peculiarly applicable to the Soviet system, it especially aptly characterizes the government of the United States which so often (not least in Hough's work) is the implicit or explicit partner in the comparison with the USSR.[44]

The fragmentation of governmental power in the United States has recently received extensive scholarly attention. Commenting on American Cabinet Secretaries' general lack of ability to manage successfully 'heterogeneous institutions with multiple and sometimes conflicting purposes' and a widespread Congressional belief that 'major bureaus should be allowed to run themselves without undue secretarial interference', Harold Seidman has remarked: 'We accept the principle of civilian control of the military profession, but not of the nonmilitary professions such as medicine, education, science and engineering.'[45] Hugh Heclo has noted that 'the administrative machinery in Washington represents a number of fragmented power centers rather than a set of subordinate units under the President,'[46] and Richard Neustadt has observed that 'alone of major modern governments, the United States has had no stiffening element in its political system, no politicized army, no preponderant party, no communist cadres, no French bureaucracy'.[47] It is, we might say, the system of 'institutional pluralism' *par excellence*.

In the Soviet Union and Soviet-type systems, ministries carry out important policy and there are areas in which they play a more important part in the policy process than their counterparts in the party apparatus. The ability of the party leadership to impose its will upon the entire government network is, however, greatly enhanced by the power of their watchdogs in the Central Committee building.

It could perhaps be argued, in the words of Jozef Lenárt in 1967 when he was Prime Minister of Czechoslovakia – he is now First Secretary of the party in Slovakia – that in the Central Committee building it is all talk, whereas in the ministries 'things get done'.[48] However, Zdeněk Mlynář, whose political memoirs are written from the unique vantage point of a political scientist and jurist who became a Secretary of the Central Committee of the Communist Party of Czechoslovakia and who reported these words of Lenárt's, is in no doubt of the power relationship between the Central Committee and the ministries. Writing of the Czechoslovak system pre-1968 when it was (as it is today) closely modelled on the Soviet one, he observes that it is clearly wrong to believe that 'a government minister is more important than a department head in the apparatus of the Central Committee' and warns against the 'big mistake' of judging 'political influence only, or chiefly, by formal position'. A head of department, he suggests, is in no way dependent on the minister, but the minister is in many ways dependent upon him, for the former is much closer to the real power centre, the Politburo. The Central Committee department head also has 'a decisive influence on the appointment, promotion or demotion of all the minister's subordinates, and ultimately of the minister himself'.[49]

Though the more technical ministries in the Soviet Union appear to acquire a significant degree of control within their area of functional specialization, it can hardly be doubted that in comparative terms, there is vastly more central direction and co-ordination within the Moscow bureaucratic establishment than in Washington. The Presidium of the Council of Ministers, the Secretariat of the Central Committee and the Politburo (for better or worse) have no functional equivalents in the United States. Certainly not the Cabinet, despite the lip-service paid to it by successive Presidents upon first entering the White House, and not even the Executive Office of the Presidency.[50] One of the problems with the former is that they are, in Hugh Heclo's words, 'a government of strangers'[51] – strangers to one another and, until they enter office, often strangers to the President himself. So far as the Executive Office is concerned, 'the Watergate record', as Harold Seidman has put it, 'graphically demonstrates the consequences of allowing the presidency to speak with many voices'.[52] Richard Rose, with some justice, concluded a recent comparative study of executive power by observing: 'The fundamental fact of American government is that political power is divided among many dozens of sub-governments in Washington, whose tentacles extend throughout the federal system. The parts are greater than the whole.'[53]

Such generalizations about the United States system of government rest upon a wealth of detailed studies of institutions and policy cases and on knowledge of the views of a great many significant participants in the policy process available to political scientists who write about Washington politics. It is important to acknowledge that we have no comparably detailed information on the relationships between institutions or on the policy process in Moscow. There is, however, more than enough evidence to enable us to conclude that the terms 'bureaucratic pluralism' or 'institutional pluralism' fit the United States much more closely than they fit, say, the executive branches of government in Britain, France or the Federal Republic of Germany.[54] Is there less co-ordination of policy and of central direction in the Soviet system than in the West European ones? It seems unlikely. After all, discipline can still be imposed fairly effectively within the single party and attempts to mobilize public opinion to support a particular department against another are impermissible. This (and almost everything else that we know about the Soviet system) suggests that power in and around the Politburo is likely to be greater *vis-à-vis* other branches of the executive (not to speak of the legislature or judiciary where it obviously is so) than the power of the highest executive organ within Cabinet systems.

Jerry Hough has recently had second thoughts about 'institutional pluralism', but, unfortunately, it is the adjective he has proposed changing, rather than the noun. Concerned that the term 'institutional' might imply that 'institutions are the only actors in the political process' when what he wishes to suggest is that the political process takes place within an institutional framework, that people wishing to exert influence must work through the official channels – the organizations designated for the purpose by the party and state authorities – he concludes that 'perhaps the phrase, "institutionalized pluralism" would convey the meaning better'.[55]

This, however, is less, rather than more, satisfactory and is open, in particular, to two objections. The first is that an inescapable connotation of 'institutionalized pluralism' is that of 'legitimized pluralism' and, as I indicated earlier, nothing is more certain than that pluralism has not been accepted as a legitimate concept by Soviet political leaders and social theorists, especially so far as attempts to relate it to the USSR are concerned. The second objection is that the notion that a wide spectrum of critical views can be presented, provided that the authors of the criticisms do not bypass the official institutional channels, sounds more like corporatism than even a qualified pluralism.

Corporatism

It is worth turning to corporatism since that concept has attracted the attention of a few comparative-minded observers of Communist politics in recent years and since there is a *prima facie* case for regarding it as just as worthy of serious attention as 'institutional pluralism'. Corporatism assumes its potential relevance as a way of conceptualizing Communist politics because it provides for particular interests to participate in the policy process without assuming competition between autonomous political groups.

Philippe Schmitter has provided the most widely accepted contemporary definition of corporatism which he characterizes as:

> a system of interest intermediation in which the constituent units are organized into a limited number of singular, compulsory, non-competitive, hierachically ordered, and functionally differentiated categories, recognized or licensed (if not created) by the state and granted a deliberate representational monopoly within their respective categories in exchange for observing certain controls on their selection of leaders and articulation of demands and supports.[56]

This Schmitter contrasts with pluralism which he defines as:

> a system of interest intermediation in which the constituent units are organized into an unspecified number of multiple, voluntary, competitive, nonhierarchically ordered, and self-determined (as to type or scope of interest) categories that are not specifically licensed, recognized, subsidized, created, or otherwise controlled in leadership selection or interest articulation by the state and that do not exercise a monopoly of representational activity within their respective categories.[57]

An extensive discussion of corporatism as such would be out of place here. It may be noted in passing that there are very different types of corporatism of which the corporatism of fascist states is but one. The most common distinctions observed are those between 'liberal' and 'authoritarian' (or 'societal' and 'state') corporatism. Among those who have hinted that the corporatist model (in an 'authoritarian' or 'state' variant) may have some relevance to Yugoslavia and possibly other East European Communist states are Schmitter,[58] Juan Linz[59] and Alfred Stepan.[60]

Corporatism, however, does not fit the Soviet case particularly well, even though in some respects it fits a number of 'pluralist' descriptions of Soviet reality better than pluralism does. Indeed, if one were forced to choose between Schmitter's definition of corporatism and his definition of pluralism (in which his emphasis on self-determination links up with Dahl's stress on autonomy), one would have to conclude that the former corresponded more closely to the Soviet political system than the latter. Schmitter himself, in fact, offers a definition of Leninist monism, based on the Soviet prototype, which is closer to, though not identical with, his corporatist definition, and which characterizes interest intermediation in such a system as one

> in which the constituent units are organized into a fixed number of singular, ideologically selective, noncompetitive, functionally differentiated and hierarchically ordered categories, created, subsidized and licensed by a single party and granted a representation role within that party and vis-a-vis the state in exchange for observing certain controls on their selection of leaders, articulation of demands and mobilization of support.[61]

In the boldest and most explicit attempt thus far to see the Soviet Union as an example of a corporatist polity, Valerie Bunce and the late John Echols follow Schmitter's distinctions between pluralism and corporatism, though they ignore his own characterization of the Soviet system as monist and his distinctions between monism and corporatism. Bunce and Echols argue that the Soviet Union may usefully be characterized as 'a mixture of corporatist types' and that 'corporatism, under the label "developed socialism", would appear to be an acceptable system with which to head into the future'.[62] They base their argument largely on the attempts at placation under Brezhnev's leadership of such powerful interests as the party apparatus, the industrial managers, the government bureaucracy, scientists and the agricultural sector, all of whom Khrushchev had succeeded in offending.[63] A leadership within an essentially monist system may, however, pursue a conciliatory policy *vis-à-vis* the most important institutional and social interests within the society without thereby introducing systemic change in the structure of power.

A transition from a Communist Party state, organized to maintain the party's control within and *vis-à-vis* every other organization, to a corporatist one is not, in principle, impossible, and one could argue that in Yugoslavia and, perhaps, even in Hungary, we have begun to see a new type of corporatism emerging. But the evidence that this is as yet happening in the Soviet Union is extremely slender. Whether we are talking about trade unions or industrial ministries, the military or the KGB, republican party organizations or research institutes of the Academy of Sciences, it is a misleading understatement to say that the respective units of interest representation accept – as Schmitter's definition of corporatism (and, for that matter, his definition of monism) has it – 'certain controls on *their* selection of leaders' (my italics) and articulation of demands.[64] It is fundamental that in all of these organizations and associations, the head is appointed from above. The system of *nomenklatura*, according to which the filling of posts considered to be of political or economic importance requires the approval of higher authority, puts certain jobs in the *nomenklatura* of more than one body – ministries and soviets as well as party committees. But in appointments to the top posts in organizations such as those mentioned above, the highest party organs have the decisive voice.[65] In no case is the leadership of the organization or association selected or elected from below, even to the extent of choosing from a limited number of candidates.

Some of these posts would be filled by governmental appointment even within pluralist or liberal corporatist systems, but the trade unions may be regarded as a test case. Can one regard as even state corporatist a system in which the head of the trade unions is appointed from outside the ranks of the trade unions with the specific aim of ensuring that the trade union movement remains a faithful executant of party policy? The case of Sándor Gáspár in Hungary, who has used his leadership of the trade unions as a support in his policy arguments with colleagues and who has defended the interests of trade unionists and of workers as he sees them, shows, perhaps, that it is possible in principle for a Communist state to make some concessions to state corporatism. There is, however, no evidence of any recent Soviet trade union leader playing as prominent a role as Gáspár, circumscribed though even that is. The chairmanship of the trade union movement in the Soviet Union has been a staging-post for a prominent party official on the way up (Grishin) or the way down (Shelepin).

It will not do to infer that the trade unions are playing a role of corporatist proportions from the fact that there has been an egalitarian trend in Soviet incomes in the post-Stalin period. Roy Medvedev has drawn attention to the fact that the call for a rapid rise in the workers' standard of living presented to the XXIV Congress of the CPSU in early 1971 showed much more concern for popular living standards than the draft prepared before December 1970. 'Undoubtedly', he notes, 'the changes were influenced by events in Poland as well as various demonstrations by workers in our country protesting against the unavailability of meat and dairy products (in Ivanovo, Sverdlovsk, Gorky and several other cities).'[66] In other words, uninstitutionalized and spontaneous protest within the Soviet Union and observation of the troubles of a neighbouring state would appear to have been the decisive influences on this occasion, rather than any influential role played by the appropriate interest-representational institutions.

Poland has provided the Soviet leaders with a number of lessons on how not to proceed and on what should be done to anticipate and prevent crises, and the latest and most serious struggle in Poland has already led the Soviet leadership to exhort trade unionists in the USSR to be more active. In the report of the Central Committee of the CPSU to the XXVI Party Congress in February 1981 (which expressed considerable concern about developments in Poland), a far from complacent account of the activities of Soviet trade unions was presented. It was noted that they 'sometimes lack initiative in exercising their broad rights' and that they 'do not always act with perseverance in questions of the fulfilment of collective agreements and the rules on labour safety, and still react feebly to cases of violations of labour legislation, to bureaucratic practices, and red tape'.[67] Exhortation from above to trade unions to be more vigilant is one thing. It would, however; be quite another if the job of heading the trade unions were to amount to more than a differentiation of functions among the party leadership in the pursuit of their collective aims or if trade unionists were to be allowed even a limited voice in the selection of their own leaders. Certainly no such developments have as yet occurred, and until they do it will be premature to see the Soviet Union as an example of a corporatist state.

                    *   *   *

Totalitarianism, a qualified pluralism, and corporatism do not by any means exhaust the ways in which the Soviet political system has been conceptualized by Western political scientists in the past twenty years. Many scholars have been content to discuss and analyse aspects of the system without feeling the need to generalize about the nature of the system as a whole. Those who have felt such a need are still, however, quite a sizeable group and it would be impossible to attempt a survey of their conclusions here. It is, though, worth noting that while one of the most popular ways of looking at the Soviet system is in terms of 'bureaucratic politics', those who adopt this approach are divided between writers who go out of their way to counterpose their 'bureaucratic' interpretation of Soviet politics to even a qualified pluralist characterization[68] and those whose study of bureaucratic politics leads them to pluralist conclusions.[69] Similarly, there are scholars who see the Soviet system as monist but not totalitarian[70] as well as those for whom it is both monist and totalitarian.[71]

II. POWER RELATIONS THROUGH SOVIET EYES

Pluralism is seen by Soviet political leaders and by official party ideologists as a threat to such pillars of the system as 'the leading role of the party' and 'democratic centralism'. This became very evident in the numerous Soviet attacks on the pluralist ideas of the Czech reformers of 1968. For these reasons, apart from any others, pluralism is not – and cannot be – explicitly commended by Soviet scholars. This does not, however, mean that the latter are confined to expressing support for a monolithic authoritarianism.

In fact, since the language of democracy is sanctified in Soviet usage, many ideas are put forward and reforms proposed in the name of strengthening democracy.[72] Sceptical Western observers may be inclined to dismiss all talk from Soviet scholars about 'democratization' as mere political rhetoric devoid of substance, but to do so would be as much of an oversimplification as to take all professions of attachment to democracy, from whatever Soviet source, at face value. Many political and social theorists in the USSR support a gradual democratization of Soviet political life in the sense of enhancing popular influence upon political decisions (partly by providing more information to the public and also by promoting more serious and systematic investigation of public opinion)[73] and through raising the level of political participation. What they do *not* advocate is *pluralism* in anything like Dahl's sense. They have shown no inclination, that is to say, to promote the existence of *organizations* which can perform actions considered harmful by 'the government' (party and state leadership) and which 'the government' cannot prevent such organizations from undertaking 'except by incurring costs so high as to exceed the gains . . . from doing so'.

Yu.A. Tikhomirov has written of 'the democratisation of state life' as the most important law of the development of the Soviet state[74] and Georgi Shakhnazarov has picked out 'democratisation' as the main development to be anticipated in the Soviet Union 'in the years to come'.[75] But in distinguishing this 'from the kind of democratisation that would eventually weaken the socialist system', the same author is indicating – as he makes explicit elsewhere – that it is not *pluralist* democracy which he has in mind.[76] While various Czech, Polish, Yugoslav, Italian and Spanish (among other) Communist theorists have regarded political pluralism as perfectly compatible with a 'socialist system', Shakhnazarov has taken pains to dissociate 'the development of socialist democracy' from any link with 'political pluralism'. In an important article in the journal, *Kommunist*, he wrote:

> In recent times one has met with the assertion that socialist democracy is also pluralist in nature. It seems hardly necessary to use an alien concept to characterise the features of the political system of socialism which for a long time have been quite adequately defined in Marxist–Leninist scholarship by such concepts as the needs and interests of classes and social groups, the unity and diversity of these interests, the coincidence or contradiction between them, their defence and expression, co-ordination, etc. So far as a general definition is concerned, to that vague and ambiguous term, 'pluralism', which may be interpreted in all sorts of ways, one ought to prefer the clear concept, 'sovereignty of the people' (*narodovlastie*).[77]

Shakhnazarov writes with some authority, for he is not only President of the Soviet Association of Political Sciences but a deputy head of the department of the Central Committee of the CPSU for relations with socialist countries. He may also be regarded as a moderate reformer within the spectrum of CPSU opinion and, along with Fyodor Burlatsky (who was first in the field),[78] he has been one of the two leading advocates in the Soviet Union of a political science that embraces not only the elaboration of political concepts and the development of Marxist political theory but also the empirical study of Soviet political life.[79]

Arguments on basic concepts

Much important discussion of concepts, including the key concept of political power,[80] has already taken place among Soviet political scientists and jurists. Indeed, the extent to which there is argument over such basic concepts as 'political power', 'the political system' and 'the state' may surprise those Western political scientists whose image of their Soviet counterparts is of an exceedingly well-drilled scholarly community. The traditional image is misleading, though not totally misleading. The view that such lack of agreement is rather unseemly is often expressed at conferences of Soviet scholars. Thus, at the conference held in the Institute of State and Law of the Academy of Sciences in Moscow in April 1979 to prepare Soviet scholars for the Congress of the International Political Science Association (held in Moscow in August of that year), L.A. Grigoryan 'underlined the significance of Yu.A. Tikhomirov's report for the elaboration of a united approach of Soviet scholar–jurists to the definition of the political system',[81] while V.O. Tennenbaum 'drew attention to the importance of working out a united ideological position of the Soviet delegation to the XI World Congress of IPSA in problems of the study of political systems'.[82]

The argument, however, goes on. In an important book entitled *State Sovereignty*,[83] V.S. Shevtsov recently criticized the views of Tikhomirov.[84] But Shevtsov's main opponent is Fyodor Burlatsky, whose record of ideological innovation includes an important part in the conception of the 'all-people's state' in Khrushchev's time and of 'developed socialism' in the Brezhnev era.[85] Burlatsky, who – along with Tikhomirov, V.G. Kalensky[86] and others – distinguishes political power from state power,[87] defines power (*vlast'*) as follows:

> Power is the practical ability to exercise one's will in social life, foisting it upon others, if necessary; political power, as one of the most important manifestations of power, is characterised by the actual ability of a given class, group or individual to implement its will, expressed in policy and law.[88]

State power for Burlatsky is an important part of political power (though with some special attributes), but is not the whole of it:

> State power is that form of political power which has a class character, which disposes of the monopoly right to promulgate laws and other directives, obligatory for the whole population, and which leans upon a special apparatus of coercion as one of the means of securing observance of these laws and directives.[89]

In distinguishing political power conceptually from state power, Burlatsky and – in greater detail – Kalensky also distinguish between two senses of the term 'state', a narrower one and a broader one.[90] In the first sense, the state is 'the apparatus of public power'[91] and excludes political parties; in the second sense, it is synonymous with the 'political system' and so includes, *inter alia*, parties. In the Soviet case, this means for both Burlatsky and Kalensky that the CPSU is not part of the state in the narrow sense, though it is part of the state in the broad sense in which it is possible to speak of the 'Soviet state' (as of a 'socialist state' or the 'American state').[92] For both authors, and especially clearly for Kalensky, it is the second sense of the term state (which goes against the traditional, legalistic definition of the state in the Soviet Union) that is the more important one. Kalensky writes of the 'completely obvious inadequacy of the interpretation of the state as the apparatus of public power, officially consolidated in legislation, for an adequate exploration of the phenomenon of contemporary statehood'.[93] This is simply impossible, Kalensky adds, 'without an analysis of political relations, of the role of ruling parties and other politico-governmental structures, political traditions, ideology, mass consciousness, etc.'[94]

Burlatsky observes that Marx used the term state not only in the narrow sense but in the broad sense,[95] though he adds that it would be 'more precise to speak of the political system' when one wishes to convey the broader meaning.[96] Indeed, in a different work from that just quoted, Burlatsky is using state in the narrow sense when, in emphasizing the importance of the study of the political system, he writes: 'The traditional basic institution of the political system is the state. But the political system cannot be reduced to the state; it includes many other political institutions which exercise functions vitally necessary for its working as an independent social sub-system, above all political parties.'[97]

What makes the work of these writers both significant and controversial in the Soviet context is their attempt (which, in Burlatsky's case, can be traced back at least as far as his famous 1965 *Pravda* article)[98] to put on the scholarly agenda the real political process and real political relations within the Soviet Union and elsewhere and to break away from the legalistic approach which has been far more dominant in Soviet writing on the state and on political institutions than the so-called 'legal–institutional' approach ever was in Western political science prior to the 'behavioural revolution'. Advocating the study of the state in the broad sense, Kalensky notes that 'political parties are not simply the most important socio-political form of organisation of classes and their leaders':

> They are the principal link between society and state power, directly orientated towards participation in its implementation, towards the representation of the interests of classes and other social groups in the very activity of the state apparatus of power. They influence, by such means, the most important politico-governmental structures of the contemporary state, as the nucleus of the mechanism of political power, understood as the totality of all those diverse forms of leadership, control and influence, in which the actual role of the ruling class is given immediate embodiment in the system of political relations.[99]

Taking the other side in the dispute is Shevtsov, who in 1976 had attacked Tikhomirov for saying that 'social organisations may in essence appear as the direct repositories, that is the subjects, of political power'.[100] Against that paraphrase of Tikhomirov's position, Shevtsov argued that 'state power, being a political power, is characterised above all by the fact that it is realised through a special apparatus, leaning on special means and measures of coercion'[101] and, further, that 'political power as such is state power and no other'.[102]

In his most recent work, *State Sovereignty*, Shevtsov goes on to criticize a number of Soviet scholars[103] for their 'mistaken positions' on political power and the state, and quotes approvingly[104] V.M. Terletsky's view that 'the relations of the party with society do not have a power character (*vlastnego kharaktera*)' and that 'the party leads society, relying on its moral–political authority (*avtoritet*)'.[105] Shevtsov reserves, however, his most damning criticism for Burlatsky. He quotes Burlatsky's statement that 'the political system implements the supreme power in society',[106] gives his own précis of Article 6 of the 1977 Soviet Constitution to the effect that 'the party is the nucleus of the political system of Soviet society'[107] and concludes: 'The CPSU appears on this [that is Burlatsky's] interpretation as a state-power social organism.'[108] Against the interpretation he attributes to Burlatsky Shevtsov posits Brezhnev's position that the party's guiding role in society is 'not by virtue of power, but thanks to its high political authority and ideational influence on the masses'.[109] Moreover, Shevtsov cites not only Brezhnev against him but Lenin, and not just any work of Lenin's but his 'Once again on the trade unions', a work devoted, as Shevtsov puts it, 'to a critique of the mistaken views of L. Trotsky and N. Bukharin'.[110]

If, Shevtsov suggests, political power and state power are not one and the same thing, then

> either in society there exist two political powers (the subject of one of which is the political system of the society as a whole, the subject of the other the state), or the political system must be regarded as the state organisation, with the party, the mass social organisations and the work collectives as components of the state.[111]

Burlatsky is, to some degree, open to this criticism by virtue of the fact that he uses the term 'state' in different senses at different times. But on the basis of the interpretation he places on the first of the two alternative meanings Shevtsov raises a spectre which hardly seems appropriate to Burlatsky's case. The name of the spectre is 'political pluralism' and, writes Shevtsov, 'the very essence of the theory of "political pluralism" and "political participation", to be found at the centre of attention of bourgeois political science' consists of the fact that 'different political groups and parties, among them even oppositional (*protivoborstvuyushchie*) ones, together implement political power by their joint efforts, and in the process of mutual struggle assist the perfecting and democratisation of the existing structure of political authority (*politicheskogo upravleniya*)'.[112] The Bulgarian scholar, Asen Kozharov, is also called as a witness against pluralism,[113] but since neither Burlatsky's use at times of the broader definition of the state, nor his subsuming at other times of the state, in its narrower sense, within the political system logically entails pluralism either as a description of or as prescription for Soviet political life, it is not clear what purpose Shevtsov's digression on pluralism serves, unless it be that of imputing guilt by association.

Shevtsov's position has its supporters among Soviet jurists and it is believed by some of them to be 'the view of the Central Committee' as well. Weight is lent to that supposition by the fact that Shevtsov holds a position within the Department of Science and Education of the Central Committee. Yet the Central Committee view is by no means so clear-cut. There are, indeed, a number of signs that Shevtsov's concept of state power has not been accorded definitive official approval. One such indication was the small print-run in which his book, *State Sovereignty*, appeared.[114] Secondly, and more significantly, his views have come under implicit criticism from Shakhnazarov (see below) who, as deputy head of the Central Committee department for relations with Socialist Countries, holds a higher rank within the Central Committee apparatus than Shevtsov, even though this position does not confer upon him party responsibilities in relation to academic life. (Nevertheless, he holds two academic offices – as president of the Soviet Association of Political Sciences and as head of the recently established Department of Theory of Political Systems and of Political Relations at the Institute of State and Law of the Academy of Sciences in Moscow – which add further institutional weight to his opinions.) Thirdly, notwithstanding Shevtsov's position within the department of the Central Committee which oversees the Institute of State and Law and his membership of the editorial board of the institute's journal, that same journal, *Sovetskoe gosudarstvo i pravo*, published a review of his *State Sovereignty* in the summer of 1981 which explicitly took issue with the author's narrow definition of state power. The reviewer, F.M. Rudinsky, observes that 'although the CPSU is not the repository of state *functions*, party organisations, acting within the framework of the Soviet Constitution, emerge in some cases as the *subjects* of *state-legal relations*' (italics mine). As an example, Rudinsky cites the part played by party organizations in the nomination of deputies in elections to soviets.[115] The nature of 'the state' and the problem of the party's place within or (according to the definition of the state adopted) *vis-à-vis* it, together with the meaning of 'political power', have, in fact, become legitimate topics of discussion among Soviet scholars, provided that certain conventions are observed.[116]

In a recent exceptionally important article (alluded to in the previous paragraph) on the development of political science in the USSR, written jointly by Shakhnazarov and Burlatsky, there is an implicit reply to Shevtsov's *State Sovereignty*.[117] In view of his considerable party standing, it is of some significance that Shakhnazarov should have established an identity of view with Burlatsky on a number of important points. Though his previously published views corresponded more closely to those of Burlatsky than to those of Shevtsov, he had not been directly involved in the debate with Shevtsov and like-minded jurists. But Shakhnazarov and Burlatsky, in their article written in 1980 and published at the end of that year, clearly resist the idea that political power is state power and nothing but state power. Thus, for instance, they write: 'The 1977 Constitution of the USSR contains a precise characterisation of the political system as embodying the power of the Soviet people. Its basic institutions are the all-people's socialist state, the CPSU, the mass social organisations, and the work collectives.'[118]

Though Shakhnazarov and Burlatsky refer once to the state 'in the broad sense'[119] (see below), they prefer to rest their case concerning the nature of political power on a broad definition of 'political system'. Having noted that 'in a certain sense of the term, the political system includes the entire sum total of strictly political relations',[120] they advance a conception of political power that is 'a logical consequence of the complex approach to problems of power and government which has been developed in legal science and the theory of scientific communism'. This 'complex approach' facilitates the overcoming of 'a certain simplification' whereby 'the entire sphere of politics was identified with the state, and the latter not infrequently reduced to the governmental apparatus'.[121] Implicitly, they would appear to be accepting that they are not going to persuade Shevtsov and jurists who share his views to accept the 'broad definition' of the state, and so they simply move the argument on. The political institutions and political relations, the entire sphere of politics with which they are concerned, have, they suggest, been given different names at different times. What was 'finally' called the 'political system' was first expressed in the concept of 'the state in the broad sense of the word' and after that in the elaboration of the concept of 'political organisation'.[122]

Shakhnazarov, like Burlatsky, has long recognized as a legal fiction the idea that all decisions of a political power character are taken by the state in the narrow sense of the term. In his important book, *Socialist Democracy*, he notes that certain areas of policy-making involve direct party decisions, notably foreign policy and especially international crises.[123] This, and the more general picture of political power offered by 'politologically minded' Soviet scholars clearly come much closer to encapsulating political realities than the legalistic version of Shevtsov, Terletsky and other jurists. A Western specialist on Soviet foreign policy has noted that the Politburo 'met during summit meetings [of the 1970s] to consider specific proposals advanced by the United States delegation'.[124] Brezhnev's own fairly detailed summary of the activities of the Politburo over the past five years at the XXVI Congress probably left few of his listeners thinking that the institution which he described as 'indeed the battle headquarters of our multi-million party' gave no more than influential advice to state institutions.[125]

Within a system of the Soviet type, as within Cabinet systems, there is, in fact, a strong tendency to push matters upwards for decision, a practice which produces so much documentation, presented to Politburo members a day or two before their meetings, that the documents prepared by the working groups have to be summarized for the members by their aides.[126] It is precisely because an authoritative decision by the Politburo can put an end to countless hours of argument between departments or ministries that ministers are often anxious to take matters which are not settled to their satisfaction by Gosplan or by the Presidium of the Council of Ministers to this highest political organ.[127] Yet a minister cannot put an item on the Politburo agenda unless (as, for example, in the case of Gromyko and Ustinov in the present Soviet Politburo) he is himself a Politburo member. The great majority of ministers who are not in that position can only get an item on the agenda by approaching the Secretariat of the Central Committee and relying on their good will and co-operation.[128] This relationship would certainly seem to reflect the political power of the Politburo (and the Secretariat) and to indicate something a good deal more than the high inspirational value of the Politburo's deliberations.

The relative autonomy of the state

Finally, it is worth noting that one other aspect of power within political systems generally (and the Soviet system by inference) has been raised recently by Soviet theorists. That is the important and sensitive question of the degree of autonomy (from society and the 'ruling class') possessed by the political leadership and/or state bureaucrats. One of the problems for the Soviet theorist is that if he accepts the notion that the highest party institutions stand at the apex of the power structure within the Soviet political system, he should, logically, include these same party institutions within the political 'superstructure'. This, however, would lead to considerable tension, to put it mildly, between the notion of the party's 'leading role' and the idea that the economic base 'in the last analysis' determines the superstructure. The problem lies with the time-worn architectural metaphor of base and super-structure, which many Soviet theorists still feel compelled to use, though the reification of a figure of speech into two concrete entities (whose relationship and relative autonomies can then be discussed) is more of a hindrance than a help in political analysis.

Shevtsov circumvents the problem in much the same way that the traditional Leninist theory of the 'dictatorship of the pro-letariat' tends to bypass this central issue. He observes that *'the political organisation in society* possesses a relative autonomy and has the possibility actively to exert influence on the whole structure of production and ideological relations' (my italics).[129] He makes it clear that by 'political organisation', he means 'the organisation of the ruling class, of its political domination' which, in the Soviet case, stands, above all, for the CPSU. By speaking of the *influence*, rather than the *power* of 'the political organisation in society' (which he distinguishes from the state), he remains true to his emphasis on state power and upon the supremacy (*verk-hovenstvo*) of the state.[130]

A rather different emphasis found in some recent Soviet writings concerns the 'enormous influence' of *state bureaucrats* on society and on *their* 'relative autonomy' from society; it is especially noteworthy that scholars who have written in this vein are among those who have pointed to the weakness of interpre-

tations of 'the state' which exclude an analysis of 'the role of
ruling parties'. Burlatsky, though his emphasis is different from
Shevtsov's, is less innovative in this respect than Kalensky. In the
book which he co-edited with V.E. Chirkin, *Contemporary
Political Systems*, Burlatsky, after duly noting Marx's demonstration 'that material production is the base which defines the
character and forms of state life,' goes on to cite Engels on the
influence 'of state power on economic development'. Persisting
with the terminology, 'base' and 'superstructure', Burlatsky
emphasizes the fact that this interrelationship does not have 'a
one-sided character'. The 'political superstructure' exerts in its
turn 'an enormous influence (*ogromnoe vozdeystvie*) on the whole
of social life'.[131] The context in which these words are written is
that of a general discussion of 'the socio-economic environment
and the political system'[132] and it must be assumed that they are
intended to be applicable to the Soviet case, though this is not
explicitly stated.

Kalensky has gone significantly further in his discussions of the
relative autonomy of the *state vis-à-vis society* and its '*ruling
class*'. Again, it should be noted, the author is writing about the
state in general, rather than about the Soviet state specifically,
but he does not appear in principle to exclude the Soviet Union
from these particular generalizations. In his very scholarly and
significant book, *The State as an Object of Sociological Analysis*,
he writes of 'the state bureaucracy' as being 'not simply a special
exclusive social stratum and caste' but as one that 'serves as the
material embodiment of state power itself' and of 'this very
stratum as that which directly operates the state mechanism and
implements public power'.[133] Kalensky, after drawing upon the
authority of Marx, Engels and Lenin for such an analysis, goes on
to observe:

> The concentration of enormous power in the hands of bureau-
> crats (*chinovniki*) has most serious political consequences, and
> leads namely to the acquisition by that special social stratum of
> a relative autonomy in relation to the ruling class as a whole,
> and to its being in certain circumstances even in conflict with
> it, thrusting upon it selfish interests of its own.[134]

In a more recent publication Kalensky develops that point and
also suggests that Marxist–Leninist teaching concerning the state

('notable for its genuine scientific objectivity and historical method') 'orients the researcher to the study of political reality in all its dialectical complexity and contradictions'. This draws attention to the possibility of a situation arising where 'the public power, even though operating in the interests of the economically dominant class, possesses, however, in relation to that class a great autonomy'.[135] Kalensky also writes of public power being at times 'implemented by representatives of other classes' (other, that is, than the 'ruling class') and here, as in his reference to the 'great autonomy', rather than the 'relative autonomy', of those who implement public power, he moves beyond the position he reached in his 1977 book.

Thus, in principle, if one were to apply this general formulation about the great autonomy of those who wield public power to the Soviet case, public power could be exercised by representatives of a class or social stratum other than the working class and such a stratum could possess a great autonomy *vis-à-vis* Soviet society as a whole and the working class in particular. In must be stressed strongly that Kalensky draws no such conclusion, but is putting forward a general proposition in the context of developing Marxist theory of the state. It is open to Kalensky's readers to draw their own conclusions, and his work (for he is simultaneously an outstanding Soviet authority on American political science[136] and a prominent historian of political thought)[137] testifies to the liveliness and interest of a significant portion of officially published Soviet writing in recent years.

III. CONCLUSIONS

The Soviet literature discussed in the foregoing pages is of considerable consequence in itself, quite apart from any bearing it may have on the writings of Western political scientists discussed in the first half of this essay. Though an excessive concern with defining terms is ultimately self-defeating, the attempts of some Soviet scholars to specify more precisely what they mean by 'the state' and 'the political system' contrasts favourably with the relatively casual way in which a good many Western political scientists decide to use one term rather than the other.[138] A more interesting contrast, however, is between the emphasis of some of the more innovative Soviet scholars on the relative autonomy of the state and the stress of Western pluralist theorists on the relative autonomy of society. They have in common the terminology, 'relative autonomy', but they are pointing in different directions. To the extent that society is autonomous from the state, pluralism is indicated; to the extent that emphasis is placed upon the autonomy from the society of the state (with its 'special apparatus of coercion as one of the means of securing observance of [its] laws and directives')[139] pluralism is seen to be curtailed or absent.[140]

From recent Soviet writing on political power and the state it seems clear that the suggestion sometimes made that criticism from 'within the ideology' is no longer possible within Soviet-type states[141] oversimplifies considerably the position in the Soviet Union itself. Many different value preferences may be detected among Soviet writers on politics, and those who wish to see a greater emphasis upon democracy and liberty and those who take a highly restrictive view of both each draw upon the works of Marx and Lenin in support of their views. Since the positive evaluations of democracy and liberty by Marx and Lenin are numerous, and since the terminology 'political pluralism', is not to be found in either of these classic sources, it is, in fact, a more straightforward matter for Soviet theorists to justify an emphasis on the importance of, and desirability of extending, democracy and liberty than to betray concern with the existence or absence of pluralism. Unlike their counterparts in some of the other Communist states, these Soviet social scientists do not make an explicit attempt to justify political pluralism in a normative sense. So far as democracy and liberty are concerned, it is worth noting Kalensky's view that in 'the comparison of political regimes[142] in socialist countries', special significance should be attached to information pertaining to 'the correlation between the degree of democratism and centralism in the political leadership, the ratio of persuasion to coercion in the methods of implementation of political power, and also [to] the level of legality and of guarantees of the basic constitutional rights and liberties of citizens'.[143]

The somewhat esoteric debate among Soviet political scientists and jurists concerns not only the meaning of words and is not only about approaches to the study of politics. Behind these disagreements lie, in many cases, also significant political differences. As a generalization, it would be fair to say that those participants in the discussion who lay most emphasis on state power and state sovereignty are more conservative Communists than those who emphasize *narodovlastie* or sovereignty of the people, even though it could be argued (and is argued by those who belong to the former grouping) that there is no contradiction between the two concepts. Similarly, those scholars who call for the empirical study of political relations in their concrete reality tend to be of a much more reformist disposition than the scholars who have remained content with formalistic and legalistic accounts of Soviet political life.

It may seem strange to categorize as conservative the view that the party can but *influence* the state and that party institutions do not wield *power* over state institutions. The evolution towards such a view in Yugoslav theory (and the trend towards curtailment of the party's role in Yugoslav practice) has, after all, been a central feature of the Yugoslav reformist 'model'.[144] Similarly, an emphasis on the party's authority, and constant need to win authority, rather than upon party power, and the enforcement of its power, is to be found in the section on 'the leading role of the Party' in the 1968 Action Programme of the Communist Party of Czechoslovakia.[145] What, then, is the distinction between, on the one hand, the standpoint of Soviet theoreticians who deny that the Communist Party of the Soviet Union exercises political power and, on the other, 'reformist' conceptions of the role of the party held by Yugoslav and 'Prague Spring' theorists? Basically, the difference is that the Yugoslavs and the Czechs faced up to the political reality that an enormous (and, in their view, excessive) power had, in fact, been concentrated in the hands of party organs. This is not at all the same thing as turning a blind eye to the exercise of power by party institutions and asserting that the party exercises its leading role in society *solely* by virtue of its great influence and authority.

The analysis of the argument among Soviet scholars on matters such as these is complicated by the fact that sometimes these academics write 'descriptively' when they would wish to write prescriptively and use an 'is' when they mean an 'ought'. Thus, in certain contexts, Soviet scholars may indeed be actually advocating a curtailment of party power when they choose to emphasize that the party cannot give orders to (for instance) soviets. It would not appear, however, in the case of the state or party power debate between Shevtsov and Burlatsky (and others)

that Shevtsov wishes to see the Politburo, Secretariat and departments of the Central Committee divest themselves of all power. If
that is no part of his intention, neither, it should be added, is it
the wish of Burlatsky and Shakhnazarov to remove political power
from party organs. What makes their standpoint inimical to the
conservative position is their desire to develop analysis of the
Soviet political system as it is, rather than as legal textbooks on
state and law have hitherto portrayed it. In essence, Burlatsky
and Shakhnazarov recognize that in the exercise of its leading
role, the party makes use of influence, authority *and* power.
While they are not suggesting for a moment that the party's
relationship with other institutions is *always* a power relationship
rather than one of influence and authority, it is, in their view, at
least as fanciful to claim that higher party organs *never* wield
political power.

The Soviet scholars engaged in the discussions noted above are
party members and they cite not only Marx and Lenin but recent
party and state documents in support of their views. But, as is
well-known and as is further illustrated by these very discussions,
the works of Marx and Lenin can be used to justify a wide range
of positions and, so far as the party or constitutional documents
are concerned, in a number of cases these scholars (some of whom
are very prominent party intellectuals) are building upon, and
extrapolating from, formulations which they themselves have
helped to legitimize by inserting in the documents. The Soviet
discussion of the state and its relative autonomy and of the
political system and political power is, then, important not only
for its intrinsic contribution to the task of conceptualizing Soviet
politics. It also amounts to one more piece of evidence (from a
sensitive ideological area) of the diversity of view to be found
within the CPSU and within various party and state institutions
even on matters of some consequence.

Yet, if we reject the picture of the monolithic unity of the
CPSU and of the Soviet state (in the broad sense) as a great oversimplification, there is no need to conclude as an alternative that
the Soviet Union has become yet another variant of a pluralist
state. While social and political forces within the broader society
and opinion groupings within the party and within various other
institutions do have an impact on public policy, the relative
autonomy of institutions other than the highest party organs is
(by comparative standards) fairly small and the relative

autonomy of the supreme holders of political power at the apex of the party hierarchy is (again in comparative perspective) very great.

Having rejected totalitarian, pluralist and corporatist conceptualizations of the Soviet system, I have no intention at this stage of producing a grand new conceptualization. Soviet reality is too complex, multifaceted and downright contradictory to be encapsulated in a word or a phrase. For those who still demand a phrase, probably less misleading, so far as the contemporary Soviet Union is concerned, than the three conceptualizations discussed in the first part of this chapter is the notion of 'diversity within monism' (to paraphrase Shakhnazarov's view of the system)[146] or the expression which Gordon Skilling once used, and perhaps prematurely discarded, 'imperfect monism'.[147]

Under such rubrics we can keep in mind the 'bureaucratic politics' aspect of the system, while noting, too, the limits that are imposed on it by the existence of a 'super-bureau' in the shape of the Politburo. Of course, the institutional rivalries and conflicts which do exist are by no means the sum total of Soviet political life. There is also an esoteric politics which includes an element of guarded debate in areas deemed by the party leadership to be of great sensitivity. This holds true, in some measure, of the debate on the state and the political system outlined above.[148] In areas of policy where the party leadership either has an interest in a relatively free debate taking place or is not itself particularly preoccupied with the issue, there is much more open political argument, some of which is ultimately reflected in policy decisions or legislation.[149] But however vigorous the discussion, the power structure remains intact, and though it would be quite wrong to rule out the possibility (among others) of corporatism or even pluralism becoming the basis of that structure and the main defining characteristic of political relationships within the Soviet Union, it is manifest that neither has happened yet.

NOTES AND REFERENCES

1. See F. Burlatsky, 'Politika i nauka', *Pravda* (10 January 1965) 4. For discussion of this article and some of the subsequent developments along the road to a Soviet political science, see David E. Powell and Paul Shoup, 'The Emergence of Political Science in Communist Countries', *American Political Science Review*, 64, no. 2 (June 1970) 572–88; Rolf H.W. Theen,

'Political Science in the USSR: "To be or *not* to be"', *World Politics*, *XXIII*, no. 4 (July 1971) 684–703; and Ronald J. Hill, *Soviet Politics, Political Science and Reform* (Oxford and White Plains, N.Y., 1980).

2. I am using 'government' generically to stand in this instance for the party and state leadership.

3. Ralph Miliband, *Marxism and Politics* (Oxford, 1977) 8.

4. Illustrations from the Soviet discussion will be given in section II of this essay. Western Marxist statements along these lines are exceedingly numerous. See, for instances, Louis Althusser, *For Marx* (Harmondsworth, 1969) 240; and Miliband, *Marxism and Politics*, 114–16. Althusser, objecting to the concept of the 'cult of personality', places Stalinism firmly in the context of the 'relative autonomy' of the 'superstructure'. Miliband, while paying attention to the 'extreme example' of Stalin (115), goes further than Althusser and writes of '*the state*' in Communist systems generally as having 'a very high degree of autonomy from *society*' (116, Miliband's italics).

5. The most prominent advocate of an 'institutional pluralist' interpretation of Soviet politics (though recently he has adopted the terminology 'institutionalized pluralism') has been Jerry F. Hough. See especially his *The Soviet Union and Social Science Theory* (Cambridge, Mass., 1977); and also Jerry F. Hough and Merle Fainsod, *How the Soviet Union is Governed* (Cambridge, Mass., 1979). Interesting 'bureaucratic pluralist' interpretations of Soviet politics include those of Darrell P. Hammer, *U.S.S.R.: The Politics of Oligarchy* (Hinsdale, Ill., 1974); and William Taubman, *Governing Soviet Cities: Bureaucratic Politics and Urban Development in the U.S.S.R.* (New York, 1973). An example of an author who uses pluralist terminology to describe institutional conflicts and rivalries within the Soviet Union but is less inclined to make this the main defining characteristic of Soviet politics is Alec Nove. Cf. his chapter, '"Centralised Pluralism": Ministries and Regional Planning', in Nove, *The Soviet Economic System* (London, 1977) 60–84, and his article, 'History, Hierarchy and Nationalities: Some Observations on the Soviet Social Structure,' *Soviet Studies*, 21, no. 1 (1969).

6. Giovanni Sartori, 'Concept Misformation in Comparative Politics', *American Political Science Review*, 64, no. 4 (December 1970) 1034.

7. Ibid., 1035.

8. Ibid., 1034.

9. Ibid., 1039.

10. Ibid., 1052.

11. Alex Inkeles, 'Models and Issues in the Analysis of Soviet Society', *Survey*, no. 60 (July 1966) 13. The *locus classicus* on totalitarianism remains Carl J. Friedrich and Zbigniew K. Brzezinski, *Totalitarian Dictatorship and Autocracy* (Cambridge, Mass., 1956) (2nd edn revised by Friedrich, 1965). See also Carl J. Friedrich, Michael Curtis and Benjamin R. Barber, *Totalitarianism in Perspective: Three Views* (London, 1969); and Leonard Schapiro, *Totalitarianism* (London, 1972).

12. For criticism along these lines, see, for example, Andrew C. Janos, 'Group Politics in Communist Society: A Second Look at the Pluralist Model', in Samuel P. Huntington and Clement H. Moore (eds), *Authoritarian*

Politics in Modern Society (New York, 1970) 437–50; Juan J. Linz, 'Totalitarian and Authoritarian Regimes,' in Fred I. Greenstein and Nelson W. Polsby (eds), *Handbook of Political Science, Volume 3: Macropolitical Theory*, (Reading, Mass., 1975) 175–411; Joseph LaPolombara, 'Monoliths or Plural Systems: Through Conceptual Lenses Darkly', *Studies in Comparative Communism*, 8, no. 3 (Autumn 1975) 304–32; and Alfred Stepan, *The State and Society: Peru in Comparative Perspective* (Princeton, N.J., 1978) (Part One, 'The Role of the State: Concepts and Comparisons'). See also Andrew C. Janos (ed.), *Authoritarian Politics in Communist Europe: Uniformity and Diversity in One-Party States* (Berkeley, Calif., 1976). For an early, perceptive and open-minded consideration of the problem, see Bohdan Harasymiw, 'Application of the Concept of Pluralism to the Soviet Political System', *Newsletter on Comparative Studies of Communism*, 5, no. 1 (November 1971) 40–54. See also Stephen White, 'Communist Systems and the "Iron Law of Pluralism"', *British Journal of Political Science*, 8, no. 1 (January 1978) 101–17; and Alexander J. Groth 'USSR: Pluralist Monolith?', *British Journal of Political Science* 9, no. 4 (October 1979) 445–64.

13. Its use is traced back to the 1920s by Leonard Schapiro in his *Totalitarianism*, 13–14.

14. David Nicholls, *The Pluralist State* (London, 1975).

15. David Nicholls, *Three Varieties of Pluralism* (London, 1974).

16. Ibid., 56.

17. See, for example, Jerzy J. Wiatr, 'Elements of Pluralism in the Polish Political System', *The Polish Sociological Bulletin* no. 1 (1966); Jerzy J. Wiatr and Adam Przeworski, 'Control without Opposition,' *Government and Opposition*, 1, no. 2 (January 1966) 227–39; Jerzy J. Wiatr, *Essays in Political Sociology* (Warsaw, 1978); Stanislaw Ehrlich, 'Le problème du pluralisme', *L'Homme et la Societé*, no. V (juillet–septembre 1967) 113–18; Stanislaw Ehrlich, 'Pluralism and Marxism', in Stanislaw Ehrlich and Graham Wootton (eds), *Three Faces of Pluralism: Political, Ethnic and Religious* (Farnborough, 1980) 34–45; and Vladimír Klokočka, *Volby v pluralitních democraciích* (Prague, 1978). For discussion of the ideas of the advocates of pluralism within the Communist Party of Czechoslovakia, see H. Gordon Skilling, *Czechoslovakia's Interrupted Revolution* (Princeton, N.J., 1976) esp. 333–72; F.M. Barnard and R.A. Vernon, 'Socialist Pluralism and Pluralist Socialism', *Political Studies*, 25, no. 4 474–90; and Zdeněk Mlynář, 'Notions of Political Pluralism in the Policy of the Communist Party of Czechoslovakia in 1968', a product of a research project under Mlynář's direction, 'Experiences of the Prague Spring 1968', Working Paper No. 3.

18. For two East European critiques of Communists' advocacy of pluralism – the first a measured and thoughtful analysis by a Hungarian scholar and the second a much more polemical, though also interesting, attack by a Bulgarian philosopher – see Peter Hardi, 'Why do Communist Parties Advocate Pluralism?', *World Politics*, 32, no. 4 (July 1980) 531–52; and Asen Kozharov, *Monizm i plyuralizm v ideologii i politike* (Moscow, 1976).

19. See, for example, G. Shakhnazarov, 'O demokraticheskom tsentralizme i politicheskom plyuralizme', *Kommunist*, no. 10 (July 1979) 107.

20. Stanislaw Ehrlich, 'Pluralism and Marxism', in Ehrlich and Wootton (eds), *Three Faces of Pluralism*, 43–4.
21. Jerzy J. Wiatr, 'The Hegemonic Party System in Poland', in Wiatr, *Essays in Political Sociology*, 188.
22. Sartori, 'Concept Misformation in Comparative Politics', 1050–1.
23. See Robert A. Dahl, *Dilemmas of Pluralistic Democracy*, forthcoming (New Haven, 1982). (I am most grateful to Professor Dahl for giving me the opportunity to read this work in manuscript and for permission to cite it.) See also Robert A. Dahl, 'Pluralism Revisited', *Comparative Politics*, 10, no. 2 (January 1978) 191–203 (reprinted in Ehrlich and Wootton (eds), *Three Faces of Pluralism*, 20–33).
24. For a summary and analysis of the evidence available up to the early 1970s, see my *Soviet Politics and Political Science* (London, 1974) ch.3, 'Groups, Interests and the Policy Process', 71–88. Much information, relevant to this theme, is to be found in H. Gordon Skilling and Franklyn Griffiths (eds), *Interest Groups in Soviet Politics* (Princeton, N.J., 1971). For more recent contributions, see Richard B. Remneck (ed.), *Social Scientists and Policy-Making in the USSR* (New York, 1977); and Peter H. Solomon, Jr, *Soviet Criminologists and Criminal Policy: Specialists in Policy-Making* (London, 1978).
25. For examples of diffusion of influence under Stalin, see Timothy Dunmore, *The Stalinist Command Economy: The Soviet State Apparatus and Economic Policy 1945–53* (London, 1981); A. Kemp-Welch, 'Stalinism and Intellectual Order', in T.H. Rigby, Archie Brown and Peter Reddaway (eds), *Authority, Power and Policy in the USSR* (London, 1980) 118–34; Peter H. Solomon, Jr, 'Specialists in Soviet Policy Making: Criminal Policy, 1938–70', in Remneck (ed.), *Social Scientists and Policy Making in the USSR* 1–33, esp. 4–6; and Solomon, *Soviet Criminologists and Criminal Policy*, esp. 32–4 and 146–7.
26. Though Gordon Skilling has been opposed to the description of the Soviet Union as a type of pluralist system, ten years ago he wrote: '. . . the system is operating differently than it did under Stalin, in part as a result of increased activity by political groups which have attained a certain degree of autonomy of action. In that sense Soviet society has shown signs of at least an incipient pluralism' (in Skilling and Griffiths (eds), *Interest Groups in Soviet Politics*, 44). Possibly misleadingly, in terms of Dahl's definition which I now accept as the best way of making pluralism a somewhat more rigorous and useful concept, I have myself written of 'elements of pluralism' within the Soviet system (Brown, *Soviet Politics and Political Science*, 74), and of 'a limited institutional or bureaucratic pluralism – in some areas of policy very limited indeed' (in Archie Brown and Michael Kaser (eds), *The Soviet Union since the Fall of Khrushchev* (London, 1975; 2nd edn [1978] 245). Like Skilling, however, I have never found it particularly useful to regard the Soviet Union as a 'type of pluralist system'.
27. See Hough, *The Soviet Union and Social Science Theory*, 14–15.
28. The work of the critics of American pluralist theorists contains many valuable insights, though evidence, too, of less than careful reading of some of the works they are criticizing. For one example, see the exchange

between Nelson W. Polsby and Kenneth Newton, *Political Studies*, 27, no. 4 (December 1979) esp. 530–1 and 543. See further William E. Connolly (ed.), *The Bias of Pluralism* (New York, 1969); and Nelson W. Polsby, *Community Power and Political Theory: A Further Look at Problems of Evidence and Inference*, 2nd enlarged edn (New Haven, Conn., 1980).

29. Hough, *The Soviet Union and Social Science Theory*, 5.

30. Ibid., 14–15.

31. Even the party daily newspaper, *Rudé právo*, was not under the full control of the party leadership, nor, indeed, that of its editor, Oldřich Švestka. One article which was an embarrassment to the Czechoslovak party leadership, in view of Soviet sensitivities, was, for example, that on the front page of *Rudé právo* on 16 April 1968, which discussed the pros and cons of whether Jan Masaryk's death in 1948 was by suicide or murder and held that the possibility of Soviet involvement was worth further investigation. See Skilling, *Czechoslovakia's Interrupted Revolution*, 381.

32. For a graph showing the pattern of popular trust in Czechoslovak politicians, 1968–9, and discussion of it, see Archie Brown and Gordon Wightman, 'Czechoslovakia: Revival and Retreat', in Archie Brown and Jack Gray (eds), *Political Culture and Political Change in Communist States* (London, 1977; 2nd edn, 1979) esp. 174–6. For more extensive coverage of opinion polling in Czechoslovakia in that period, see Jaroslaw A. Piekalkiewicz, *Public Opinion Polling in Czechoslovakia, 1968–69: Results and Analysis of Surveys Conducted During the Dubček Era* (New York, 1972).

33. Thus, for example, links were established between the district committees of Prague 1 (an intelligentsia-dominated party organization in the district in which the university and a number of research institutes were located) and Prague 9 (a predominantly working-class district).

34. Even with regard to appointments which it supposedly covered, the *nomenklatura* became a dead letter for much of 1968. It was not formally abolished, but was generally ignored.

35. See, for example, on these two organizations Skilling, *Czechoslovakia's Interrupted Revolution*, esp. 546–8; Vladimir V. Kusin, *Political Grouping in the Czechoslovak Reform Movement* (London, 1972) 176–91; and Galia Golan, *Reform Rule in Czechoslovakia: The Dubček Era 1968–1969* (Cambridge, 1973) 80–2.

36. For a good general account of developments within Czechoslovakia during the 1970s, see Vladimir V. Kusin, *From Dubček to Charter 77: Czechoslovakia 1968–78* (Edinburgh, 1978).

37. For an authoritative Soviet view of these concessions, see, in particular, the letter of the Central Committee of the CPSU to the Central Committee of the Polish United Workers' Party, *Pravda* (12 June 1981) 2.

38. By January 1981 one-quarter of party members were members also of Solidarity; by April the proportion had grown to one-third. For a useful brief account of party–Solidarity relations up to the end of January 1981, see Z.A. Pelczynski, 'Stalemate and after in Poland', *New Society* (5 February 1981) 232–3.

39. See Hough and Fainsod, *How the Soviet Union is Governed*, 547.

40. H. Gordon Skilling, 'Interest Groups and Communist Politics', *World*

Politics, 18, no. 3 (April 1966) 449. As early as 1954, Karl Deutsch drew attention to the need of totalitarian regimes 'to combat their own automatic drift towards pluralization and disintegration'. So far as the USSR was concerned, he concluded, however, that the 'imperfect data . . . seem to suggest that the Soviet dictatorship in Russia still disposes of substantial resources to stave off its own disintegration or pluralization for some time'. See Karl W. Deutsch, 'Cracks in the Monolith: Possibilities and Patterns of Disintegration in Totalitarian System', in Carl J. Friedrich (ed.), *Totalitarianism* (New York, 1964) 331.

41. While recognizing *Interest Groups in Soviet Politics* as a landmark in the study of the Soviet political system, I have expressed some reservations about, for instance, the 'conceptual stretching' aspect of the work in my 'Problems of Interest Articulation and Group Influence in the Soviet Union', *Government and Opposition*, 7, no. 2 (Spring 1972) 229–43, and in *Soviet Politics and Political Science*, 71–4.

42. Not least in his first book, *The Soviet Prefects: The Local Party Organs in Industrial Decision-Making* (Cambridge, Mass., 1969).

43. 'Institutional pluralism' and 'bureaucratic pluralism' are generally used interchangeably in the literature, though the latter term may focus attention more exclusively on the major party and state bureaucratic structures, whereas 'institutional pluralism' may call to mind not only ministries, departments of the Central Committee of the Party, the military, the KGB, and so on, but also such institutions as research institutes of the Academy of Sciences.

44. 'Institutional pluralism' is not, of course, the only form of pluralism to be found in the United States. Indeed, T.H. Rigby has suggested that the limitations of 'institutional pluralism' are best appreciated if we accept the fact that '"bureaucratic crypto-politics" are found in the government machine of the capitalist democracies as well' as in the Soviet Union and then try to 'imagine what it would mean for "pluralism" and the structure of power generally if this were the *only* politics operating in these countries, if the whole public competitive political process were absent, and the spokesmen of all official and voluntary organisations, all communications media and all "representative bodies" presented a unanimous front of support for the current policies of the government' (T.H. Rigby, 'A Conceptual Approach to Authority, Power and Policy in the Soviet Union', in Rigby, Brown and Reddaway (eds), *Authority, Power and Policy in the USSR*, 25).

45. Harold Seidman, *Politics, Position and Power: The Dynamics of Federal Organization*, 3rd edn (Oxford and New York, 1980) 322.

46. Hugh Heclo, *A Government of Strangers: Executive Politics in Washington* (Washington, D.C., 1977) 12. See also Heclo on 'issue networks' (a concept that might well have some application in the Soviet context) in Anthony King (ed.), *The New American Political System* (Washington, D.C., 1978) 87–124.

47. Richard Neustadt, *Presidential Power: The Politics of Leadership From FDR to Carter* (New York, 1980 edn) 242.

48. Zdeněk Mlynář, *Night Frost in Prague: The End of Humane Socialism* (London, 1980) 111.

49. Ibid., 53; and the slightly fuller version in Zdeněk Mlynář, *Mráz přichází z Kremlu* (Cologne, 1978) 69.
50. See Seidman, 'Coordination: The Search for the Philosopher's Stone', in Seidman, *Politics, Position and Power*, 200–17.
51. Heclo, *A Government of Strangers*. See also Heclo in King (ed.), *The New American Political System*, esp. 122.
52. Seidman, *Politics, Position and Power*, 94.
53. Richard Rose, 'Government against Sub-governments: A European Perspective on Washington', in Richard Rose and Ezra N. Suleiman (eds), *Presidents and Prime Ministers* (Washington, D.C., 1980) 294.
54. See Rose and Suleiman (eds), *Presidents and Prime Ministers*, ibid.
55. Hough and Fainsod, *How the Soviet Union is Governed*, 547. See also 543–55.
56. See Philippe C. Schmitter, 'Still the Century of Corporatism?', *Review of Politics*, 36 (January 1974) 85–139, esp. 93–4; and 'Models of Interest Intermediation and Models of Societal Change in Western Europe', *Comparative Political Studies*, 10, no. 1 (April 1977) 7–38, esp. 9. Among those who have used Schmitter's definition (though several of them also express certain reservations) are Linz, 'Totalitarian and Authoritarian Regimes,' 307; Stepan, *The State and Society*, 66; Leo Panitch, 'The Development of Corporatism in Liberal Democracies', *Comparative Political Studies*, 10, no. 1 (April 1977) 64; and Linn A. Mammergren, 'Corporatism in Latin American Politics: A Reexamination of the "Unique" Tradition', *Comparative Politics*, 9, no. 4 (July 1977) 466.
57. Schmitter, 'Still the Century', 96; 'Models of Interest Intermediation', 9.
58. Schmitter, 'Still the Century', 99–100.
59. Linz, 'Totalitarian and Authoritarian Regimes', 312 (though see also 346 where he writes of Yugoslavia as an 'authoritarian regime' in which 'the different degree of autonomy granted to different groups fits well with our notion of limited pluralism').
60. Stepan, *The State and Society*, 15.
61. Schmitter, 'Still the Century', 97; 'Models of Interest Intermediation', 30.
62. Valerie Bunce and John M. Echols III, 'Soviet Politics in the Brezhnev Era: "Pluralism" or "Corporatism"?', in Donald R. Kelley (ed.), *Soviet Politics in the Brezhnev Era* (New York, 1980) 1–26, esp. 19–20.
63. Ibid., 14.
64. Schmitter, 'Still the Century', 94; 'Models of Interest Intermediation', 9.
65. On the *nomenklatura*, see Bohdan Harasymiw, '*Nomenklatura*: The Soviet Communist Party's Leadership Recruitment System', *Canadian Journal of Political Science*, 2, no. 4, 493–512; Rolf H.W. Theen, 'Party and Bureaucracy', in Gordon B. Smith (ed.), *Public Policy and Administration in the Soviet Union* (New York, 1980) 18–52, esp. 38–44; and Michael Voslensky, *La Nomenklatura* (Paris, 1980).
66. Roy A. Medvedev, *On Socialist Democracy* (London, 1975) 404.
67. L.I. Brezhnev, 'Otchet tsentral'nogo Komiteta' (report of the Central Committee of the CPSU to the XXVI Congress), *Pravda* (24 February 1981) 8.
68. Daniel Tarschys exemplifies such an approach. See his *The Soviet Political Agenda: Problems and Priorities 1950–1970* (London, 1979) esp. ch. 2,

'The Soviet Political System: Three Models', 10–39, in which he compares and contrasts totalitarian, pluralist and bureaucratic models.

69. William Taubman is a prominent representative of this tendency. See his *Governing Soviet Cities* and his 'The Change to Change in Communist Systems', in Henry W. Morton and Rudolf L. Tőkés (eds), *Soviet Politics and Society in the 1970's* (New York, 1974) 369–94. Gordon B. Smith's 'Bureaucratic Politics and Public Policy in the Soviet Union' in Smith (ed.), *Public Policy and Administration in the Soviet Union*, adopts a similar position.

70. This is a position that emerges clearly in, for example, the numerous articles of T.H. Rigby over the past two decades. See, in particular, his 'Politics in the Mono-Organizational Society', in Janos (ed), *Authoritarian Politics in Communist Europe*, 31–80.

71. Leonard Schapiro is the most prominent among the scholars who adhere to this position. See especially his 'Reflections on the Changing Role of the Party in the Totalitarian Polity' in his *The Communist Party of the Soviet Union*, 2nd edn (London, 1970) 619–29.

72. For some examples, see Hill, *Soviet Politics, Political Science and Reform*.

73. See, for example, F.M. Burlatsky, *Lenin, Gosudarstvo, Politika* (Moscow, 1970); G. Shakhnazarov, *Sotsialisticheskaya demokratiya: nekotorye voprosy teorii* (Moscow, 1972); and R.A. Safarov, *Obshchestvennoe mnenie i gosudarstvennoe upravlenie* (Moscow, 1975).

74. Yu. A. Tikhomirov, 'Razvitie nauchnykh znaniy o sotsialisticheskom gosudarstve', in D.A. Kerimov, V.E. Chirkin and G. Kh. Shakhnazarov (eds), *Politika mira i razvitie politicheskikh sistem* (Moscow, 1979) 37.

75. G. Shakhnazarov, *The Destiny of the World: The Socialist Shape of Things to Come* (Moscow, 1978) 153.

76. Ibid.

77. G. Shakhnazarov, 'O demokraticheskom tsentralizme i politicheskom plyuralizme', *Kommunist*, no. 10 (July 1979) 107. This passage appears also in Shakhnazarov's book, *Fiasko futurologii (Kriticheskiy ocherk nemarksistskikh teoriy obshchestvennogo razvitiya)* (Moscow, 1979) 279.

78. See note 1.

79. After writing separately over many years, they joined forces to write an article in which they call, *inter alia*, for the establishment of a separate institution for the study of political science in the Soviet Union. See G. Kh. Shakhnazarov and F.M. Burlatsky, 'O razvitii Marksistsko–Leninskoy politicheskoy nauki', *Voprosy filosofii*, no. 12 (December 1980) 10–23, esp. 23.

80. Cf. ibid., 17, where Shakhnazarov and Burlatsky write of 'political power' as 'the key indicator' in political science.

81. See N.B. Pakholenko and N.N. Efremova, 'Nauchnoe soveshchanie sovetskoy assosiatsii politicheskikh nauk, "razvitie politicheskikh sistem v sovremennom mire"', in Kerimov, Chirkin and Shakhnazarov (eds), *Politika mira i razvitie politicheskikh sistem*, 266.

82. Ibid. The idea that a united front in such matters is a 'good thing' dies hard, despite the fact that nothing would have impressed Western political scientists more than the public airing at the IPSA Congress of disagreements among their Soviet counterparts, even the very same disagreements

which already find expression within specialized publications in the USSR.

83. V.S. Shevtsov, *Gosudarstvennyy suverenitet (Voprosy teorii)* (Moscow, 1979). Shevtsov's book was passed for typesetting in June 1979, and though the official publication date is 1979, it was on sale only from early 1980. The *tirazh* is small: 2400. (Tikhomirov's views are criticized on pages 16 and 157). Shevtsov, a prominent jurist and party ideologist, is also an official within the Department of Science and Education of the Central Committee of the CPSU and a member of the executive committee of the Soviet Association of Political Sciences. His most recent books, apart from *Gosudarstvennyy suverenitet*, are *Natsional'nyy suverenitet (problemy teorii i metodologii)* (Moscow, 1979); *Citizenship of the USSR (A Legal Study)* (Moscow, 1978); and *Sotsial'no-politicheskie osnovy edinstva sovetskogo naroda* (Moscow, 1975).

84. As expressed in Yu. A. Tikhomirov, *Mekhanizm upravleniya v razvitom sotsialisticheskom obshchestve* (Moscow, 1978); and 'in 'Sotsializm i politicheskaya vlast'', *Sovektskoe gosudarstvo i pravo*, no. 5 (1974) 11–19.

85. Burlatsky is a philosopher by academic background and head of the Department of Philosophy of the Academy of Social Sciences attached to the Central Committee of the Party. He also holds an appointment at the Institute of the International Workers' Movement of the Academy of Sciences and is a Vice-President of the Soviet Association of Political Sciences. As a young member of the party apparatus, he was remarkably influential in the late Khrushchev years. When he and some of his colleagues first put forward the idea of the 'all-people's state', the high-level party reaction was one of shock and the proposal was condemned as revisionist from within even the ranks of the leadership. Before long, however, the concept was given the highest possible official endorsement in the 1961 Party Programme, though it was to suffer a partial and temporary eclipse in the early Brezhnev years. (See Roger E. Kanet, 'The Rise and Fall of the "All-People's State": Recent Changes in the Soviet Theory of the State', *Soviet Studies*, 20, no. 1 [July 1968] 81–93.) The idea has been fully rehabilitated only since the appearance of the 1977 Constitution, though even then with an emphasis on the relative continuity between the 'all-people's state' and the stage of the 'dictatorship of the proletariat' which was absent in Khrushchev's time. On Burlatsky and his contributions to the formulation of the concepts of the 'all-people's state' under Khrushchev and of 'developed socialism' under Brezhnev, see also Hough, *The Soviet Union and Social Science Theory*, 112 and 256; and Hough and Fainsod, *How the Soviet Union is Governed*, 255.

86. See especially V.G. Kalensky, *Gosudarstvo kak ob'ekt sotsiologicheskogo analiza (ocherki istorii i metodologii issledovaniya)* (Moscow, 1977); and 'Problemy sotsiologii gosudarstva v istorii politiko-pravovoy mysli', *Sovetskoe gosudarstvo i pravo*, no. 5 (1979) 117–22.

87. See, for example, F.M. Burlatsky, 'Politicheskaya sistema razvitogo sotsializma', *Voprosy filosofii*, no. 8 (1977) 18; Fyodor Burlatsky, *The Modern State and Politics* (Moscow, 1978) 47–51; and F.M. Burlatsky and V.E. Chirkin (eds), *Politicheskie sistemy sovremennosti* (Moscow, 1978) 26–7.

88. Burlatsky and Chirkin (eds), *Politicheskie sistemy sovremennosti*, 26.

89. Ibid., 27.
90. See, for example, Burlatsky, *The Modern State and Politics*, 50; Kalensky, *Gosudarstvo kak ob'ekt sotsiologicheskogo analiza*, 179; and Kalensky, in Burlatsky and Chirkin (eds), *Politicheskie sistemy sovremennosti*, 34–5.
91. Kalensky, in Burlatsky and Chirkin (eds), *Politicheskie sistemy sovremennosti*, 34.
92. Burlatsky, *The Modern State and Politics*, 50; Kalensky, *Gosudarstvo kak ob'ekt sotsiologicheskogo analiza*, 179.
93. Kalensky, *Gosudarstvo kak ob'ekt sotsiologicheskogo analiza*, 179.
94. Ibid.
95. Burlatsky, *The Modern State and Politics*, 50.
96. Ibid., 50–1. L.S. Mamut in his *Karl Marks kak teoretik gosudarstva* (Moscow, 1979) notes (166) that Marx used the concept of public power in a variety of different senses. Referring (178) to G.N. Manov, *Gosudarstvo i politicheskaya organizatsiya obshchestva* (Moscow, 1974) and to Burlatsky's 'Politicheskaya sistema razvitogo sotsializma', Mamut notes that 'the state' is regarded by these authors 'as one of the institutions of the political organisation, of the political system', and for 'such a formulation of the problem', he adds, there are 'now weighty reasons'. 'However,' he goes on, 'the problem of distinguishing the state and the political organisation of society, the state and the political system, the problem of their links and relations, so controversial today, had hardly been raised so sharply in Marx's time. Therefore he did not specially single it out and analyse it.'
97. Burlatsky, 'Politicheskaya sistema razvitogo sotsializma', 23. Indeed, as long ago as his *Pravda* article on 'Politika i nauka' (10 January 1965), Burlatsky made, *inter alia*, essentially this point.
98. Burlatsky, 'Politika i nauka'.
99. Kalensky, *Gosudarstvo kak ob'ekt sotsiologicheskogo analiza*, 180.
100. V.S. Shevtsov, 'Politicheskaya vlast' v sisteme politicheskoy organizatsii sovetskogo obshchestva', in D.A. Kerimov (ed.), *Mezhdunarodnye otnosheniya, politika i lichnost'* (Moscow, 1976) 35–44, esp. 40.
101. Ibid.
102. Ibid., 41.
103. Among them, Tikhomirov (16 and 157), L.S. Mamut (23) and A.K. Belykh (158). Shevtsov, *Gosudarstvennyy suverenitet*.
104. Ibid., 158.
105. V.M. Terletsky, *Leninskoe ideynoe nasledie i problemy sovetskogo stroitel'stva* (Kiev, 1974) 214–15.
106. Burlatsky, in Burlatsky and Chirkin (eds), *Politicheskie sistemy sovremennosti*, 9.
107. The full article (which some might think implies the exercise of political power on the part of the Communist Party) reads:

> The leading and guiding force of Soviet society and the nucleus of its political system, of all state organisations and public organisations is the Communist Party of the Soviet Union. The CPSU exists for the people and serves the people.
> The Communist Party, armed with Marxism–Leninism, determines

the general perspectives of the development of society and the course of the home and foreign policy of the USSR, directs the constructive work of the Soviet people, and imparts a planned, systematic and theoretically substantiated character to their struggle for the victory of communism.

All party organisations shall function within the framework of the Constitution of the USSR.

(*Constitution of the USSR*, Moscow, 1977, 21)

108. Shevtsov, *Gosudarstvennyy surverenitet*, 159.
109. Ibid.
110. Shevtsov, ibid., 160.
111. Ibid., 158.
112. Ibid., 160.
113. The reference is to A. Kozharov's article, 'O kontseptsii ideyno-politisheskogo plyuralizma', *Problema mira i sotsializma*, no. 1 (1977); see also Kozharov's *Monizm i plyuralizm v ideologii i politike*.
114. See note 84.
115. *Sovetskoe gosudarstvo i pravo*, no. 7 (July 1981) 142–4, esp. 143.
116. The Soviet literature on 'Political power in Soviet society' was reviewed in a 1977 Moscow dissertation, in which the author placed Soviet scholars in three different groups in terms of their use of the concept of power 'as a general sociological category'. In this particular classification, the distinctions are between (1) those who see power as the leadership, direction and co-ordination of people's actions; (2) those (whom the author sees as composing the largest group and in which he includes Burlatsky) who define power as the 'right and possibility' or 'ability' to subordinate the wills of individuals to the predominant wishes in a given association; and (3) those who identify power directly with coercion or subordination. See V.L. Usachev, *Politicheskaya vlast' v Sovetskom obshchestve (avtoreferat dissertatsii na soiskanie uchenoy stepeni kandidata yuridicheskikh nauk)* (Moscow, 1977) esp. 4.
117. Shakhnazarov and Burlatsky, 'O razvitii Marksistsko–Leninskoy politicheskoy nauki'. I discuss this and other recent developments in Soviet political science in a forthcoming article, 'Political Science in the Soviet Union: A New Stage of Development?'
118. Shakhnazarov and Burlatsky, 'O razvitii Marksistsko–Leninskoy politicheskoy nauki', 17.
119. Ibid.
120. Ibid.
121. Ibid.
122. Ibid. For an example of a book which takes a similar view of power within the political system, while using the terminology, 'Political organisation of Soviet society' for what should now, in Shakhnazarov's and Burlatsky's terms be 'the Soviet political system', see M.N. Marchenko, *Politicheskaya organizatsiya sovetskogo obshchestva i ee burzhuaznye fal'sifikatory* (Moscow, 1973) esp. 40 and 69–70.
123. Shakhnazarov, *Sotsialisticheskaya demokratiya* 86–7. This distinction by Shakhnazarov of the party's role according to area of policy is also noted by

Hill, *Soviet Politics, Political Science and Reform*, 124.

124. David Holloway, 'Foreign and Defence Policy' (49–76) in Brown and Kaser (eds), *The Soviet Union since the Fall of Khrushchev*, 73.
125. *Pravda* (24 February 1981) 8.
126. Mlynář, *Nightfrost in Prague*, 136. Mlynář is writing about the Presidium of the Central Committee of the Communist Party of Czechoslovakia, the meetings of which he attended in 1968 as a Secretary of the Central Committee and later as a full Presidium member. He notes that 'the decision-making process was essentially the same under Dubček as it had been under Novotný' so far as this highest party organ was concerned. In an interview with the present author in Oxford on 2 June 1979, Mlynář expressed the opinion that the same practices and procedures were followed in the Soviet Union.
127. My source for this statement is a senior Gosplan official.
128. Mlynář interview.
129. V.S. Shevtsov, 'Politicheskaya vlast' v sisteme politicheskoy organizatsii Sovetskogo obshchestva', in Kerimov (ed.), *Mezhdunarodnye otnosheniya politika i lichnost'*, 35–36.
130. Ibid., 39.
131. Burlatsky, in Burlatsky and Chirkin (eds), *Politicheskie sistemy sovremennosti*, 18.
132. Ibid., 17–23.
133. Kalensky, *Gosudarstvo kak ob'ekt sotsiologicheskogo analiza*, 122.
134. Ibid., 123.
135. Kalensky, 'Problemy sotsiologii gosudarstva v istorii politiko-pravovoy mysli', 122.
136. Apart from numerous articles, he published a well-informed book on American political science which Rolf H.W. Theen took as his major point of reference for an entire article on Soviet political science. See V.G. Kalensky, *Politicheskaya nauka v SShA: kritika burzhuaznykh kontseptsiy vlasti* (Moscow, 1969); and Theen, 'Political Science in the USSR: "To be or not to be"' (note 1).
137. His latest book is devoted to the political thought of James Madison. See V.G. Kalensky, *Medison* (Moscow, 1981).
138. Jack Hayward has suggested that both the terms 'state' and 'society' have 'a misleadingly monolithic ring about them', that this is especially true of the former, and that this is 'one reason why many political scientists eschew the term, "state" and prefer "political system"'. See Jack Hayward and R.N. Berki (eds), *State and Society in Contemporary Europe* (Oxford, 1979) 23.
139. Burlatsky, in Burlatsky and Chirkin (eds), *Politicheskie sistemy sovremennosti*, 27.
140. 'Institutional pluralism', in so far as it may exist, is, of course, a special case of 'stretching' of the concept of pluralism. In Dahl's definition of the relative autonomy of organizations, the 'government of the state' is implicitly treated as *one* organization. Institutional groupings and conflicts *within* government would not, in his terms (or, indeed, in those of most other pluralist theorists), count as pluralism at all.
141. A view expressed, for example, by Zdeněk Mlynář, 'The Rules of the Game: The Soviet Bloc Today', *Political Quarterly* 50, no. 4 (October–December 1979) 407.

142. 'Political regime' is a concept that has been elaborated in an interesting way by Soviet scholars in recent years. I have more to say about it in a forthcoming article, 'Political Science in the Soviet Union: A New Stage of Development?'

143. Kalensky, *Gosudarstvo kak ob'ekt sotsiologicheskogo analiza*, 171.

144. For the best account of this evolution, see Dennison Rusinow, *The Yugoslav Experiment 1948–1974* (London, 1977).

145. See *Akční program Komunistické strany Československa* (Prague, 1968) 15–18, esp. 15–16.

146. See, for example, Shakhnazarov, 'O demokraticheskom tsentralizme i politicheskom plyuralizme', 108.

147. See Skilling, 'Interest Groups and Communist Politics', 449. Cf. H. Gordon Skilling, 'Pluralism in Communist Societies: Straw Men and Red Herrings', *Studies in Comparative Communism*, 13, no. 1 (Spring 1980) 84.

148. Discussion in print of Soviet foreign policy is of an even more esoteric nature with differences of view expressed in somewhat veiled terms and policy changes shrouded in a mantle of continuity. See, for example, Jerry F. Hough, 'The Evolution of the Soviet World View', *World Politics*, 32, no. 4 (July 1980) 509–30; and Morton Schwartz, *Soviet Perceptions of the United States* (Berkeley, Calif. and London, 1978). Other writers continue to see only the undifferentiated view of 'Moscow's spokesmen'. See, for example, Stephen P. Gibert, *Soviet Images of America* (London, 1977).

149. This holds true for many areas of social policy from reform of family law to the problem of alcoholism and to protection of the environment. For useful brief accounts of debates in these areas of policy, see Peter H. Juviler, 'Family Reforms on the Road to Communism', in Peter H. Juviler and Henry W. Morton, *Soviet Policy-Making: Studies of Communism in Transition* (London, 1967); Peter H. Juviler, 'Whom the State has Joined: Conjugal Ties in Soviet Law', in Donald D. Barry, George Ginsburgs and Peter B. Maggs (eds), *Soviet Law after Stalin*, Part I (Leyden 1977); Solomon, *Soviet Criminologists and Criminal Policy*, esp. ch. 6, 81–90; Donald R. Kelley, 'Environmental Policy-Making in the USSR: The Role of Industrial and Environmental Interest Groups', *Soviet Studies*, 28, no. 4 (October 1976) 570–89; and Thane Gustafson, 'Environmental Policy under Brezhnev: Do the Soviets Really Mean Business?', in Kelley (ed.), *Soviet Politics in the Brezhnev Era*, 129–49.

5 Political Pluralism and Markets in Communist Systems*

WŁODZIMIERZ BRUS

I. INTRODUCTORY REMARKS

The aim of this essay is to examine the relation between the increase in the role of the market mechanism in East European communist economies and the prospect of evolution of their political systems toward pluralism. The question asked is: whether or to what extent should 'marketization' of the economy be regarded as a factor contributing to 'pluralization' of the polity?

In many respects the problem is similar to the one posed by Benjamin Ward in his article, 'Political power and economic change in Yugoslavia'.[1] However, Ward was more ambitious: he wanted to 'get behind the institutional forms of the realities of political decision making' and asked whether 'since the reforms of the early 1950s Yugoslavia has become more democratic'.[2] Ward employed quite an elaborate criterion:

A polity will be said to have become more democratic, *ceteris paribus*, when the range of issues over which the government is challenged or can reasonably expect to be challenged expands,

---

* The author wishes to acknowledge with thanks comments upon an earlier version of the paper received from members of the seminar on 'Politics and Markets' run by R.W. Johnson and S.M. Lukes (University of Oxford), as well as from Professor Gregory Grossman (University of California, Berkeley).

or when the intensity of challenge increases. By challenge is meant an attempt to defeat or substantially modify the proposal with some significant probability of success.[3]

Here the approach is more institutional – some would say, formal. I speak not of democracy but of *political pluralism*, a concept that I take to correspond to *polyarchy* as it appeared first in Dahl and Lindblom (1953),[4] and as it was later refined by Lindblom in his book *Politics and Markets*.[5] In the latter source the following 'familiar rights and prerogatives' are listed as ('imperfectly') included in 'all polyarchical authority systems': freedom to form and join organizations; freedom of expression; the right to vote; eligibility for public office; the right of political leaders to compete for support; the right of political leaders to compete for votes; alternative sources of information; free and fair elections ... which decide who is to hold top authority; and the establishment of institutions for making government policies depend on votes and other expressions of preference.[6] The elements of polyarchy can, of course, be worded differently (for example in a more aggregated manner, as in Peter Wiles's 'empirical criteria for the existence of *political* freedom'[7]) but the essence remains roughly the same. Thus, pluralization of the political system is understood to mean acquisition of the features of polyarchy. There seems to be no reason to exclude the possibility of gradual or only partial institutionalization of the 'familiar rights and prerogatives', with the result that pluralization can also be a gradual or incomplete *process*.

None of the existing communist polities, including Yugoslavia, is classified by Lindblom[8] as polyarchic, although the Yugoslav economy ('and perhaps Hungary') is counted among the market-oriented ones. If we accepted this view, would not our investigation be redundant from the very outset? I think not, because what we are looking for are dynamic tendencies influenced by factors that can be necessary but still insufficient. Differences over time and between individual countries deserve an examination in this context.

How should we designate the communist non-polyarchies? There are few signs of hesitation in this respect in the independent East European literature ('samizdat') or in the writings of East European political scientists who are publishing abroad (one of the recent examples being Mlynář[9]): the communist political systems are described as *totalitarian*, and the present writer, having attempted to elaborate on the matter,[10] regards himself as belonging to the same 'camp'. However, many Western political scientists reject the 'totalitarian syndrome', invoking, *inter alia*, the interest-group approach pioneered by H. Gordon Skilling.[11] The differences go well beyond terminology, but there is no need to discuss them here. For the sake of terminological symmetry with polyarchy, and following some earlier leads (S. Ossowski's 'monocentric order'[12] and T.H. Rigby's 'mono-organizational society'[13]) the communist polities will in this paper be called 'mono-archies' (if I may coin the term).

The concept of 'marketization' seems generally unambiguous. It refers to the introduction or extension of the market as a mechanism of allocating goods and services. However, in the evolution of the communist systems such an all-embracing definition may be of little use. It seems particularly important to distinguish between the purely formal application of passive market categories[14] as in the Soviet *khozraschet*, where monetary flows merely follow the physical flows determined by administrative decisions, and the market in an economic sense, with price relations presenting real alternative choices. Even the second case must be further qualified: price relations may reflect preferences of the planners who use the market as an instrument (a regulated market), or they may reflect the horizontal interactions of independent economic agents (a free market). Thus, marketization is not only a matter of the width of the market but also of its depth, the latter being inversely related to the degree of government involvement. 'An economy will be said to have become more marketized, *ceteris paribus*, if over some range of issues government involvement in the decisions is reduced.'[15] This formula may be subject to various detailed interpretations, but in the main it brings out the real issue. It is primarily from this point of view that we shall have to look at the political consequences of differences in the scope of consumer and labour markets, and particularly at the scope of changes in the system of functioning of the *public* economy: comprehensive transformation, as in the Yugoslav case, or the limited changes resulting from economic reforms in the Soviet-bloc countries. The market-oriented economic reforms have been regarded by many as harbingers of political pluralism. The failures of most of them have been explained (at least in part)[16] by political fears of the ruling élite and the supporting apparatus. How well founded were, and still are, these expectations and fears? This may be another way of asking the question we have set out to answer in this essay.

II. 'POLITICS IN COMMAND'

The history of communist systems offers quite a number of instances when marketization of some sort coincided with a form of political liberalization. We may look as far back as the change in the USSR from 'war communism' to NEP in 1921 (which included resuscitation of the rural–urban market, a private sector outside agriculture, commercial principles of operation for state enterprises, and so on). The NEP not only meant direct restoration of freedom of choice in the economic sphere for the peasant, consumer and job-seeker, but was also accompanied by notable relaxation in culture and ideology, in personnel policy, in foreign contacts, and to some extent in the operation of the state administration itself (particularly local administration in the countryside).[17] Conversely, the end of NEP went hand-in-hand with the onset of extreme forms of Stalinist tyranny. Soviet and East European post-war history, on the whole, does not apparently offer such sharp distinctions, although one could suggest that correlation exists between the post-Stalin ameliorations in exercising the mono-archy, and the lifting of many restrictions in consumer and labour markets. The lifting of these restrictions allowed shifts from administrative to market-type rules in relations between the state and the *kolkhozy* and brought a more positive attitude to individual farming plots, or even (in the Polish case) to private agriculture as such. There has been a significant extension of personal liberties in Yugoslavia parallel to the first steps towards market socialism in the 1950s, and some writers[18] claim that such a parallel development continued in the process of marketization of the Yugoslav economy. Hungary does not yet provide adequate evidence for comparisons over time, although it is often said to be relatively more liberal than most of its less marketized partners in the Soviet bloc.

On the other hand, this parallelism ought not to be stretched too far: lack of it, or even developments in opposite directions, are quite frequent. It was during NEP that the remnants of intra-party pluralism and trade union autonomy were effectively eradicated (the latter occurred contrary to Lenin's own insistence on the need to revive the trade unions in view of the commercialization of state enterprises).[19] Indeed, the political foundations of Stalinism were laid at just this time. Market freedoms failed to provide any defences against the decision to bring the NEP to an end; and, conversely, when some reprieve had to be granted to the market in the 1930s (in the form of a *kolkhoz* market and the de-rationing of consumer goods) these same market freedoms did not in the least curtail the grinding power of the political terror machine. Another twist took place during the war: a relaxation occurred in the intellectual sphere and a major breakthrough (under the circumstances) came in human rights with the opening of the churches. This breakthrough did not, of course, have any relation to changes in the economic mechanism. Likewise, one could hardly detect liberalization accompanying the East German 'New Economic System' in the mid-1960s or any change in the political climate after the fall of Khrushchev and the reforms launched in the Soviet Union by Kosygin.

Looking behind the instances of positive correlation between marketization and liberalization in a search for possible traces of a causal relationship, we find in most cases a rather predictable sequence of events: political developments (sometimes of an explosive character) precede both marketization and liberalization. To use the Chinese phrase, politics is usually in command. NEP is the first clear case in point, followed by the Soviet–Yugoslav break, the Hungarian uprising (with delayed but lasting effects), and the succession of Polish revolts from 1956 to 1980. The Czechoslovak Spring was comparatively peaceful but politically the most comprehensive development so far, and fully deserves to be called 'the interrupted revolution'.[20] One could venture to add China to this list, after the overthrow of the 'gang of four'.

To state in general terms that political liberties are won through political struggle is trivial; after all, none of the existing polyarchies can be claimed to be a spontaneous outcome of the operation of the market, *laissez-faire* or otherwise. But such a statement is perhaps less trivial when applied to communist systems for several reasons. First, there is the still hovering millennial view of communism as being, by definition, a free society and one devoid of political conflicts (the author will be forgiven for failing to discuss this point); and, second, there is the amalgamation of strictly political with economic power which makes the communist mono-archy so special. The latter aspect seems very relevant to our problem and calls for a brief examination.

The communist systems have emerged not as a result of gradual evolution in the course of which spontaneous change in economic institutions transformed the political set-up step by step, but as a result of the revolutionary establishment of a new state which embarked upon construction of an economic system according to a preconceived design (or according to what was supposed to be a design). With the takeover by the state of most of the productive apparatus and the introduction of central planning, the conventional boundaries between the political and economic spheres, if they have not disappeared completely, have at least become very blurred indeed. Political decisions concern primarily economic matters and the question of power in the economy is of paramount and direct political significance. In addition there has been (and still is) a strong ideological bias against the market, the overcoming of which (the German term *Aufhebung* fits better philosophically) is regarded as a condition of or even tantamount to attainment of the ultimate goal of communism proper.

Several corollaries seem to follow. First, any systemic change along the road to marketization requires prior political decision (which may be reversed as well!). Second, every such decision means a contraction of the sphere under direct control of the mono-archy, quite apart from the indirect consequences for the polity in a strict sense (which may or may not happen, as we have yet to ascertain). And third, it presents ideological difficulties.

Why then should marketization occur at all under a communist mono-archy? Under some conditions it presumably becomes, or promises to become, advantageous for the mono-archy, or at least appears to be a lesser evil. In many instances a belief in the 'lesser evil' was clear. The transition from 'war communism' to NEP was a matter of life and death for the regime; private plots and *kolkhoz* markets in the 1930s were indispensable for averting an

ultimate economic disaster with potentially severe political
consequences. Post-war cases were perhaps less dramatic, but
their essence was often similar: the aim was to preserve or
strengthen the mono-archy by giving in to economic exigencies.
Concessions became an increasingly vital factor for securing, if
not active support, at least passive acquiescence on the part of the
populace. 'Kadarism' is probably the most outstanding example
of this kind to date. Long memories of the revolution of 1956
made a better deal for the consumer absolutely imperative. When
it came to be recognized that such a change required a complex,
market-oriented reform, the necessary step was taken, but with
the utmost care not to undermine the mono-archy proper. (With
the Polish experience of 1980 in mind, Brezhnev and others must
have blessed the hour in which they decided not to thwart the
Hungarian experiment.) This does not mean that marketization
must always remain the bitter medicine forced upon a reluctant
power élite by extreme conditions. In some circumstances the
initiative may come from above (for example, when marketization is regarded as an effective weapon in factional struggle).
The clearest case of marketization initiated from above came in
Yugoslavia after 1948. At first, the change was apparently considered mainly in the context of economic policies designed to
secure domestic support in the battle against the Stalinist threat,
and perhaps to facilitate external reorientation as well. But soon
marketization developed into the economic foundation of the
ideology of self-managed socialism. In Czechoslovakia during
1968 (as by the 'revisionists' in Poland during 1956) market-
oriented economic reforms were regarded as part and parcel of
the programme of political pluralization. Thus, it would not be
correct to say that marketization was in all cases undertaken solely
as a form of 'dynamic petrification'[21] of mono-archy. Nevertheless, in many cases (perhaps most), this was indeed the intention.

What a paradox: the market emerges not as the gravedigger
but as the saviour of communist mono-archy! But does it work as
intended? Or, intentions notwithstanding, does marketization in
the long run become a factor promoting the transition to
polyarchy? We are again at our original question – this time, let
us hope, with a better understanding of the framework in which
communist mono-archies might consent to enlarging the role of
the market.

III. MARKETS AS CONSTRAINTS

As mentioned in the first section, the concept of marketization in communist economies must be made more specific for the purposes of our analysis. We shall therefore attempt to distinguish between three 'degrees' of marketization which have appeared in the communist experience so far: first, there are consumer and labour markets in an otherwise centralistically managed economy, approximated in practice by the Soviet-type systems; second, there are centrally planned economies with a regulated market mechanism,[22] approximated by the Hungarian New Economic Mechanism (NEM); and, third, there is market socialism, approximated by the post-1965 Yugoslav system. It goes without saying that each of the subsequent degrees subsumes the preceding one. Peasant markets complicate somewhat this neatly arranged sequence, as do 'irregularities' in the scope and intensity of the 'second economy' (understood here as activity outside the official rules). Whenever possible these complications will be taken into account, but basically we shall proceed by the indicated degrees.

Consumer and labour markets

The existence of a consumer (retail) market and of a labour market (the latter term remains banned in the USSR and a few other communist countries) nowadays is taken for granted but it was not always so. The marketless model of 'war communism' was once looked upon nostalgically as the proper form of communist economy.[23] At the XVII Congress of the CPSU in 1934, Stalin had to defend the legitimacy of 'Soviet trade' after proclaiming fulfilment of the tasks of the transition period from a multi-sectoral (in socio-economic terms) to a socialist system.[24] Leaving aside the 'imperfections' caused by formal and informal rationing of some consumer goods and services, or restrictions on freedom of choice of occupation and place of work, do these markets exert any influence on the way the state authority operates?

I think they do. Let us take the consumer market first. Its existence means that the consumers' share in national income finds its expression predominantly (that is, apart from public services in kind) in monetary purchasing power. The aggregate of this purchasing power, created by the state as paymaster and purchaser of agricultural produce, constitutes some sort of obligation on the part of the state to provide a corresponding volume of goods and services at established prices. This obligation, as we all know very well, is by no means always fully honoured (shortages occur), but even so it remains a matter of concern to the planners and policy makers who cannot look with indifference at market disequilibria which give rise to obvious dissatisfaction and to black-market phenomena. To try to close the gap simply by way of price increases is quite difficult politically and makes failure to fulfil the obligations quite obvious.

The difference between a retail market on one hand, and the direct distribution of consumer goods and services on the other, becomes even more pronounced when the structure of supply (or the product-mix) is taken into consideration. True, the centralized model of the Soviet-type economy corresponds by and large to the situation in which 'freedom of choice in consumption does not imply that production is actually guided by the choices of the consumers'.[25] Planners can, to a large extent, allocate resources between production of various consumer goods according to their own scale of preferences, imposing this structure on the possessors of unspecified purchasing power (money) by an appropriate manipulation of retail prices. Nevertheless, they can do so only within limits, as anyone familiar with the concept of price-elasticities of demand will appreciate theoretically, and as anyone familiar with the coexistence of shortages and excessive stocks in East European warehouses will corroborate empirically. Thus the planners, in their production decisions, must at least give some consideration to consumer preferences: the arbitrary power of the mono-archy is somewhat curbed by the existence of the retail market.

The labour market seems to have even greater effect from this point of view. The central plan determines to some extent the structure of demand for jobs (through planning of education) and more directly regulates the overall structure of job openings (through investment and employment policy). The latter can hardly be changed from below on any significant scale. What can be affected, however, under conditions of free choice of occupation is both the size of the work force at the margin (for example family members join or leave the work force in response to the kind of jobs available), and the earning differentials.

Despite the fact that the setting of wage scales in the plan is one of the most important state functions, under the impact of spontaneous labour turnover those scales almost inevitably deviate from the established norms. In a supply-determined labour market freedom to change jobs becomes quite a powerful informal bargaining factor and is used as a sort of substitute for orderly institutionalized bargaining. In some sociological investigations of the Soviet labour market it is claimed that resistance of unskilled and semi-skilled workers to the Shchekino-type incentive schemes (strongly focused on productivity increases) has been motivated mainly by the fear of losing this bargaining power.[26] The 'second economy' in employment (moonlighting) also acts against effective control of time utilization on the regular job, particularly with regard to work intensity. And the individual plots in *kolkhozy*, closely linked with peasant markets, exert perhaps an even stronger influence on the intensity and quality of work in collective farming. Obviously, in relation to private farming (as in Poland) or to more genuinely cooperative farming (as recently in Hungary), the market constraints are even greater: not only are price elasticities of output high, but neglect of proper 'terms of trade' between agriculture and industry may lead to harmful changes in occupational structure on a macroeconomic scale, as witnessed, for example, in Poland towards the end of the 1970s.

One should, of course, beware of exaggeration. In a centralized model the direct economic power of the communist mono-archy is enormous. The authorities control macroeconomic decisions concerning both aggregate accumulation-consumption ratios and the allocation of investment and consumption funds between sectors. They also control microeconomic decisions up to the enterprise level through detailed target planning and physical allocation of resources. Similarly, they have control over appointments to positions of authority throughout the economy, while the Party apparatus supervises economic activity on all levels. The sphere of operation of the market is not only circumscribed but also has many peculiar features which make it fall far short of a system of popular control'.[27] Nonetheless, even in such a restricted form the consumer and labour markets provide some limitation on the mono-archy's economic power and make it less arbitrary.

Regulated market mechanism

A centrally planned economy with a regulated market mechanism, as approximated by the Hungarian NEM, means that concentration of all economic decisions within the socialized sector at the central level gives way to a *multiplicity of decision-making levels*. In a simplified two-tier model (centre–enterprise) the centre takes *directly* the *fundamental* macroeconomic decisions, while the current or *standard* decisions (what and how to produce, in the first place) are taken by the enterprises themselves. This model entails abolition of both obligatory target planning and of the hierarchical subordination of operative (annual) plans. It also eliminates the vertical allocation of goods and services between enterprises in physical terms. Enterprises enter freely into contractual (horizontal) relations with each other, reacting as buyers and sellers to alternative choices reflected in prices (money becomes active within the state economy). Effective central planning is expected to be maintained by:

1. the general framework created as a result of fundamental decisions taken directly at the centre;
2. 'rules of behaviour' for the enterprises (the maximand – profit, rate of profit, value added, and so on – and the link between the chosen maximand and personal incentives, supply of factors, and so on) determined in such a way as to make the pursuit of microeconomic objectives contribute to the attainment of macroeconomic goals; and
3. control over the parameters entering into the enterprises' calculation (prices, taxes, interest rates, credit availability, custom tariffs, rates of exchange, and so on) which enables the centre to guide the autonomous agents in the desired overall direction.

Even without going into more detailed analysis, it seems clear that despite the retention of overriding economic powers by the centre, we have here a substantial extension of the market: it operates now *within the state economy as well*, and not only in relations between the state and the households. How does this extension affect the economic position of the state?

In the first place, it reinforces the constraints represented by the consumer and labour markets. Profit-oriented enterprises must pay more attention to consumer preferences than do plan-oriented enterprises. It would be too much to say that production is actually 'guided by the choice of consumers' (the structure of capacities is largely determined by the plan, and an active price policy may still be pursued), but the change in this direction is substantial and the situation cannot any longer be described as offering no more than freedom to choose between fixed alternatives. This still is not a case of 'consumer sovereignty', but after all such sovereignty is a myth everywhere. As for the labour market, economic considerations in an enterprise's personnel policy must gain in weight at the expense of political ones and operational autonomy should also lead to greater flexibility in implementing wage policy. Overall there occurs a reduction in the degree of imperfection of this market.

Second, a regulated market mechanism within the state economy replaces commands and administrative methods in plan implementation by *rules* and *economic* instruments. Rules can be changed, of course, but neither simply nor frequently. Use of economic instruments requires consideration of the cost consequences of government decisions, including compensation to enterprises if their position is adversely affected. On both counts the degree of arbitrariness has to be curtailed. Furthermore, since the plans of enterprises are no longer formal segments of plans worked out by the state hierarchy, the latter (at least to some extent) has to treat enterprise plans and actual performance as independent variables and to enter into a process of mutual exchange of information and mutual adjustments.

Third, the autonomy of the enterprises (this term seems preferable to 'independence' because of the implications of effective central planning) creates the preconditions for employee participation in management, which in turn may evolve into full-fledged self-management. Self-management is an *institutional* change that might be of political significance in a system where the economy is dominated by the state. In itself it cannot be regarded as the direct outcome of introducing a regulated market mechanism; separate decisions are required. However, without autonomy of the enterprises both participation in management, and even more so self-management, are meaningless. There is very little to be co-managed. Conversely, creation of such an autonomy generates pressure for participation in management. Moreover, for the same reasons which Lenin advanced at the outset of NEP, commercial attitudes on the part of enterprises may also evoke legitimate claims to independent employee representation (trade unions, workers' councils).

Fourth, the introduction of a regulated market mechanism into the state economy must influence the position of non-state enterprises. As can be seen in Hungary, this tendency applies in a most interesting way to the co-operative sector, which becomes visibly more autonomous and market-oriented. Private enterprises acquire a great deal more security, which is essential for a longer-term orientation of business activity. After some period of orderly application of rules both within and outside the state sector, one may expect both a diminished role for the 'second economy' and at the same time the emergence of genuine choice between alternative (legal) sources of livelihood in the state, co-operative or private sector. Even on a relatively modest scale this tendency acts as another constraint on the mono-archy's arbitrariness.

Fifth, we must not omit the development of foreign economic relations. In theory these relations could be regarded as being connected only remotely with domestic economic reforms. In practice, however, a strong feedback appears to be the rule rather than the exception. Introduction of a regulated market mechanism decentralizes contacts with foreign partners (in trade transactions proper, in technical and scientific co-operation, and so on) and this change may affect the political sphere. Marketization is by no means the only factor helping to increase the flow of people and information across the frontiers, but some interrelation certainly exists.

Market socialism

The main distinction between a centrally planned economy with a regulated market mechanism and *market socialism*, as defined by this author, is that the latter shifts the responsibility for capital formation ('expanded reproduction' in Marxist terminology) away from the state to enterprises themselves. In principle the division of net revenue into retained and distributed portions, as well as the decision to save or to expand productive capacities out of the retained revenue, is to be left to the enterprises. These choices can be more or less influenced by some form of indicative planning (so far, not adequately defined in Yugoslav practice), or by the usual fiscal and/or monetary policies. Nevertheless, the choices are supposed to be taken on economic rather than on political grounds, a requirement that entails wide-ranging extension of the role of the market. In the first place, some sort of capital market, however imperfect or unconventional, must take over from the state budget the function of inter-enterprise, inter-sectoral and inter-regional redistribution of investment funds. An obvious requirement is a change in the role of the banking system, which can no longer act merely as a financial arm of the central planner (as in the case of central planning, with even a regulated market), but instead has to operate on a commercial basis. Prices and other market categories function in what may be called the conventional way, and the creation of conditions conducive to competition becomes essential. These conditions must include a high degree of openness to the world market. Such openness may be compatible with some type of controls, but it cannot be reconciled with the orthodox rules of a 'monopoly of foreign trade'. The economy can be said to remain socialist in so far as private ownership of capital is eliminated, or at least in so far as the public sector maintains its predominant position in the economy. However, the question of how an economy consisting of fully commercialized public enterprises can be made to serve some overall social welfare objectives, to conform to a desired pattern of income distribution, and to take account of externalities, and so on, is a tricky one. Compared with what has been presented here as the 'second degree' of marketization, market socialism operates not only without the general framework created by the so-called fundamental decisions, but also without 'rules of behaviour' dictated from above. In this case the 'rules of behaviour' derive from the market and from the particular way in which the entrepreneurial function is defined – whether it is vested in professional management on behalf of the state, in shareholders' representatives, or in employee self-management. The latter is the case in Yugoslavia, and because this is the only communist country with an economy resembling market socialism, we can disregard the other theoretically possible versions.

It seems that there is no need to go point by point over the previously discussed market constraints in order to prove that all of them are substantially reinforced under market socialism. In so far as the market replaces direct controls, government involvement in the economy changes its forms and becomes more restricted. This is true, as we have seen, even for the centralized system and applies all the more forcefully to central planning with a regulated market. Market socialism represents not merely another step in the same direction, but for reasons that should be clear from our brief characterization of the model, it may probably claim to represent what in Marxist dialectics is usually called a 'qualitative change'. Even looking at the practice of implementing the model in Yugoslavia – with all the 'imperfections' caused by informal state and party controls – one sees a large-scale reduction of government involvement in the economy. The ideology of self-managed socialism firmly emphasizes the fundamental character of this direction: depoliticization of the economy is presented as the true manifestation of the 'withering away of the state'. 'Social ownership of the means of production creates the possibility of eliminating not only the private owner, but in the final analysis also the state as intermediary between the producer and the means of production.'[28]

One aspect that perhaps deserves separate mention is the new dimension opened by market socialism for pursuit of local (especially regional) interests as a result of the decentralization of investment decisions. Local interests are now able to manifest themselves not only in pressing the centre for favourable allocations, but also in the promotion of development plans backed by their own resources. An element of independence is hereby created with potential significance for political pluralization, particularly when regional aspects interact with national (ethnic) ones, as is often the case in Yugoslavia.

IV. MARKETS – ENGINE OF PLURALIZATION?

A more extensive market means less *economic* power for the state. This conclusion follows from our examination of different degrees of marketization in communist systems and is hardly astounding. In the light of this conclusion the rationale for *political* resistance to market-oriented economic reforms becomes understandable even when economic reforms do not involve the polity as such. At least two reasons seem important in this connection: first, reduction of authority in such a basic area is likely to be regarded as a loss in itself; and, second, substantial vested interests, including direct material ones, are at stake. The overgrown bureaucracy in the party and state economic administration faces not only the prospect of overall trimming but also that of changed rules of recruitment and tenure. 'Active money would deprive many Party functionaries of their present functions, powers and benefits.'[29] Reinforced by ideological prejudices and perhaps by genuine pragmatic reservations about the results – whether these reservations are justified or not is irrelevant in this context – the opposition to economic reforms is to be expected.

It turns out that the question posed at the end of the first section of this paper may still not be sufficiently precise. The fears of the ruling élite and its supporting apparatus can be well founded, but for reasons that still fall short of answering our problem. What we want to know, specifically, is not whether and how much marketization constrains or reduces the *area* of mono-archal power, but whether *by doing so* it becomes a factor working toward transformation of the system of power as such; that is, whether it contributes to setting the mono-archy on a pluralistic trajectory toward acquisition of a polyarchal institutional character. General references to liberalization will not help us much – even truly pluralistic changes will not do – unless they can be shown to be linked with marketization. Perhaps this approach is excessively pedantic in the sense that it is not possible to make a clear distinction between the constraints imposed upon mono-archy and its transformation. Nevertheless, we shall try below to trace the link that we are seeking. As it is rather pointless to look for such a link in the transition from 'war communism' to the centralized model, we shall concentrate on the implications of change from our 'first degree' to higher degrees of marketization.

The *first element* to consider is *the role of political devices in the resolution of conflicts*. Reduction of government involvement in the economy as a result of marketization leads in a direction opposite to the one aptly described by Lindblom:

... strains may be exacerbated by the steady tendency of polyarchal governments to move certain decisions out of the market into government. The distribution of income, for example, is increasingly decided by government decisions on taxes, public education, public housing, health care, pensions, disability, and unemployment compensation, and other transfer payments. As these decisions move from market to government, there is more to fight about in politics and a greater burden, consequently, on whatever political devices there are to keep the peace.[30]

Not all the examples given will show a reverse tendency in the transition to communist market-oriented systems, but there is enough evidence to indicate that along with marketization governments gradually cease to be held responsible for everything that happens in the economy: some unpopular economic developments are more likely to be treated as non-political. One has to be very cautious in view of the intangibles involved, but it would seem that in Yugoslavia upward price movements are seldom described in typical East European fashion: '*they* raise prices'. In Hungary the government is much more exposed in this respect. Nevertheless, it has so far proved to be politically less vulnerable not only compared with the Polish government which was thrice thwarted on the issue of price increases, but also compared with other East European governments which in most cases did not dare to increase prices even under conditions of economic exigencies. Similar tendencies may be observed with regard to other economic issues.   .

With the sphere of tensions narrowed, the ruling élite may feel less threatened by liberalization or even by institutional reforms of a potentially pluralist character. This tendency is particularly discernible in the Yugoslav case where self-management expanded from a purely syndicalist into an overall political concept. Whatever its limitations, such a concept provides somewhat greater room for institutions that make government policies 'depend on votes and other expressions of preference' (the second rather than the first comes to mind), as well as for freedom of expression, alternative sources of information and so on. When marketization is coupled with self-management, conflicts are inevitable on a scale beyond the local level, and particularly on a national one. These conflicts cannot be resolved by simple imposition of decisions from above, and must involve compromise and persuasion; this need in turn prompts institutional solutions that, so far, have hardly reached polyarchal standards, but perhaps may be regarded as stepping stones of pluralization. If we were to accept the proposition that at least some fundamental macroeconomic problems would require government decisions, the system of autonomous self-managed enterprises might in the long run be expected to lead even more directly toward polyarchal forms of control over central decisions affecting collective interests at lower levels.[31]

The *second element* deserving examination is the impact of marketization on the *potential for political activity and on the attitudes of various social strata* (or classes, if one does not feel constrained by orthodox Marxist definitions). The connection most often stressed has to do with the new position of industrial managers who are seen as the main beneficiaries of marketization in terms of power. Managers acquire greater scope for decision-making, greater personal independence in view of depoliticization of career prospects and so on. Taking into account the weakening of the administrative apparatus for the same reasons, the political opportunities of the 'managerial class' do indeed look better, and opportunities usually engender ambitions. The managers are supposed to coalesce with the non-industrial intelligentsia and perhaps with some upper strata of the workers to form a new kind of middle class anxious to break the power monopoly of the party élite. The technocratic challenge, as it is frequently described, does indeed seem to be linked to marketization and to be directed against some features of mono-archy, especially against suppression of alternative sources of information (freedom to voice different expert opinions). On the other hand, the very extension of the role of the market and enterprise autonomy (depoliticization of the economy) may be enough to satisfy managerial interests without generating pressures for pluralization of the polity (the more so when top technocrats join the power élite). Some social scientists even advance the hypothesis that East European managers operating in a market environment would be positively interested in the maintenance of mono-archy in order not to face the workers alone. 'The managerial class, while freed from control from above, will nonetheless need to depend on, and will therefore support the police powers of the state in order to overcome dissent caused by the inequality of distribution and lack of control over production.'[32] The inequality of distribution need not necessarily become an automatic source of conflict between workers and managers of a particular enterprise in market conditions, but manifold conflicts will certainly arise and the security provided by a mono-archal state, standing behind the managers, may be felt desirable. A Hungarian author even goes so far as to claim that the managers were in fact against a consistent marketization with full independence for themselves, and opted instead for a half-way house in order to retain the sheltering power of the state.[33] Paradoxically, the same sheltering power of the state may be sought by the workers against the managers, or more generally by the working people at large against the operation of a market unrestricted by effective policies designed to defend the interests of employees and consumers. As a result, the mono-archy could find itself in a position of social arbiter, and thereby be favourably situated from the point of view of its own concern to preserve power. Of course, the alternative would be the emergence of independent institutions countervailing the power of both government (including local government) and management. These independent institutions would be genuinely representative trade unions and/or workers' self-management organs. In so far as marketization, with the ensuing conflicts and the new framework of conflict resolution, could be claimed *to spur effective action* for creating such institutions (or to imbue the existing empty forms with a new spirit, a tendency that may apply also to the pseudo-parliaments and their local equivalents, to the 'national fronts', to the façade of non-communist political parties, and so on) we would get another, indirect, link between marketization and pluralization of the political system. The para-doxical outcome of this alternative might be some restraint in use of the market mechanism: social considerations combined with awareness that independent institutions check state and managerial arbitrariness could provide the foundation for a better balance between the plan and the market, or between social preferences and commercial attitudes.

But does marketization really spur actions that effectively promote political pluralism? Here we come to the *third element* of the possible link: *marketization is supposed to create conditions more conducive to the struggle for political rights* because it makes people less economically dependent on the mono-archal state, and because it enhances the opportunities for entering into horizontal relations, for gaining better access to information, and for learning to invoke rules against abuses of authority and so on.

This proposition is most difficult to test. It is true that people must feel personally less constrained when the command system gives way to the market-oriented one, but whether this fact in itself becomes a spur to political action is another matter; greater economic independence from the state may well have the opposite consequence of promoting both non-political attitudes and the pursuit of strictly private interests, particularly after a string of frustrating political experiences. I could not find anything illuminating on this score in the socio-political literature concerning the two most relevant countries – Hungary and Yugoslavia. The post-1968 Hungarian experience would rather vouch for a more pessimistic scenario – veto rights granted to trade unions were hardly conceived by members as an instrument of institutionalized independent bargaining, and one unique case-study shows quite a depressing lack of militancy among industrial workers.[34] However, it may well be that in Hungary special countervailing forces are connected with the lingering effect of the 1956 trauma which provided the basis for the 'kadarist' compromise. So far, these countervailing forces have had a greater political impact than the economic reform. As for Yugoslavia, such effects of economic reform may have been more pronounced because greater economic independence in this case goes hand in hand with group interests that are institutionalized in an industrial, regional and especially in the national context. The political implications of these institutions have been mentioned earlier (in the third section). No obvious correlation could be found between the degree of economic independence and political militancy if one were to apply the test to Polish peasants on the one hand, and workers on the other.

These are the main elements of the possible link between marketization and pluralistic political change as seen by this author. The connection looks quite complex, often tenuous, and in some aspects simply dubious. Ought we then to conclude that the expectations of some and fears of others with regard to the political significance of the market are misconceived? Intuitively, one would not be prepared to accept such an unequivocal statement, especially when the reverse side of the coin springs to mind: is it possible to visualize polyarchy reconciled with a fully fledged centralized command-economic system? When the question is posed in this way[35] one tends to say 'no' without much hesitation. There is also the fact that in most cases when people in communist countries are able to voice their demand for political pluralization, a market-oriented economic reform is closely associated with or even regarded as an integral part of changes in the polity. Perhaps the political value of marketization lies therefore not so much in its active role as an engine of destruction of mono-archy but in the creation of an economic environment more propitious for the maintenance of polyarchal elements won in direct political struggles. This interpretation looks plausible in light of our analysis. It affords new significance to the role of the market as a factor reducing the *area* of political authority and hence providing greater independence for the individual, as well as a basis for the grouping of interests. The positive feed-back with pluralist polity should be, obviously, more pronounced if direct rank-and-file control over economic decisions (self-management) were institutionalized. At the same time, by putting the role of market into a broader context, this interpretation may accommodate better the posture of workers' movements during some of the crises in communist countries: the simplistic formula 'we want more say in political matters, hence we want a more extensive market' is nowhere to be seen; there is strong insistence on political pluralization and basic support for market-oriented economic reforms, but hardly for the unrestricted operation of market forces without proper consideration for social preferences. To some extent this pattern could be observed in Czechoslovakia in 1968, and was made particularly explicit in the list of demands drawn by the Gdansk strike committee in the course of the Polish Summer of 1980.

*   *   *

This paper has consistently omitted all side issues, however signi-ficant in themselves – for instance, the economic merits of marketization or the viability of compromise solutions for the plan-market dilemma. But despite this singlemindedness, firm conclusions – an outcome usually attractive for the reader and rewarding for the author – have hardly been reached. The relationship between markets and political pluralism in communist systems turns out to be more complicated than con-ventionally assumed. Market-oriented economic reforms do not necessarily (and certainly do not automatically) chart the way towards polyarchy, although they may make the struggle for pluralism somewhat easier and create a more favourable economic environment for maintaining and developing political liberties once they are won. On the other hand, under some circumstances the ruling élite may institute economic reforms in its own self-interest, with the purpose of strengthening mono-archy at the cost of partially relinquishing direct controls. The general conclusion therefore must be that the effects of marketization of the economy for the pluralization of the polity are in the last resort determined by the scope and outcome of political struggles.

NOTES AND REFERENCES

 1. Benjamin Ward, 'Political Power and Economic Change in Yugoslavia', *American Economic Review: Papers and Proceedings*, 58 (May 1968) 568–85.
 2. Ibid., 568.
 3. Ibid., 569.
 4. Robert A. Dahl and Charles E. Lindblom, *Politics, Economics, and Welfare* (New York, 1953).
 5. Charles E. Lindblom, *Politics and Markets: The World's Political–Economic Systems* (New York, 1977).
 6. Ibid., 133.
 7. P.J.D. Wiles, *Economic Institutions Compared* (Oxford, 1977) 459.
 8. Lindblom, *Politics and Markets*, 161, table 12.1.
 9. Zdeněk Mlynář, 'Notions of Political Pluralism in the Policy of the Communist Party of Czechoslovakia', *Experiences of the Prague Spring 1968*, Working Paper No. 3 (Vienna, 1979) (mimeographed).
10. Włodzimierz Brus, *Socialist Ownership and Political Systems* (London, 1975).
11. H. Gordon Skilling and Franklyn Griffiths (eds), *Interest Groups in Soviet Politics* (Princeton, N.J., 1971).
12. Stanislaw Ossowski, *Osobliwosci Nauk Spoecznych* [Singularities of Social Sciences] (Warsaw, 1962).
13. T.H. Rigby, 'Stalinism and the Mono-Organizational Society,' in Robert C. Tucker (ed.), *Stalinism: Essays in Historical Interpretation* (New York, 1977) 53–76.
14. Włodzimierz Brus, *Ogolne problemy funkcjonowania gospodarki socjalistycznej* [General Problems of Functioning of the Socialist Economy] (Warsaw, 1961) English edn: *The Market in a Socialist Economy*, trans. Angus Walker (London, 1972).
15. Ward, 'Political Power and Economic Change', 572.
16. Włodzimierz Brus, 'The East European Reforms: What Happened to Them?', *Soviet Studies*, 31 (April 1979) 257–67.
17. Moshe Lewin, *Russian Peasants and Soviet Power: A Study of Collectivization* (Evanston, Ill., 1968).
18. Wiles, *Economic Institutions Compared*.
19. Vladimir I. Lenin, 'O roli i zadachakh professionalnykh soyuzov v usloviakh novoy ekonomicheskoy politiki' [On the Role and Tasks of Trade Unions in Conditions of the New Economic Policy], *Polnoe Sobranie Sochinenie*, 44 (Moscow 1964) 341–53.
20. H. Gordon Skilling, *Czechoslovakia's Interrupted Revolution* (Princeton, N.J., 1976).

21. Władysław Bienkowski, *Problemy teorii rozwoju spoecznego* [Problems of the Theory of Social Development] (Warsaw, 1966).

22. Brus, *Ogolne problemy funkcjonowania*.

23. See Lev Kritsman, *Geroicheskiy period Velikoy Russkoy Revolutsii: Opyt analiza tak nazivaemogo voennogo kommunizma* [The Heroic Period of the Great Russian Revolution: A Contribution to the Analysis of So-called War Communism] (Moscow, 1926) and Laszlo Szamuelyi, *First Models of Socialist Economic Systems* (Budapest, 1974).

24. Joseph Stalin, 'Report to the Seventeenth Congress of the CPSU (b) On the Work of the Central Committee', in *Problems of Leninism* (Moscow, 1947) 492–6.

25. Oskar Lange (with Fred Taylor), *On the Economic Theory of Socialism* (Minneapolis, 1938) 95–6.

26. Viktor Zaslavsky, 'The Regime and the Working Class in the USSR', *Telos*, 42 (Winter 1979–80) 5–20.

27. Lindblom, *Politics and Markets*, 144.

28. League of Communists of Yugoslavia, *Program Saveza Komunista Jugoslavije* [The Programme of the League of Communists of Yugoslavia] (Belgrade, 1958) 128.

29. Gregory Grossman, 'Gold and the Sword: Money in the Soviet Command Economy', in H. Rosovsky (ed.), *Industrialization in Two Systems: Essays in Honour of Alexander Gerschenkron* (New York, 1966) 235.

30. Lindblom, *Politics and Markets*, 353.

31. Włodzimierz Brus, 'Political System and Economic Efficiency: The East European Context', *Journal of Comparative Economics*, 4 (March 1980) 40–55.

32. Zygmunt Bauman, 'Second Generation Socialism', in L. Schapiro (ed.), *Political Opposition in One-Party States* (London, 1972), 233.

33. Marc Rakovski, *Towards an East European Marxism* (London, 1978), ch. 2.

34. Miklos Haraszti, *A Worker in a Worker's State* (London, 1977).

35. Radoslav Selucky, *Marxism, Socialism, Freedom: Towards a General Theory of Labour Managed Systems* (London, 1979).

6 Regime–Dissenter Relations after Khrushchev: Some Observations

FREDERICK C. BARGHOORN

I. INTRODUCTION

Dissent is endemic to political systems. As Robert Dahl has noted, 'No government receives indefinitely the total support of the people over whom it asserts its jurisdiction.'[1] Political systems vary, however, in the limits they place on thought and behaviour critical of official policy and in the severity of the sanctions they mete out for transgression of the established limits or boundaries.

Very early in Soviet history, dissent was equated with opposition and opposition tended to be treated as tantamount to treason. The most extreme manifestations of hostility to dissent and opposition were, of course, Stalin's purges and show trials. According to the rules governing those trials, 'having mildly oppositionist intent was equivalent to carrying out acts with violently counterrevolutionary objective consequences'.[2] The function of labelling Bukharin and other critics of Stalin's policies as criminals was, writes 'Ernest Clark' (Thomas Remington) 'to reinforce community normative boundaries against deviance'.[3] In all political systems, the placement of these boundaries reflects official policy on the rights of citizens *vis-à-vis* the authorities and prescribes the channels through which citizens can legitimately and safely communicate demands. In Stalin's Russia, the narrowness of the boundaries created a political system which was probably among the most restricted and exclusionary ever known. In this paper I argue that although there is no longer a regime of mass terror in Soviet Russia, the behaviour of the regime toward dissenters suggests that the official *attitude* toward overt dissent has not changed significantly.

In the post-Khrushchev era, the correlation between the regime's attitude and its policy toward overt dissent is not as direct as it was under Stalin; there are several factors which intervene to constrain or inhibit the regime's free hand. This essay will focus on three of these factors. First, there is the increasing difficulty of reversing past policies. In the history of regime–dissenter relations in the Soviet Union, the Khrushchev period may be characterized as a period of relative leniency. That leniency raised expectations not only among the intelligentsia, but in society at large, expectations which have proven to die hard. In the second section of this essay, I will review the record of dissent after Khrushchev as an instance of the theory of 'relative deprivation'. Second, there is the problem of the obsolescence of established margins. In articulating and enforcing limits of acceptable thought and conduct, the regime simultaneously defines who and what will be considered deviant in Soviet society. The discrimination between 'insiders' and 'outsiders' works only so long as the strategic groups can clearly be classified as 'insiders'. When relations develop between 'outsiders' and strategic 'inside' groups, the established boundaries may give rise not only to theoretical problems, but to actual problems in the regime's social base of support. In the third section of the paper, I examine two such new relations: the linkage of dissenters and workers which has already been forged and the nascent relation between dissidents and the scientific-technical intelligentsia. And third, there is the problem of the unanticipated consequences of policy formulation. In meting out severe sanctions for deviant behaviour, the regime aims both to punish infringements of the established limits of acceptable thought and action and to deter similar transgression of boundaries. In the fourth section, I examine the extent to which the severity of regime sanctions has had the opposite effect – namely the effect of galvanizing and crystallizing further dissent.

The term 'dissent' as used in this essay refers to the public, uncensored expression by Soviet citizens of independent thought, implicitly or explicitly critical of official policy, practices or ideology.

Now I do not mean to suggest that overt protest is the only significant form of dissent in the USSR. Perhaps unpublished dissent 'within the system' can, as Roy Medvedev asserts, 'in many cases' do more to promote 'liberalization' and 'democratization' than dissent from 'outside' the system.[4]

Nor should one omit mention of the proposals by Soviet social scientists for reform in the political system. These proposals, surveyed by Ronald Hill, have been published mostly in obscure journals and have seldom been acted upon by the authorities.[5] But they are of potential significance. Perhaps relatively compliant reformers, even 'closet' critics, patiently waiting for more favourable circumstances to speak their piece, as well as those who articulate a variety of preferences can, in Cohen's words, 'contribute to the growth of reformist ideas and thus to the enlightenment of future officials'.[6]

But overt dissent is of particular interest because it alone requires not only a broadening of participation in Soviet political life but a widening of the boundaries of legitimate expression of opinion.

The spectrum of unauthorized, unpermitted attitudes cir- culated in *samizdat* is broad, very broad indeed. Its main currents (within each of which there are subcurrents) include the views of the Soviet 'democrats' or 'defenders of rights' (*pravozashchitniki*), the very important Russian 'nationalist' groups (both official and dissident), the articulators of the interests and values of non-Russian ethnic groups, the religious dissenters ranging from Pentacostalists, Adventists and non- conformist Baptists to Russian Orthodox protestors against what they regard as government violation of the constitutional rights of the Church,[7] the Marxist perspectives of Roy Medvedev, and the views of former Marxists such as General Petr Grigorenko.

Despite the breadth of opinion expressed, the authors constitute only a tiny minority of critically thinking Soviet people, not to speak of the Soviet population as a whole. They were very special people; they had succeeded in asserting and affirming independent self-hood against the enormous pressures for conformity and uniformity exerted by the Soviet socialization and communication mechanisms. They were mostly very strong personalities who resented official pressure on them to suppress their personal moral convictions, but they were not egotistical individuals. For the most part, they were capable both of compassion for persons who fell victim to official violence and repression, including fellow participants in the struggle for what they perceived as truth and justice, and of a high degree of solidarity for fellow participants in this struggle, regardless of differences of philosophy or point of view.[8]

Some of these people, such as Vladimir Bukovsky and Andrei Amalrik, had begun in early childhood to fashion their independent, nonconformist perspectives. Others, such as Andrei Sakharov, only consciously broke with the official philosophy and political culture in middle age, after clashes with authority that revealed to them the gulf between official norms and their own personal moral convictions.

Whatever the pattern of their radicalization, their current ideological orientation and their policy recommendations for the future, the overwhelming majority of Soviet dissidents have advocated peaceful and lawful change, by means of respectful petitions to the authorities, peaceful demonstrations, and, when all else has failed, by publication abroad of their analyses and recommendations. There have of course been some violent episodes, such as in the Novocherkassk strike in 1962, or in the mutiny on a Soviet Baltic Fleet warship in 1975.[9]

In speculating about the origin and persistence of peaceful and legal dissent in the USSR, one is inclined to attribute this pattern in part to a widespread revulsion against violence – at least, among intellectuals and probably in other social strata – after the violent Stalin years. As the computer scientist, Valentin Turchin, who labels himself an 'evolutionist' and a 'gradualist', has written, 'The result of the Bolshevik revolution taught us not to believe in the fiery call to destroy the ruling class at one stroke, to smash the state machine and build on its ruins a new, just and flourishing society.'[10] Turchin asserts, in the paragraph in which the above statement occurs, that the majority of educated Soviet people share his views. Interestingly, a few pages later, Turchin writes that he has always sought to be guided by Mahatma Gandhi – and was guided by him in the writing of his book.[11]

But an equally, if not more important reason for the dissidents' adoption of the method of peaceful, legal protest was pragmatic. This seemed to be the only method that promised any success in persuading the authorities to obey the laws: to respect the rights of freedom of speech and emigration, the right to peaceful demonstrations, the right to the formation of organizations – rights that were formally provided by Soviet law but were nullified by administrative practice.

In his major study, *The Politics of Nonviolent Action*, Gene Sharp argues, 'The result of using nonviolent weapons against violent action may be a significant increase in the actionists' total combat effectiveness.'[12] Such a judgement tallies with the observations made by the late Andrei Amalrik to his KGB interrogators in 1970 before he was sentenced to three years of internal exile and forced labour in Eastern Siberia. Their gist, as I recall them, was that the KGB was foolish to persecute peaceful protestors such as Amalrik and likeminded people, since such persecution might lead future protesters to turn, in desperation, to violent methods. However, Amalrik noted that as far as the KGB was concerned, violent protest was easier to deal with than the nonviolent variety.[13] Of course, nonviolent resistance is no easy course of action for those who pursue it – as the experience of men like Ginzburg, Plyushch, Orlov, Moroz, Bukovsky and many others has shown. Vladimir Bukovsky has asked:

> Now, when I hear from all sides so many high-sounding words and assurances of sympathy and support, when I hear condemnation of dishonest Soviet psychiatrists . . . I involuntarily find myself wondering: who among you, if you suddenly lived in the Soviet Union, would choose the freedom to be different? Would many of you be so eccentric as to want to be persecuted for the sake of an abstract honesty before your conscience?[14]

But, as Sharp points out, 'The time comes when passivity, acquiescence and patience give way to open nonviolent struggle.'[15]

A major weakness of the dissenters' reliance on legal protest was, however, that the authorities sometimes chose to categorize the advocates of the strategy as psychiatric cases. This categorization is of a piece with the insistence by Soviet authorities that all appropriate opportunities for legitimate political participation and expression of opinions are available to Soviet citizens. Those citizens who insist on voicing opinions that the rulers deem objectionable or on using channels of participation that are not sanctioned must be 'mentally unbalanced'.

The new sanctions meted out by the regime have forced the dissenters to develop new ways of coping, as will be illustrated in the fourth section. But the dissenter–regime relationship is an

136   *Pluralism in the Soviet Union*

interactive one. Even as it presents great difficulties for those at the margin, so too the relationship challenges the regime itself. It is to that challenge I now turn.

II. THE DIFFICULTY OF REVERSING THE PAST: AN INSTANCE OF THE THEORY OF RELATIVE DEPRIVATION

Khrushchev's de-Stalinization campaign generated great hope among the Soviet people, not only among the survivors of Stalin's camps and their friends, but among the intelligentsia in general. The release of millions of victims of Stalin's slave labour system, the legal reforms, the decision to abandon terror as an instrument of rule and the relaxation of censorship led to the surfacing of hitherto suppressed aspirations in Soviet society. Of course it cannot be denied that there was considerable repression of non-conformist thought under Khrushchev. One recalls the hounding of Boris Pasternak, the exiling of the poet Joseph Brodsky for 'parasitism', the persecution of the non-conformist Baptists, and the harsh treatment of young protesters such as Vladimir Bukovski around 1960. But Khrushchev did encourage, however unsystematically and hesitantly, overt re-examination of the ideological rationale of the traditional Soviet policy of strict, tight boundaries to expression and conduct. And in comparison with what was to follow, the Khrushchev era was one of remarkable tolerance for advocates of within-system change.

For example, under Khrushchev there was a long period of publication in the pages of the leading literary journal, *Novy Mir*, of what Dina Spechler, in an interesting essay, has called 'permitted dissent'. Spechler describes this body of writing as being of increasing openness and boldness. It began in the early post-Stalin years with 'administrative pragmatism', or 'exposure of defects in the system of bureaucratic rule and administration', and culminated around 1965 in the expression of the 'stronger, more challenging types' of dissent, 'moral humanism' and 'historical revisionism'.[16]

The tone of the loyal, reformist dissent somewhat fitfully tolerated by Khrushchev, but almost entirely rejected by his more conservative (except in the sphere of applied technology) successors, is well illustrated by an article published by the poet, and editor in chief of *Novy Mir*, Aleksandr Tvardovsky, in the first issue of that journal in 1965. The statement, published in honour of the magazine's fortieth anniversary, appeared during the brief interlude before the neo-Stalinist impulses of the Brezhnev-Kosygin leadership had fully manifested themselves. It might well be regarded as the swan-song of the hopeful anti-Stalinist reformism articulated under Tvardovsky's skilful editorship of *Novy Mir*.

Tvardovski noted that the jubilee issue included pieces by Yevgeny Yevtushenko, Ilya Ehrenburg and Viktor Nekrasov – all of whom had been abusively criticized by Khrushchev, but not punished, in 1962–3 – as well as poems by Boris Pasternak and Anna Akhmatova. He pointed out that *Novy Mir* had experienced 'the pernicious influence of well-known phenomena in our life – illegal repression, the spirit of distrust and suspicions'. It was, he said, impossible to forget that many of the most talented Soviet writers had been wrenched out, morally and physically, from literature. But, he went on, an end had been put to 'arbitrariness' in 'the life of the country and party', thus opening new 'fruitful possibilities' for the future. He hailed the publication of Ehrenburg's memoirs, and of Aleksandr Solzhenitsyn's *One Day in the Life of Ivan Denisovich*. He expressed confidence that Solzhenitsyn would make even more significant contributions in the future, a confidence that he based in part on the deliberations of the Twentieth Congress of the Communist Party of the Soviet Union, in 1956 – most of the results of which were to be honoured more in the breach than in the observance by Khrushchev's successors.

Perhaps the most important of the many weighty, but unfortunately soon to be discarded, judgements contained in Tvardovsky's jubilee article concerned the use that 'bourgeois enemies' of the Soviet Union could make of revelations in Soviet literature of the negative aspects of Soviet life and history. Tvardovski agreed that enemies could interpret such material to their advantage. However, he insisted, 'the direct and open truth' was much more useful to the Soviet people than to foreign enemies. As a loyal communist, Tvardovsky quoted Lenin in support of his views about truthful disclosure, but obviously his interpretation of Lenin differed drastically from the one that was soon to become dominant in the intellectual life of the USSR. He expressed delight that Soviet readers were becoming more sophisticated and critical. In this connection, he asserted that the increasing responsiveness of *Novy Mir*'s readers was creating 'powerful, truly democratic' support of 'public opinion', without which there could be no vital literary life. And, near the end of the article, he rejoiced in the appearance in *Novy Mir* of a number of new, young critics, including Andrei Sinyavski.[17]

As Stephen Cohen has noted, the overthrow of Khrushchev 'brought an end to reform and even some counter-reform in most areas of Soviet society'.[18] The narrowing of the bounds to dissent and the regime's determination to maintain them were signalled by a series of well-known events: the arrests of Sinyavsky and Daniel in 1965 (and their trial in 1966); the severe repression against writers of protest letters and organizers of peaceful demonstrations in 1968; and thenceforth systematic application of selective terror against dissenters, which achieved its greatest intensity in the repression inflicted on the Helsinki monitoring groups and associated organizations in 1977–81.

These developments were in no small part a reaction against the threat to the stability (ideological and political) of the Soviet bloc that Leonid Brezhnev and his Politburo colleagues perceived in the Czechoslovak experiment in 'socialism with a human face'. To be sure, the favourable response to the Czechoslovak events by such 'liberal' Soviet scientists as Andrei Sakharov only increased the perceived threat.

As is well known, the first moves in the post-Khrushchev campaign to suppress dissent occasioned a surge of protest. I believe that this outbreak of protest owes much of its force to the contrast between the new rigid, arrogant and punitive attitude toward independent thought and the relatively relaxed stance of Khrushchev, at least *vis-à-vis* those whom he regarded as loyal Soviet citizens. As I have argued elsewhere, the frustration and resistance evidenced in the outbreak of protest can be explained as an instance of 'relative deprivation' in the sense articulated by Gurr.[19] Building largely on the 'frustration–aggression' hypothesis of John Dollard and his collaborators, Gurr defined 'relative deprivation' as a 'perceived discrepancy between men's value expectations and their value capabilities'. Gurr posits that 'conditions that increase the... level of intensity of expectations without increasing capabilities', or 'decrease... value position' without decreasing expectation, 'increase deprivation, hence the intensity of discontent'. (Gurr has also suggested that 'short-term deterioration in...conditions of life' can produce similar effects'.[20] We will explore the applicability of this insight to the Soviet setting in the next section.)

Gurr's propositions seem to me extremely helpful in understanding the reactions of some Soviet intellectuals not only to the intensified repression of Khrushchev's successors, but also to the roller-coaster character of Khrushchev's own cultural policy. At the same time, Gurr's notion of 'relative deprivation' may be a useful shorthand device to refer to one of the constraints under which the post-Khrushchev leadership operates in formulating its policy on dissent.

III. THE 'INSIDER'–'OUTSIDER' DEMARCATION: A PROBLEM IN BOUNDARY PERSISTENCE

As part of the process of articulating boundaries of acceptable thought and behaviour, a regime attempts to stigmatize or brand as 'outsiders' those who violate the boundaries. The maintenance of the demarcation between 'insiders' and 'outsiders' is becoming increasingly complex in the contemporary Soviet Union because of growing relations between dissident intellectuals on the one hand and certain strategic social groups on the other.

The democratic movement and Soviet labour

Relations between blue-collar workers (and non-intellectuals generally) and Soviet democratic dissidents have traditionally been characterized by remoteness, even mistrust. However, the gulf between the two groups has not by any means been as wide as is sometimes believed by Western observers, nor has the alleged indifference of the civil rights activists to workers' concerns been as great as some critics of the democrats have charged. In fact, an increasing convergence of intellectual and worker protest activity was one of the most important sociopolitical trends of the 1970s in the USSR. The significance of intellectual–worker rapprochement and co-operation must as yet be regarded as potential rather than actual because repression by the regime has inflicted such heavy blows on dissident activity in the last four or five years that protest activity of all kinds has been considerably weakened. However, the precedents set in the second half of the

1970s, perhaps especially in the area of workers' rights, may well cast a long shadow into the future.

Some of the most significant developments were as follows. First, the role of workers in the civil rights movement bulked ever larger over time. Second, prominent dissidents, such as Sakharov, Turchin and others, indicated their interest in and concern regarding the problems, needs and rights of workers. Third, as several members of the Moscow Helsinki monitoring group have reported, workers in considerable numbers approached them with requests for information and help.

Before commenting on the above topics, it will be appropriate to deal with two aspects of labour unrest, namely, sporadic, largely spontaneous strikes, and the unprecedented efforts in 1977–8 to set up trade unions independent of the national party-dominated, Moscow-centred trade union network.

Information about worker dissatisfaction in the USSR, and in communist countries generally, except for Poland, is relatively limited. Particularly in the USSR, workers in any given factory were until very recently unable to communicate their grievances to fellow workers of other factories, let alone to those in other parts of the Soviet Union. By and large this lack of opportunity for communication persists, severely hindering development of organized activity by workers in defence of group interests (and depriving the outside world of information on the problems of Soviet workers).

Nevertheless, the available information attests to a fairly large number of strikes, demonstrations and riots by Soviet workers. Montias has observed that 'dissatisfaction with economic conditions is the prime force behind' such manifestations of worker dissatisfaction.[21]

In the post-Stalin period, the situation of workers *vis-à-vis* the more privileged strata of Soviet society has improved, but expectations may have risen faster than tangible improvements. Under Khrushchev the rights of the official trade unions were increased and Stalin's severe rules on lateness to or absence from work were relaxed. Also, Khrushchev (and Brezhnev) rejected Stalin's heavy emphasis on selection of intelligentsia members for recruitment into the ruling party. However, labour unrest grew. Indeed its most explosive single manifestation to date occurred under Khrushchev: the strike in the Novocherkassk Electric Locomotive Plant in June 1962, which was followed by demonstrations of support by hundreds of townspeople.

The Novocherkassk incidents followed strikes in Murom, in central Russia and in TemirTau, Kazakhstan. The protest in Novocherkassk was suppressed by military force and casualties were heavy.[22] Solzhenitsyn calls this event 'a turning point in the modern history of Russia'. He may be right. The events there set an example of resistance to the combination of a sudden increase in food prices and lowering of wages that apparently triggered the workers' protest. Henceforth the regime was to pursue policies designed to avoid stretching the patience of workers beyond breaking point. In particular, although the standard of living of Soviet workers remains very far below that of their counterparts in 'capitalist' countries, it has slowly improved since 1962 – although since the late 1970s there have been numerous reports from travellers and exchange students of food shortages even in Moscow, Leningrad and other large cities, and of considerably tighter supplies, especially of meat, fish, eggs and cheese, in provincial towns. However, the policy, introduced by Khrushchev, of buying grain abroad, coupled with other related measures, has reduced the probability of a recurrence of a Novocherkassk-style disturbance.

Nevertheless, labour dissatisfaction has persisted, occasionally becoming acute enough to erupt in brief strike actions, many of which doubtless remain unknown outside the USSR.

Plyushch in his autobiography reported a 1967 protest by factory workers in Priluky, seventy kilometres from Kiev, sparked by police brutality, as well as a 1969 protest against poor living conditons by workers of a Kiev hydro-electric power station. In the latter case, says Plyushch, angry women rushed to the platform of a meeting hall and called out the names of the mistresses for whom the station's director had allegedly found good living quarters, while workers' families and their small children huddled in barracks.[23]

In May 1976 in Riga, Latvia, port workers struck, following introduction of several meatless days a week in public eating places – apparently throughout the USSR. In connection with the strike four workers, judging by their names three of them Russians and one Jewish, were sentenced to camps for 'slanderous statements defaming the Soviet state and social system'.[24]

According to the *Chronicle of Current Events* there was a brief strike at the Kaunas (Lithuania) rubber-goods factory on 14 December 1977, after the management – with the consent of the official trade union – had suddenly lowered the permitted rate of spoiled goods, resulting in a sharp lowering of wages. KGB officials arrived to admonish the strikers; some were arrested and one was beaten, but the old spoilage rate was restored.[25]

Perhaps one of the most important strikes in years reportedly took place at the huge Togliatti factory (until 1964, Stavropol) on the Volga river southeast of Moscow, for two days in early May 1980. According to *The New York Times* correspondent Anthony Austin, 'a Soviet citizen who is knowledgeable about such matters' linked the strike to 'an unofficial worker leadership' at the plant that had in recent years successfully protested against unsatisfactory conditions. Austin cited the same source as having said that there had been similar protests in other places and that 'Moscow's policy in all such cases' (that is those involving food shortages) had been 'to move swiftly to meet the workers' grievances and to restore order'. According to Austin's source, the Togliatti workers were less passive than were most Soviet workers, who were unwilling to defy the taboo on strikes in the 'classless' society and usually acted on their discontent by finding another job, thus aggravating the 'acute problem of high labor turnover'.[26]

In addition to the Togliatti events, there was a considerable number of other strikes in 1980 and 1981.[27] The evidence indicates persistent and increasing discontent among Soviet workers, and also a disposition to act to redress grievances.

In 1977–8 a number of blue-collar workers, some persons with occupational background that in the West would be categorized as lower-middle class, and a few veteran human rights activists collaborated in forming labour unions not controlled by the Communist Party of the Soviet Union. This may have ushered in a significant new stage in the development of working-class consciousness. It certainly constituted a bold effort to forge new and effective instruments for articulating the interests of working people.

In September 1977 Vladimir Klebanov, a former Donbass coal miner, and several score other workers and engineers published an 'Open Letter to world public opinion regarding the true situation of workers and employees on the eve of the sixtieth anniversary of the USSR'. They criticized KGB chief Yuri Andropov for a speech he had delivered. The speech, given over largely to denouncing dissidents, sought to create the impression of perfect solidarity between Soviet workers and the Soviet regime. The letter asserted that the signatories were forced to appeal to the 'so-called bourgeois press', since their complaints against corrupt practices by officials, illegal dismissals of workers, management violation of safety regulations, for example, at their former places of employment had resulted only in the complainants' being fired from jobs, committed to mental institutions, and so on. Thus these former workers were saying that by its harsh, restrictive policies the regime had forced them to become open critics. In perhaps the most striking sentence of the letter, the group called themselves 'the numerous army of the Soviet unemployed' – unemployed because they had, justifiably, complained.[28]

On 1 February 1978, a few days after a press conference at which Klebanov and a few associates indicated their intention of forming an independent union, the formation of the union, called The Association of the Free Trade Union in the Soviet Union – better known simply as the Free Trade Union – was announced, all its statutes were published, though not, of course, by the official Soviet press. One hundred and ten persons signed the announcement of the formation of the Free Trade Union. About fifty identified themselves as workers; three as collective farmers; twenty-four as employees (*sluzhashchie*); eighteen as professionals (mostly engineers) and a few either gave no occupational identification or described themselves as pensioners, invalids and so on. A note to the list of members pointed out that a number, presumably prospective members, had asked that their names not be given. The Free Trade Union's announcement was in the form of an 'appeal' to the International Labour Office and 'to the trade union organizations of the workers of the Western countries'. It stated, among other things, that there were in the USSR thousands of workers in the same situation as the members of the new union.[29]

In terms of implementing the goals proclaimed in its statutes, such as defending the rights of workers and employees harassed by the authorities, helping them with housing needs and promoting trade union democracy, the Free Trade Union was unable to do much, beyond publicizing the issues. Klebanov and other members quickly fell victim to repression: Klebanov and some of his colleagues were committed to psychiatric hospitals. By the end of March 1978 the Free Trade Union, though never formally disbanded, 'had been virtually neutralized as a result of persecution by the authorities'.[30]

A similar fate befell the Free Interprofessional Union of Working People or SMOT (its Russian acronym), founded in Moscow in October 1978 at the initiative of Vladimir Borisov and a group of workers and veteran human rights activists. Borisov himself belonged to both of the above categories. An electrician by trade and a computer specialist, he was one of the founders of the well-known Initiative (or Action) Group for the Defence of Civil Rights in the USSR in 1969. Although blue collar workers accounted for a smaller percentage of the membership of SMOT than of the Free Trade Union, SMOT's *modus operandi* and ideological stance were similar to those of its predecessor organization – and so was its fate! However, before it succumbed to repression (in 1980 Borisov was deported to the West) SMOT succeeded in distributing five 'information bulletins' in the period December 1978 through July 1979, which described searches, arrests, trials and sentencing of its members. The criminal charges against some of these individuals were based, *inter alia*, on possession of works of Andrei Sakharov and, in one case, of Aleksandr Solzhenitsyn's *Gulag Archipelago*. SMOT appealed to various foreign groups and organizations, such as 'honest psychiatrists of the world', the International Confederation of Free Trade Unions (MOT, in Russian acronym) and Amnesty International, and it called on the Soviet authorities to observe the human rights provisions of the Final Act of the 1975 Conference on Security and Co-operation in Europe. Its statements were concerned with social injustice, inequality, and the poverty of Soviet workers.[31]

One of the most interesting perspectives on the relations between the dissidents and workers was offered by Ludmilla Alekseeva, the veteran civil rights activist and Helsinki Watch member and now the foreign representative of the Moscow Helsinki group. In a paper delivered in the United States in October of 1979, Alekseeva reminded her audience that the Soviet movement 'in defence of rights' (*pravozashchitochnoe dvizhenie*) began as a movement of the Moscow humanistic intelligentsia and then attracted support from the scientific and technical professionals. Of more than 700 signers of letters in defence of Aleksandr Ginzburg and Yuri Galanskov in 1968, only 6 per cent were workers. Some 'worker' participants in the rights movement in that period were persons of intelligentsia origin, like Ginzburg himself, who had been forced to become workers because they were denied the opportunity to complete their higher education in consequence of their dissident activity. But according to Alekseeva the segment of the Soviet working class most likely to be drawn into the civil rights movement is the increasing percentage of workers with full secondary or partial higher education. Turning to data on persons sentenced for *samizdat* activity, demonstrations 'under the banner of civil rights,' participation in independent organizations, and so on, Alekseeva reports that from 1965 to 1976 the percentage of workers ranged from 24.5 to 28.5 per cent, but in 1976–9 it amounted to 41.3 per cent. However, the workers sentenced in a series of trials in 1978–9 were, she asserts, not highly educated workers, but 'workers from the provinces' with a typical working-class education of not more than eight years. She adds that ordinary workers with limited education now, as in the past, constitute a very large proportion of the membership of such mass protest movements as those of the Crimean Tatars, the Soviet Germans and the non-conformist Baptists and Pentecostalists. The latter two groups, she adds, account for 28.4 per cent of all political prisoners, and are almost entirely composed of workers; they have long been denied access to higher education.

Alekseeva emphasized the lack of correlation in Soviet dissident activity between class identity and movement demands. What is happening, especially since the advent of the Free Trade Union and SMOT is that a social component is being added to the previous preoccupation of the human rights movement with civil rights. She sees the 'movement for social rights' as 'one of the currents of the dissident movement'. Its participants, like those of the older civil rights movement, share similar problems and characteristics: all Soviet citizens are working people (*trud-yashchiesya*) and all work for one employer, the state. Hence the interests of all are similar, and peaceful legal protest in the struggle against the very powerful Soviet state is the only hope of improvement in the situation.

Alekseeva points out that some of the organizers of the Free Trade Union knew about the civil rights movement and 'had found a path to its activists'. She bases her argument on the fact that Document 8 of the Moscow Helsinki group, which deals with dismissals from work, psychiatric committal (and other such sanctions) of persons who had complained to higher authorities about violations of regulations committed by their employers, was based on information supplied by the victims; and the document was published more than a year before the union's organization![32]

Besides Vladimir Borisov, whose activity in the worker protest movement has already been mentioned, even more prominent Soviet civil rights advocates have demonstrated their concern about the rights of workers and, in general, about the situation of underprivileged Soviet people. Andrei Sakharov devoted a considerable part of his book, *My Country and the World*, to poverty, lack of the right to strike, inequality, social injustice and other problems affecting Soviet working people.[33] In the address that Sakharov sent to the Second International Sakharov Hearing held in Rome in November 1977, he urged investigation of Soviet workers' rights, including the 'right to strike, the problem of guaranteeing workers' fair pay and social status'.[34] Sakharov's contribution to the dissidents' efforts to alleviate the situation also, of course, includes ceaseless appeals to the Soviet authorities and to world opinion on behalf of 'ordinary people with grievances the system has not addressed or resolved' and this has been true even since the authorities forcibly exiled him and his wife to the provincial city of Gorky, in January 1980.[35] In the fall of 1976, and in February 1978, respectively, Valentin Turchin, the distinguished computer scientist (who was forced to emigrate in 1977) and Elena Bonner Sakharov's wife and a founding member of the Moscow Helsinki group, wrote for the group separate studies on problems of workers. Turchin presented data on low wages and other factors that impelled four workers to seek to emigrate from the USSR. Bonner and four collaborators expressed satisfaction with the establishment of the Free Trade Union under Vladimir Klebanov's leadership, and they sought to link the FTU with the principles contained in the Helsinki Final Act.[36]

Considerations of space have required the foregoing account to be brief, but it is sufficient to demonstrate a rising tide of Soviet worker dissatisfaction in recent years and a growing tendency toward co-operation in the pursuit both of workers' goals and of goals common to workers and democratic dissidents, especially after the establishment of the Soviet Helsinki Watch movements.[37]

In the post-Khrushchev period, there have been important bridges built between the dissenters and other groups in Soviet society – religious groups and non-Russian ethnic groups to name just two instances.[38] In terms of the volume of protest activity, *samizdat* output, and arrests and sentencing of their proponents, these two groups figure much more importantly than do the workers on whom this section has focused. But both religious groups and non-Russian nationality groups cannot be considered strategic groups inside Soviet society and therefore their relations with the civil rights movement will likely not provoke the re-drawing of the 'insider' – 'outsider' demarcation in the way in which the *rapprochement* between the civil rights activists and the workers may well do.

The democratic movement and the scientific–technical intelligentsia

At this juncture, those in the democratic movement have more developed relations with representatives of the working class than they do with representatives of the scientific–technical intelligentsia. But signs point to the likelihood of increasing ties between civil rights activists and those concerned with scientific and technical progress.

The logic behind this latter connection is most clearly articulated in the writing of Barbara Wolfe Jancar. Jancar argues that the process of modernization is associated with tendencies to social pluralization. She explains that economic development and differentiation promote a growth in the number of 'individuals with sufficient skills and social access to maneuver and succeed in society'.[39] This process in turn gives rise to conflict 'over whether to push forward economic growth through liberalization at the expense of political power, or whether to continue in a modified Stalinist course'.[40] But, as a result of the appearance in the political arena of groups whose co-operation is necessary for con-tinued economic development, the ruling group must allow for some dissent, 'because terror is dysfunctional to economic progress'.[41]

In examining the effect upon dissent of the process of modern-zation, Jancar pays attention to the changing self-image of the workers. She explains that as the economy and society become more developed, dissenters learn that organization and communi-cations resources become increasingly available to opposition elements, including dissident workers. Workers, in contrast to peasants, are not 'outside the modernization process'.[42] And of course, their share of the population grows with industrial development. Jancar generalizes that 'Modernization means that political expertise is no longer the prerogative of the few, but through mass education and the organized living pattern of urbanized modern life, it has been diffused throughout all society.'[43] It seems likely that as urbanization and industrialization proceed further, the trends perceived by Jancar will intensify, as will the difficulties for the regime of maintaining the established boundaries.

Perhaps more important than the discussion of the growing involvement of workers in dissident activity is the light Jancar throws on the increasing reflection in dissident literature of the concerns of the scientific–technical intelligentsia, surely one of the (if not the) key group in contemporary Soviet society. Jancar explains that in the post-Stalin era, the goals of dissent have tended to change from 'overthrow of the Stalinist system', to 'rationalization of the system in terms of free access to information, flexible decision-making, and adaptation to change as the communist countries move into the post-industrial society'.[44]

There is a considerable body of statements by Soviet dissidents which would corroborate the growing importance of technical, organizational concerns in dissent. The Soviet dissident material is often quite explicit in its criticisms of economic failures and in prescribing remedies, such as greater freedom of information and 'democratization'.

In March 1970, the celebrated nuclear physicist Andrei Sakharov, the historian Roy Medvedev and the physicist and computer scientist Valentin Turchin (who now lives in the United States) addressed a very important letter to Brezhnev, Kosygin and Podgorny. This letter seems to have been the last respectful petition in which Sakharov and Turchin joined. Recalling that petition some three years later, Sakharov stated, 'The subject of the letter was the interdependence of democratization and techno-economic progress.'[45] In his well-known earlier essay 'Reflections on Progress, Peaceful Coexistence and Intellectual Freedom', Sakharov had pointed to the linkage between intellectual freedom and 'democratization' on the one hand and creativity and welfare on the other, but his treatment of the question in the essay was less specific and fully developed than in the 'letter of the three'. In that letter, there are references to declining economic growth, to Soviet backwardness in the chemical industry and to 'immeasurable' backwardness *vis-à-vis* the United States in computers. In later petitions to the Soviet authorities and in statements such as his Nobel Peace Prize Lecture, read in Oslo by his wife Elena Bonner (he was denied the exit visa necessary to deliver it in person), Sakharov reverted to the same theme. In the Nobel Lecture, entitled 'Peace Progress and Human Rights', for example, Sakharov developed the thesis that 'freedom of conscience together with other civic rights, provides both the basis for scientific progress and a guarantee against its misuse to harm mankind, as well as the basis for social and economic progress, which in turn is a political guarantee making the effective defence of social rights possible'.[46]

Sakharov has not been alone in this. As Feldbrugge notes, dissidents belonging to several ideological currents attributed the unsatisfactory state of the Soviet economy to much the same causes as those pinpointed by Sakharov – excessive centralization, party domination, bureaucratic privilege and inertia. Some sources, among them the statutes of the All-Russian Social Christian Union for the Liberation of the People, offer specific suggestions for structural reform of the economy, with provision for a sphere for private enterprise, 'at least in the production of consumer goods and in services'.[47]

Whatever their criticisms of the inefficiency and backwardness of the Soviet socio-economic system, Sakharov and his fellow physicists Yury Orlov and Valentin Turchin are united in their view that that system is extraordinarily stable and durable.[48] They attribute the ability of the Soviet leadership to shrug off public pressures for change to a combination of selective coercion practised by Stalin's successors (whose memories of Stalin's terror are still fresh) and to the continued effectiveness of censorship. Orlov, for example, argues that in the USSR, the authorities deprive the workers of the right to strike, publicly protest, and so on, but they grant them the right to work poorly. What results is demoralization, but demoralization cannot undermine the social order.[49]

That the concerns of the scientific–technical intelligentsia are reflected in dissident literature is beyond question; what remains to be seen is whether representatives of that intelligentsia will gravitate in any substantial numbers to the dissident movement.

Were they to do so, the regime would be faced with a most formidable challenge to the established demarcation between 'inside' and 'outside' groups.

IV. UNANTICIPATED CONSEQUENCES OF POLICY

Dysfunctions of the regulative–coercive complex

Every political system must exert some control over the behaviour of individuals and groups in the society. Here I will give the name 'regulative–coercive complex' to the structures and practices the function of which is to prevent disapproved conduct such as open dissent and, if prevention fails, to suppress such conduct.[50] In the Soviet Union, prevention proceeds with the aid of such devices as socialization into official norms, rewards for compliant behaviour; suppression proceeds with the aid of such sanctions as dismissal from work, prosecution, and if necessary, sentencing to prison and labour camps or even committal to mental institutions.

If a major purpose of the activity of the regulative–coercive complex is to suppress dissent, an unintended consequence of its operations is the generation of protest and criticism. Indeed, there is a great deal of evidence indicating that indignation aroused by harassment and persecution of dissenters and compassion for them as perceived victims of injustice has probably been the most potent single factor shaping post-Stalin Soviet dissent. I do not mean to imply that articulation of dissent is directly proportional to official repression. Obviously, severe repression – and the threat thereof – can sharply reduce overt protest, as happened for example as a result of the KGB campaign of 1968 against approximately 1000 signers of protest letters and petitions.[51] Similarly, dissent has been weakened by the exceptionally severe repression inflicted by the Soviet authorities on dissenters of all kinds since the Belgrade conference of 1978 (called to review compliance with the Final Act of the 1975 Helsinki Conference). One need only compare the long lists of signers of Helsinki group documents in 1976 and 1977 with those issued in 1980 and 1981, often signed only by Elena Bonner and a dwindling handful of fellow members.[52]

Nevertheless, though diminished in volume the voice of the

civil rights protesters continued to be heard in 1981. For example, on the occasion of the exiled Sakharov's sixtieth birthday (21 May 1981) a group of Moscow writers and scholars paid tribute to him in a collection of essays. There can be little doubt that those who in the face of burgeoning repression thus hailed Sakharov's struggles for his ideals were themselves expressing commitments and accepting risks similar to or greater than those confronting the renowned scientist living under conditions of strict isolation and police surveillance.[53]

Nor was the May 1981 gathering an exception. Indeed, the protest activity we are concerned with in this essay began as a response to the arrests and trials of 1967 and 1968, organized by the Soviet authorities in retaliation for protests against the trial and sentencing of Sinyavsky and Daniel in 1966.[54]

Insight into the relationship between the repression of dissident activity and further outbreaks of dissent has been provided by Karel van het Reve, a Dutch expert on Russian literature, who spent a year as a Moscow correspondent. During his stint in Moscow, van het Reve became well acquainted with Pavel Litvinov, who compiled the record of the trials of Vladimir Bukovsky and others who had demonstrated in January 1967 against the arrest of Aleksandr Ginzburg and Yury Galanskov who themselves had compiled a 'white book' on the Sinyavsky–Daniel trial. Van het Reve records that as a boy Litvinov had been 'an admirer of the late Joseph Stalin'.

> His difficulties in matters of faith seem to have begun with the trial of Daniel and Sinyavski. He was mildly curious . . . but did not dare go near the court building. Wanting to know what those writers were tried for, he started to read their works. Being honest, he was struck by the gross injustice of sentencing writers to five and seven years hard labour for a couple of stories and an essay on socialist realism, and he decided to join those who wanted to do something about it.[55]

Former General Petr Grigorenko, one of the most important civil rights activists, twice victim of committal to psychiatric institutions and champion of the vain efforts of the Crimean Tatars to return from the exile to which Stalin sent them during the second world war, has written that the Sinyavsky–Daniel trial 'was a kind of signal to the whole thinking public of the country to defend the right to think'.[56] Grigorenko tells us that the linguist and dissident activist Tatyana Khodorovich came to him in the spring of 1969 and said, 'I am the mother of four children, but I cannot keep silent any longer.'[57] Khodorovich was one of fifteen persons who shortly after Grigorenko's second arrest – a few weeks after her above-mentioned conversation with him – formed the important Initiative Group (often also called Action Group) for the Defence of Civil Rights in the USSR. One of the best known of her actions on behalf of victims of police arbitrariness was her editorship of a book, 'documenting the harrowing case of Leonid Plyushch', a brilliant Ukrainian mathematical biologist and, along with Khodorovich, a founder of the Initiative Group.[58] Plyushch was objectionable to the authorities because he was a persistent critic of violations of human rights. Perhaps even more infuriating to Moscow was Plyushch's identification with the fate of the Ukrainian people. There is also much evidence in Plyushch's autobiography that one of the aspects of Soviet life that most repelled him – and caused him to conclude that the USSR is 'the country of man's maximum alienation' – was violations of legal rights, callous treatment of political prisoners, and so on. He was stunned by Khrushchev's revelations at the Twentieth CPSU Congress regarding Stalin's crimes and concerned about what he saw as the rebirth of Stalinism under Brezhnev. He saw evidence of this 'rebirth' in 'the invasion of Czechoslovakia, the illegal trials, and the persecution of people for demostrating, circulating *samizdat* and participating in the Ukrainian national revival', as he told the notorious psychiatrist Snezhnevsky in prison, before his transfer to a mental institution.[59]

Some of the titans of Soviet dissent, such as Solzhenitsyn, Grigorenko, and certainly Sakharov, undoubtedly set an inspiring example to their fellow free-thinkers, and thus may themselves be regarded as factors in sustaining the struggle for freedom. Of his master work, *Gulag Archipelago*, Solzhenitsyn himself has written, 'I dedicate this to all those who did not live to tell it.'[60]

Leonid Plyushch reports that after receiving a warm reply from Solzhenitsyn to greetings sent in 1967 on his fiftieth birthday, 'We were happy in the thought that our culture existed again and hopeful that it would not be destroyed once more.'[61] Solzhenitsyn, of course, was only one of many Soviet dissenters who protested against the crippling effects of censorship and persecution on Soviet cultural life.[62]

A special word should be said about the role of Lidiya Chukovskaya in protesting for many years against the persecution of independent-minded writers. Chukovskaya spoke out about every major event in the life of the Russian intelligentsia about which 'it was unthinkable to remain silent'.[63] The fact that her husband perished in Stalin's jails at the height of the purges may well have been a motivating force in her protests against the persecution of her fellow writers and critics. The fact that Chukovskaya is the daughter of the famous, highly respected literary critic, Kornei Chukovsky, perhaps saved her from arrest. But she was subjected for years to administrative pressures and sniping in the press, to which, in conformity with standard Soviet practice, she was not permitted to reply. Finally, in 1974, the ailing, half-blind author and critic was expelled from the Union of Soviet Writers at a session which none of her friends and supporters was allowed to attend.[64] Subsequently, other distinguished writers and literary scholars and critics, including Lev Kopelev – outstanding expert on German literature, who spent ten years in prison camps for objecting to rape and pillage by Soviet forces in Germany – Vladimir Voinovich, and a handful of others, were expelled from the Writers Union, and Georgy Vladimov, author of the well-known novel – unpublished in the USSR – *Faithful Ruslan*, resigned in protest. The expulsions of several writers, including Kopelev, occurred after the signing by the USSR of the Final Act of the Conference on Security and Co-operation in Europe, the signatories of which, ironically, pledged respect for freedom of thought.[65]

Coping with the regulative–coercive complex

Thus far, we have examined the constraints on the policy of the regime toward dissenters. But the relationship with the regime presents no less serious dilemmas for the dissenters. In a polity which severely restrains dissent, they must choose between whatever limited channels of articulation of opinion are made available by the authorities and they must devise new and untried channels.

The recourse to legality

One of the outstanding features of the contemporary dissent movement is the strong concern of dissidents with legality. Indeed more *samizdat* items have been concerned with what their authors regarded as official violations of individual and group legal rights than with any other category of dissent.[66]

Apparently the lion's share of credit for devising a strategy of peaceful, legal resistance to repression of dissent must go to the mathematician, symbolic logician and poet, Aleksandr Yesenin-Volpin. Vladimir Bukovsky reports that in 1961, when he and a small group of his friends had engaged in such actions as holding poetry readings in Mayakovsky square in Moscow and attempting to form a club under the aegis of the Komsomol, the official youth league, they began to be interrogated by the KGB. At that point, says Bukovsky, ' . . . I learned for the first time about a witness's legal rights. Aleksandr Sergeyevich Yesenin-Volpin, recently released from the Leningrad Special Mental Hospital, read us a whole lecture on the subject.'[67] Bukovsky adds that 'Alik [nickname for Aleksandr] Volpin was the first person we had ever come across to speak seriously of Soviet laws', and when he and his friends made fun of him for taking Soviet laws seriously, Volpin would reply, 'That's the whole problem – that no one pays any attention to them.' Volpin, 'brandishing his criminal code like a magic wand', had persuaded the guards at the trial of some young friends of Bukovsky to allow their friends to hear the sentences pronounced. This incident, according to Bukovsky, 'was the beginning of our civil rights movement and the movement for human rights in the USSR'.[68]

Some years ago, I was told by an American who had had long conversations with Volpin in Moscow that the latter had told him that he had arrived at the legalist mode of behaviour by a process of elimination, it being, under Soviet conditions, the only means by which dissidents had any hope of coping with the enormous difficulties confronting anyone who sought effectively to claim the rights formally granted by the Soviet constitution and Soviet laws.

One weakness of the legalist approach developed by Volpin, Valery Chalidze and others is that respect for law is so weak in the ranks of those – such as KGB officials – whose duty, supposedly, is to enforce the law, that the latter sometimes regard zealous and persistent defence by citizens of their legal rights as evidence of contumacy, or even of mental illness.

The appeal to world opinion

A second coping mechanism prevalent among dissenters has been the effort to publicize broadly information about the abuses of rights in the USSR and recommendations designed to promote the cause of peace and freedom not only in Russia but throughout the world. In the pursuit of this aim, Soviet dissenters have appealed to what Biddulph has termed 'four different external publics': foreign communist parties, Western intellectuals, international agencies and world opinion.[69] Of these, it is the appeal to world opinion which is assuming increasing significance of late. By now most of the leading dissidents have resorted to such appeals. One may mention, for example, 'democrats' such as Sakharov, 'legalists' like Aleksandr Yesenin-Volpin and Valery Chalidze, participants in the Jewish Emigration movement and in the Crimean Tatars' struggle to return to their ancestral homeland, leaders of the Christian Committee for the Defence of the Rights of Believers in the USSR. Even Roy Medvedev, the leading Soviet 'Marxist–Leninist' dissident who has been severely critical of many dissidents for the 'extremist' language of their statements and their practice of forming organizations,[70] seems to regard granting interviews to representatives of the 'bourgeois' press as admissible. He himself has frequently been interviewed by foreign correspondents and his 1980 book, *On Soviet Dissent*, consisted mostly of interviews with correspondents of the leading Italian newspaper, *Corriere della Sera*.

The first major instances of such appeals occurred after Khrushchev. In 1967, Pavel Litvinov and Andrei Amalrik 'decided to make a regular practice of approaching Western correspondents in Moscow'.[71] The aspects of the human rights struggle that most attracted Litvinov were its demand for openness and public information about political trials, and the public disclosure by participants therein of their identities – in a word, its non-conspiratorial nature. And since the authorities did not permit publication of protest statements in the official press, the concept of openness (*glasnost*) logically entailed their publication in the foreign press.[72]

In January 1968, Litvinov and Larisa Bogoroz, who were both

six months later to take part in the Red Square demonstration against the Soviet bloc invasion of Czechoslovakia, distributed to 'the Western progressive press' an appeal 'To World Public Opinion', which protested violations of Soviet law in the trial of Ginzburg and Galanskov. The appeal was broadcast on the same day in English and Russian by the BBC from London, and, reported Litvinov, 'found a wide response among Soviet citizens and also among people of progressive views in the West'.[73]

The practice of appealing to external publics, established in the late 1960s and early 1970s by people like Amalrik, Litvinov and Bukovsky, was maintained by many other dissenters. As is well known, coverage of the statements and activities of dissenters by foreign newspeople was broadcast back to the USSR by foreign radios. This, despite Soviet jamming of such radios as the American Radio Liberty, made a major contribution to dissemination of dissenters' views inside the USSR, and lifted their spirits. Indicative of the significance attributed by informed dissidents to Western support is Pavel Litvinov's statement that 'we have survived because the West exists and in it a Western press'.[74]

Probably the greatest contributions to the continuation of the effort initiated by Litvinov and Bogoroz to gain foreign support for Soviet human rights activists and thus generate pressure on the Soviet authorities to grant the activists' requests, or at least to refrain from prosecuting them, were made by Solzhenitsyn, Sakharov and the men and women who in May 1976 and subsequently created the Moscow-based Public Group to Promote the Fulfilment of the Helsinki Accords (*Obshchestvennaya Gruppa Sodeistviya po Vypolneniyu Khelsinkskikh Soglashenii*), and its numerous affiliated organizations, including religious and labour groups, and the four groups set up in the Ukraine, Lithuania, Georgia and Armenia.[75] It will be recalled that Academician Sakharov was a friend of many members of these groups, that his wife, Elena Bonner, was one of the founders of the Moscow group, and that some of the Moscow group's press conferences were held in the Sakharovs' apartment.

In the fall of 1973, Solzhenitsyn and Sakharov were engaged in a dramatic struggle with the Soviet leadership, which Solzhenitsyn, using a term taken from the language of military strategy, called the 'encounter battle'.[76] The spirit of Solzhenitsyn's participation in this struggle is suggested by his statement that

'The battle was raging in view of the whole planet, its sympathies were on our side: what if our best regiment was surrounded – that wasn't fatal! It was only for a time!'[77] Referring to his and Sakharov's press conferences in August and September 1973, Solzhenitsyn says, 'This was the first time in fifty-five years, I think, that people hounded by the Soviet press had dared to bark back.'[78] He quotes Yevgeny Barabanov, a fellow dissident and friend – who contributed to Solzhenitsyn's book, *From Under the Rubble* – who said 'sending a manuscript abroad was no crime, but an honorable act, because it saved the manuscript's life'.[79]

Solzhenitsyn's account of the 'encounter battle' is vivid. It reflects his joy in ideological combat, his sense that he was an instrument of destiny waging a righteous struggle. Also, his account is clearly that of a man who believed that the appeal to world opinion was a necessary tactic in a struggle for survival.

In contrast, Sakharov's statements on the same subject seemed to be those of a man driven by a sense of his duty to help victims of injustice and persecution in the USSR, and to warn the West of the dangers of a 'false detente', while urging serious negotiations between 'East' and 'West' to regulate the arms race and lessen the danger of outbreak of a nuclear war. As Alfred Friendly Jr points out, Sakharov and the majority of his fellow dissenters did not 'act in the real expectation of influencing policy and events. Instead their inner compulsion is a moral one. ... It makes them optimists without concrete hope.'[80] However, Sakharov on occasion indicated that he placed reliance if not for his own, at least for his family's safety, in the support of his scientific colleagues abroad and of 'international public opinion', which, he noted, had 'defended us' in 1973 – this last was a reference, no doubt, to such actions as the warning issued by Mr Philip Handler, President of the US National Academy of Sciences, during the press campaign against Sakharov in 1973, that American–Soviet scientific co-operation would be imperilled if measures such as detention of Sakharov were taken.[81]

The Helsinki groups and their affiliated organizations were more purposeful, explicit and bold than any other post-Stalin dissidents in appealing for foreign support for their activities and in attempting to convert it into pressure on the Soviet regime. This is not surprising in view of the inclusion in the Final Act of the Conference on Security and Co-operation in Europe (CSCE) of principles pledging respect for 'human rights and fundamental freedoms', including freedom of thought, conscience and religion, and for 'equal rights and self-determination of peoples'. To be sure, as Yaroslav Bilinsky and Tonu Parming note in an outstanding paper, the Soviet negotiators at Helsinki succeeded in getting incorporated into the text of the Final Act significant reservations and limitations to these principles – but they provided very useful justification for Soviet advocates of individual and of group rights.[82]

A glance at the documents issued by the Soviet Helsinki groups and their territorial and functional affiliates reveals their determination to communicate information about what they regarded as violations by the Soviet authorities of a wide range of rights. The announcement on 12 May 1976 by the eleven founders (the physicist Yury Orlov, Bonner, the computer specialist and Jewish activist leader Anatoly Shcharansky, as well as other veteran rights advocates such as Grigorenko and Ludmilla Alekseeva) proclaimed the intention to 'appeal to heads of government and to public opinion'.[83]

In July 1976 the group prepared a 'short digest' for Western media, asserting that the course of Soviet internal policy since the signing of the Final Act indicated that the USSR was not going to fulfil the 'international obligations' it had undertaken by signing it.[84]

The high point in the determination of the members and friends of the Helsinki groups to press their appeal to the West was the exchange of letters between Sakharov and President Jimmy Carter in January 1977.

In view of the tactic of public appeals and of the tendency of worker–activists, nationality rights proponents, and representatives of religious groups to join forces, it is not surprising that the Soviet leaders took severe action to nip in the bud possible growth of tendencies that obviously angered and frightened them. It is well known that most of the leaders of all of the groups that coordinated their efforts in the vigorous campaign to reach world opinion in the years 1976–8 are now either in Soviet prisons and camps, or in internal exile, or in enforced emigration. However some activity by the handful of Helsinki activists who remain a liberty or, like Sakharov and Bonner, are in exile in the USSR continues.[85]

The exiling of Sakharov to the provincial city of Gorky in January 1980, and imposition on him and his wife of a severe surveillance regime after he had criticized the Soviet invasion of Afghanistan, was carried out to show that despite his enormous international stature, the civil rights fighter and 'father of the Soviet hydrogen bomb' was not immune to administrative reprisals. This outcome should not, however, by construed as proof that the appeals to foreign opinion undertaken over the years by Sakharov and others were vain gestures. Considerable evidence can be cited indicating that, for example, Western protests in response to appeals made by Solzhenitsyn, Sakharov and others ameliorated the position of Barabanov, who seemed certain to be sentenced to seven years in prison, but merely lost his job instead; appeals also led to Grigorenko's transfer from a special to an ordinary psychiatric hospital and may have, at least partly, been responsible for the release of Plyushch and Bukovsky.[86]

What the exiling of Sakharov and, before it, the truly ferocious repression visited on the majority of the members of the Helsinki groups – and indeed, the majority of formerly active dissidents – indicates is that there are limits to the effectiveness of any kind of help and support given by foreign opinion, or foreign governments, to Soviet dissenters.[87]

What does seem to make some difference in the Soviet treatment of dissent is whether Soviet leaders think (as a few years ago) that there might be some rewards, such as favourable terms of trade and access to Western oil and gas, computers and other especially needed types of technology which could be jeopardized by the excessively repressive treatment of dissidents, especially those with international reputations.

V. CONCLUSION

In the post-Khrushchev period, the Soviet regime has contained dissent, but at a very great cost. By its harsh repression of dissenters, the Soviet regime has suffered moral defeat, in the eyes of substantial segments of Western public opinion, and probably of Soviet opinion also. The dissenters have projected a far more positive image than has the Soviet regime, whose agents, not the dissidents, have been seen to be engaging in lawless and illegal behaviour.

Why has the Soviet leadership pursued a policy so repressive as to blacken the image of the USSR in wide circles of foreign opinion, particularly liberal socialist, and even in many cases, communist opinion? The answer seems to lie in the political and ideological insecurity of the Soviet leaders. They are apparently afraid that if they do not hold the line against any and all challenges, as they see them, to such basic principles of 'Leninism' as the Communist Party's monopoly of policy formation and implementation, control over all organized public activity, and strict censorship of public communication, disintegration will set in. Such insecurity presumably reflects a consciousness that, while only the tiniest minority of Soviet citizens are prepared to risk the consequences of overt dissent, as long as penalties remain harsh enough, a far larger number are dissatisfied and might support protest activities if they are not nipped in the bud before they can get out of control. Indeed, the growing tendency in the 1970s toward co-operation between dissatisfied working people, religious groups and non-Russian minority groups on the one hand and the veteran civil rights activists on the other, may appear to the regime to be a timely warning.

In fact, however, realism requires taking into account the vast assets still at the disposal of the Soviet regime in its effort to suppress dissent. The most important is doubtless the vast machine of bureaucracy and police power that keeps alive the heritage of fear inculcated by Stalin over several decades. In addition, there is the self-interest of an élite that values its advantages all the more because of the very modest level at which the vast majority of the Soviet people live. Even among intellectuals, there is still apparently considerable fear of the potential for violence and class hatred of the common people, and a concomitant tendency to tolerate, even to value, tough, centrally administered 'law and order'. Also, there is the complicated Soviet nationality problem. For Russians and Russianized non-Russians, particularly of élite status, the democrats' concern over the political rights of non-Russians might appear a threat to the centralized, multi-national, Russian-dominated Soviet state with which many of them still identify and which they regard as the source and guarantee of their power and privileges.

But as this essay has argued, the regime does not have a totally free hand in the shaping of policy toward the dissenters. Failure on the part of the Soviet leadership to correct the defects and evils that dissidents consider it their duty to expose will feed the moral indignation that has underlain the public protest of the last fifteen-odd years. Protest could probably be smothered by a return to Stalin-style terror, but this seems unlikely to occur as long as the Soviet rulers feel constrained by the need to take account of public opinion in countries, particularly in Western Europe, from which they hope to acquire know-how and equipment needed to enhance Soviet economic and military power, not to mention Moscow's continuing effort to project as favourable an image as possible to groups it still counts on manipulating in its global struggle against the United States and Communist China.

Hence one is inclined to conclude that as far as we can peer into the future a stalemate pitting committed and determined but relatively powerless dissidents against the enormous power of the KGB and the Soviet propaganda machine will continue. That is, the Soviet regime will be able to contain the dissident movement, but not to eliminate it.

No one understands the David-and-Goliath position of the dissenters as well as they themselves. They understand that, as Turchin points out, unless they can greatly increase their numbers, in the foreseeable future Soviet dissenters are very unlikely to become more than an embarrassment to the Soviet Union in the conduct of its foreign relations or a potential threat to Soviet domestic stability.

On their own future, the dissidents are anything but optimistic. Anyone familiar with the writings of dissidents such as Sakharov, Orlov, Turchin, Bukovsky and others knows that they are not optimistic about an early flourishing, or even about survival, of dissent in the present period. However, these writings, and, more important, the behaviour of their authors convey an impressive determination to persevere in what to lesser men and women would have seemed a lost cause, and a calm faith that their struggle has not been in vain. As Valentin Turchin says, in *The Inertia of Fear*:

The dissidents' importance to societal life within the USSR consists in the fact that they are creating a new model of behavior which, merely by the fact of its existence, affects each member of society. Under the present conditions, being a dissident in the USSR means that one necessarily drops out of the system. But in the final analysis, the fate of the system depends on those who remain in it. Slight changes in the thinking and behavior of many people are what is most needed today.[88]

But even if the Soviet democrats were never to accomplish more than they have to date, their achievements would have been remarkable. And there is reason to think that their efforts will bear fruit in the future. The vitality of the movement they created is apparent in the continued appearance of such *samizdat* publications as *A Chronicle of Current Events*, continued, though reduced, activity of the Soviet Helsinki groups, and most important, the steady stream of *samizdat* material contained in the *Materialy samizdata* series. Even more hopeful, despite the near-decimation of dissenters by the fierce repression of recent years, there has been an increase of protest activity in some areas – for example, Lithuania, Georgia, and most recently Estonia. And, hearteningly, the dissident movement is now recruiting second-generation activists[89] – sons and daughters of those original thinkers who struck out so bravely in defence of their right to think for themselves.

NOTES AND REFERENCES

1. Robert A. Dahl, *Regimes and Oppositions* (New Haven, Conn., 1973) 1.
2. Ernest Clark [Thomas Remington], 'Revolutionary Ritual: A Comparative Analysis of Thought Reform and the Show Trial', *Studies in Comparative Communism*, 9 (Autumn 1976) 232. Professor Remington kindly authorized me to reveal his identity. On the equating of dissent in the Soviet Communist Party with opposition, and both with treason, see Leonard Schapiro 'Putting the Lid on Leninism' in Leonard Schapiro (ed.), *Political Opposition in One-Party States* (London, 1972) 33–57.
3. Clark, 'Revolutionary Ritual', 234.
4. Roy Medvedev, *On Soviet Dissent: Interview with Piero Ostellino* (New York, 1980) 127.
5. Ronald J. Hill, *Soviet Politics, Political Science and Reform* (New York, 1980).
6. See Stephen F. Cohen, 'The Friends and Foes of Change: Reformism and Conservatism in the Soviet Union', *Slavic Review*, 28 (June 1979) 202.
7. On the diversity of overt dissent, see appropriate parts of, for example, the following: Peter B. Reddaway, *Uncensored Russia* (New York, 1973); Ferdinand Feldbrugge, *Samizdat* (Leyden, 1975); Frederick C. Barghoorn, *Detente and the Democratic Movement in the USSR* (New York, 1976); *The Political, Social and Religious Thought of Russian 'Samizdat'* – *An Anthology* (Belmont, Mass., 1977).

8. The foregoing is based on unpublished material by Marta Zahaykevich entitled, 'The Development of Moral Resistance in Soviet Human Rights Activists', a topic on which Ms Zahaykevich is writing a dissertation. I am indebted to her for furnishing me a copy of this material and to Professor Peter Juviler of Barnard College for bringing her research to my attention.
9. On the mutiny, see *Arkhiv Samizdata* 2767, Radio Free Europe (July 1975). On the Novocherkassk events, see Aleksandr Solzhenitsyn, *Gulag Archipelago* (New York, 1976) 506–14.
10. Valentin Turchin, *Inertsiya strakha* (New York, 1977) 5.
11. Ibid., 8. He concludes the introduction to the book with a long quotation from Gandhi's *My Life*.
12. Gene Sharp, *The Politics of Nonviolent Action* (Boston, 1973) 453.
13. Amalrik made the remark I report above in a panel of a conference, at which I was present, at Stanford University that led to publication of the book *The Soviet Union: Looking to the 1980's* ed. Robert B. Wesson (Stanford, Calif., 1980).
14. In Bukovsky's Foreword to Sidney Bloch and Peter Reddaway, *Russia's Political Hospitals* (London, 1977).
15. Sharp, *Politics of Nonviolent Action*, 521.
16. Dina Spechler, 'Permitted Dissent in the Decade after Stalin: Criticism and Protest in *Novy Mir*, 1953–1964', in Paul Cocks *et al.* (eds.), *The Dynamics of Soviet Politics* (Cambridge, Mass., 1976) 28–50.
17. Aleksandr Tvardovsky, ('On the occasion of the Jubilee') *Novy Mir*, 1 (1965) 3–18.
18. Cohen, 'Friends and Foes of Change', 193.
19. Frederick C. Barghoorn, 'The Post-Khrushchev Campaign to Suppress Dissent', in Rudolf L. Tőkés (ed.), *Dissent in the USSR* (Baltimore, 1975) 53.
20. Ted Robert Gurr, *Why Men Rebel* (Princeton, N.J., 1970) 13, 47, 113.
21. He is careful, however, to point out that strikes and riots cannot be correlated with changes in real wages. J.M. Montias, 'Economic Conditions and Political Instability in Communist Countries', *Studies in Comparative Communism*, 13 (Winter 1980) 285. Montias focuses mainly on Eastern Europe, especially Poland, but one of the nine cases he examines is the strikes and demonstrations at Novocherkassk, in the Don region of Russia, in June 1962.
22. See Jay D. Sorenson, 'Soviet Workers: The Current Scene', *Problems of Communism*, 13 (January–February 1964) 25–32; Albert Boiter, 'When the Kettle Boils Over...', ibid., 33–43; and Aleksandr Solzhenitsyn's vivid, detailed account in *Gulag Archipelago*, 506–14.
23. Leonid Plyushch, *History's Carnival* (New York, 1979) 122–4, 171. See also Julian Birch, 'The Nature and Sources of Dissidence in Ukraine', in Peter J. Potichnyj (ed.), *Ukraine in the Seventies* (Oakville, Ont., 1975) 307–30 (on 'economically based dissent' 321). Birch cites *A Chronicle of Current Events*, No. 8, reporting that the hydroelectric-station workers sent a delegation with an appeal concerning poor housing to the CPSU Central Committee. It appears from Birch's data, and material in Reddaway *Uncensored Russia*, 288–91, that a number of the organizers of this protest were arrested. Birch also reports two other – apparently successful – strikes in Ukraine.

24. See 'dopolnenie' (supplement) to Document 7 of *Documents of the Helsinki Watch Group in the USSR* (in Russian), Vypusk vtoroi (New York, 1977) 19–20. Signed by group members Ludmilla Alekseeva, Aleksandr Ginzburg, Malva Landa and Yury Orlov. Of these five, only Alekseeva escaped arrest, and she was forced to leave the USSR early in 1977.

25. *A Chronicle of Current Events*, Amnesty International Publications, No. 49 (London, 1978) 51.

26. Anthony Austin, 'Workers in Soviet Said to Strike at Two Large Automobile Factories', *The New York Times*, 14 June 1980. Austin's dispatch also mentioned a 'rumour' that 200,000 workers had struck at a car and truck plant in Gorky. Austin also noted that one report on the Togliatti affair described it as an action in solidarity with a strike of drivers of buses linking the plant and the town of Togliatti. *Posev*, No. 1(1980) published a report on a bus drivers' strike in Togliatti, which, however, referred to events that reportedly occurred in August 1979.

27. See, for example, Paul Langner, 'Soviet strikes irk leaders – unionist', *Boston Globe*, 16 March 1981, based on telephone interview with veteran human rights activist, and organizer of an unofficial trade union, Vladimir Borisov. Borisov, expelled from the USSR in June 1980, told Langner that coal miners in the Vorkuta area had been on strike a few days before the interview. He also referred to four other strikes – including the one at Togliatti. It is interesting that Borisov told Langner that the Prague spring in 1968 was 'the highest point of the Union movement in Russia'. He also was reported as saying that the current Soviet tactic for dealing with strikes was to 'give in to the demands of the workers, and later, over a long time' to arrest the leaders, and that a new 'motorized militia' was being trained to deal with strikes. He also reported 'clandestine contacts between Poland's Solidarity and the Soviet free trade unionists'. This last statement takes on added interest in light of a UPI item in the *The New York Times* for 23 October 1980 entitled 'Estonian Dissidents Report Two-Day Factory Strike', according to which a strike in a tractor factory in Tartu was 'inspired' by labour unrest in Poland. According to a Reuters dispatch, reprinted in *Novoe Russkoe Slovo* for 25 July 1980, Borisov told of a strike in Minsk in April 1980, due to a food shortage, and said that Soviet workers were becoming less passive than they formerly had been. An unsigned dispatch in *Novoe Russkoe Slovo* for 18 November 1981, dateline Stockholm 17 November, reported that according to the well-known exiled dissident leader Sergei Soldatov his Estonian Democratic organization was urging its followers in the USSR to begin on 1 December a series of half-hour strikes 'on the Polish model'. The dispatch also reported that Soldatov's organization had no less than 2000 activists linked with workers in Moscow, Leningrad, Vilnius and Riga.

28. Text, with three lists of signers, including one list of twenty-three stating they had, 'in protest against a rightless situation', informed the Presidium of the USSR Supreme Soviet of their intention to renounce Soviet citizenship, in Valery Chalidze (comp), *SSSR-Rabochee dvizhenie?* (New York, 1978) 34–54. On p. 9 of his introduction to this valuable collection of materials, Chalidze asserted that while there was not yet a labour movement in the USSR, 'all the conditions for the beginning' of such a movement existed:

worker dissatisfaction with their poor economic–social situation, consciousness of the gulf between their subordinate position in society and the claims of Soviet propaganda, intensified by listening to foreign radio broadcasts, and so on. See also Chalidze, 'A Workers' Movement in Russia?', *Wall Street Journal*, 16 May 1978.

29. Announcement and statutes, with commentary by Chalidze on latter, in *SSSR-Rabochee dvizhenie?*, 55–80.

30. Julia Wishnevsky, 'Members of Unofficial Trade Union Harassed', Radio Liberty Research RL 132/80 (2 April 1980) 1. See also Elizabeth Scheetz, 'Disaffected Workers Publicly Defend their Rights', RL 47/78 (28 February 1978), and Julia Wishnevsky, 'Persecution of Independent Soviet Trade Unionists', RL 154/79 (18 May 1979).

31. See *SMOT, informatsionnye byulleteni* (Frankfurt-Main, 1979), and also the above-cited report by Julia Wishnevsky. According to the *Posev* publication, the International Confederation of Free Trade Unions, in 1979, criticized the USSR for repression of SMOT's members.

32. See Alekseeva, 'Lyudi stali menshe boyatsya, chem prezhde', interview with West German television, in *Posev*. 3, 3 March 1977 (almost immediately after Alekseeva's forced emigration), in which she pointed out that the Helsinki group members were aware that 'ordinary people' knew about their activities. In *Novoe Russkoe Slovo*, beginning in the 15 March 1977 issue, Alekseeva narrated the history of the group under the title 'Moskovskaya Gruppa Sodeistviya'. See her statement that 'we were especially pleased that among those who appealed to the group were not only intellectuals but workers and peasants', in ibid., 27 March 1977. See also Alekseeva's article in ibid., 7 April 1981, on the extremely severe sentence passed on Helsinki group member Tatyana Osipova, in which Alekseeva also describes the flood of letters and requests from workers with which Osipova and her husband, Ivan Kovalev, also a member of the group, had to deal. It is worth noting that Alekseeva here also cited the extremely harsh treatment of Osipova as evidence of a new trend toward very severe sentences for dissenters. Alekseeva has also provided evidence on worker–Helsinki group relations in other statements.

33. Andrei D. Sakharov, *My Country and the World* (New York, 1975) 11–41.

34. Andrei D. Sakharov, *Alarm and Hope*, (eds) Alfred Friendly Jr and Efrem Yankelevich (New York, 1978) 130.

35. Ibid., 128. See *Materialy Samizdata*, 1980 and 1981 issues, for numerous appeals by Sakharov and, more frequently, by his wife Elena Bonner on behalf of a wide variety of victims of repression.

36. AS2755, 1976; AS3215, 1978.

37. Considerable additional material on the subjects discussed above is contained in works cited earlier, especially Chalidze *SSSR-Rabochee dvizhenie?*, and in Albert Boiter (ed.), *Sobranie Dokumentov Samizdata*, vol. 30, *Khelsinkski Samizdat iz SSSR* (Munich, 1978) 475–506, 710–16, 719–24.

38. An excellent treatment of religious dissent is in Barbara Wolfe Jancar, 'Religious Dissent in the Soviet Union', in Tőkés (ed.), *Dissent in the USSR*, 191–230. On nationality dissent, including resistance to Russification, Jewish and German emigration demands, the Lithuanian struggle to

preserve their Catholic heritage, and so on, see Helene Carrere d'Encausse, *Decline of an Empire: The Soviet Socialist Republics in Revolt* (New York, 1979, 1980), and Teresa Rakowska-Harmstone, 'The Nationalities Question', in Wesson (Ed), *The Soviet Union: Looking to the 1980's,* 129–54. For recent data on the especially heavy incidence of repression of nationalist protest and exceptionally severe sentences, see data in 'Three Years of Repression in the USSR', *Freedom Appeals,* No. 9 (New York, March–April 1981) 29–31, and in Yaroslav Bilinsky and Tonu Parming, 'Helsinki Watch Committees in the Soviet Republics: Implications for Soviet Nationality Policy', *Nationalities Papers,* 9 (Spring 1981) 1–25. See also *Sobranie Dokumentov Samizdata,* vol. 30; Sakharov, *Alarm and Hope;* Alekseeva's earlier cited West German television interview; and parts of my chapter in Wesson (ed.), *The Soviet Union: Looking to the 1980's.*

39. Barbara Wolfe Jancar, 'Modernity and the Character of Dissent', in Charles Gati (ed.), *The Politics of Modernization in Eastern Europe: Testing the Soviet Model* (New York, 1974) 340.
40. Ibid., 341.
41. Ibid., 345.
42. Ibid., 344.
43. Ibid., 350.
44. Ibid., 350, 354.
45. See Andrei D. Sakharov, *Sakharov Speaks,* ed. Harrison E. Salisbury (New York, 1974) 39. Text of the letter is on 115–34.
46. Sakharov, *Alarm and Hope,* 5. Text of lecture on 3–18.
47. Feldbrugge, *Samizdat,* 68, 107, 128. Quotation on 128.
48. See Sakharov's 1977 essay, 'Alarm and Hope', in *Alarm and Hope,* 99-111; Yury Orlov, 'Vozmozhen li sotsializm netotalitarnogo tipa', in Pavel Litvinov, M. Meerson-Aksenov and Boris Shragin, *Samosoznanie* (Insights) (New York, 1976) 279–304; Turchin, *Inertsiya strakha.*
49. Orlov, 'Vozmozhen li sotsializm netotalitarnogo tipa', 285.
50. On 'regulative performance', see Gabriel A. Almond and G. Bingham Powell Jr, *Comparative Politics: A Developmental Approach* (Boston, 1966) 307–14, quotation on 307. On the Soviet system for suppression of dissent see, for example, Frederick C. Barghoorn, 'The Post-Khrushchev Campaign to Suppress Dissent', 35–94, and Peter Reddaway, 'Policy Towards Dissent Since Khrushchev' in T.H. Rigby, Archie Brown and Peter Reddaway (eds), *Authority, Power and Policy in the USSR* (New York, 1980) 158–92. Very important is Bloch and Reddaway, *Russia's Political Hospitals* (London, 1977).
51. Reddaway, 'Policy Towards Dissent Since Khrushchev', 168, asserts that 'about three-quarters' of the signers yielded to pressure, 'their dissent henceforth becoming either passive or covert'.
52. See 'Three Years of Repression in the USSR –A Statistical Survey', in *Freedom Appeals* (March–April 1981) 29–31, and issues of *Materialy Samizdata* for 1980 and 1981.
53. See 'Sakharovsky sbornik' unsigned, in *Russkaya Mysl* (Paris) 21 May 1981.
54. For a succinct account of the major events, see Karel van het Reve's introduction to Pavel Litvinov, *The Demonstration in Pushkin Square* (Boston, 1969) 1–10.
55. Ibid., 63.

56. Petr Grigorenko, *Sbornik statei* (New York, 1977) 63.
57. Ibid., 74.
58. Bernard W. Hudson, 'Dissent in a Strait-Jacket' *The Times Literary Supplement*, 18 April 1975.
59. Plyushch, *History's Carnival*, 295–6. Plyushch's statement about alienation is on 262.
60. See the fifth unnumbered page of volume I, *Gulag Archipelago*, for the dedication; and 19, 134–7, on the reason for Solzhenitsyn's arrest.
61. Plyushch, *History's Carnival*, 124. See also Lidiya Chukovskaya, 'Breakthrough', hailing the publication of the first volume of *Gulag* in 1973 as an event the immensity of the consequences of which could only be compared with the death of Stalin, in *Aleksandr Solzhenitsyn*, 456–7.
62. See, for example, Grigory Svirsky, *Na lobnom meste* (At the Execution Square) (London, 1979).
63. N. and S. Shuleiko (eds), *Otkrytoe slovo* (The Open Word) (New York, 1976) 7.
64. As Chukovskaya said at this session, she had been condemned to nonexistence as a writer, but she took comfort in the fact that she shared the fate of Mikhail Zoshchenko, Anna Akhmatova, Boris Pasternak, Aleksandr Solzhenitsyn, Aleksandr Galich and Vladimir Maksimov. See her 'Poslednee slovo' in *Otkrytoe slovo* (New York, 1976) 99.
65. For a discussion of post-Helsinki Soviet behaviour in the area of freedom of expression and literary cultural communication, see Robert Bernstein 'A Publisher Looks at Helsinki', *Index on Censorship*, 6 (November–December 1977) 39–43.
66. This point was made in 1975 in Feldbrugge, *Samizdat*, 7, and has undoubtedly been still more valid since, as dissidents, under increasing pressure by the KGB, have been more and more concerned with police searches, arrests, trials, and so on.
67. Vladimir Bukovsky, *To Build a Castle – My Life as a Dissenter* (New York, 1977) 160.
68. Ibid., 162–3.
69. Biddulph in Tökés (ed.), *Dissent in the USSR*, 110–12.
70. He believes that these practices unnecessarily irritate the authorities and are self-defeating. See Roy Medvedev, *On Socialist Democracy* (New York, 1975) 70–1, 80–2; Barghoorn, *Detente and the Democratic Movement*, 74; Roy Medvedev, *On Soviet Dissent* (New York, 1980) ch. 10.
71. Pavel Litvinov, 'The Human Rights Movement in the USSR', *Index on Censorship* (Spring 1975) 14.
72. See Litvinov, 'O dvizhenii za prava cheloveka', in *Samosoznanie*, 82.
73. Pavel Litvinov (comp) and Peter Reddaway (ed.), *The Trial of the Four* (New York, 1972) 225–7.
74. See 'Press Statement of Pavel Litvinov on 22 March 1974', *Radio Liberty Dispatch*, 17 April 1974, for full text of the statement in which the above quotation appears.
75. The fullest documentation on the Helsinki – often called Helsinki Watch, or Monitor – groups is in the 750-page third volume of the *Archiv Samizdata* (Munich, 1978), and, most recently, in 'Implementation of the Final Act of the Conference on Security and Cooperation in Europe: Findings and Recommendations Five Years After Helsinki', by the

Commission on Security and Cooperation in Europe, 96th Congress, 2nd
Session (Washington, D.C., 1980). See also portions of Reddaway's chapter
in Rigby *et al.* (eds), *Authority, Power and Policy in the USSR*, and of
Barghoorn's chapter in Wesson (ed), *The Soviet Union: Looking to the
1980's*.

76. See his exciting account in *The Oak and the Calf*, 346–60.
77. Ibid., 349.
78. Ibid., 351.
79. Ibid., 356.
80. *Alarm and Hope*, Introduction, xv.
81. Ibid., 98; Barghoorn, *Detente and the Democratic Movement*, 178–9.
82. Bilinsky and Parming, 'Helsinki Watch Committees in the Soviet
Republics'.
83. The wide range of interests of the groups, including defence of the rights of
non-Russian minorities, of Jews to emigrate, of workers to emigrate on social
and political grounds, of all citizens to be freed of the threat of political
abuse of psychiatry, and so on, is revealed even by looking at the table of
contents of *Archiv Samizdata*, volume 30, cited earlier. AS2542. Text on
3–5 in AS vol. cited earlier.
84. AS2651.
85. See, for example, 'Moscow Helsinki Watch Group: Document 138', in *The
Wall Street Journal*, 14 October 1980.
86. Solzhenitsyn, *The Oak and the Calf*, 356; Alfred Friendly Jr, Introduction
to *Alarm and Hope*, xvi.
87. Roy Medvedev pointed out to the Italian correspondent Zucconi, in
February 1980, that detente 'was pretty much ruined with the invasion' of
Afghanistan. Roy Medvedev, *On Soviet Dissent*, 143. Of course, I do not
mean to suggest that Western men and women who care about human
rights and are concerned about the future of a country the development of
which is so important to world peace and welfare should ever stop doing
what can be done to promote the cause that Sakharov and others have so
devotedly served. Soviet dissidents, in emigration and at home, keep
reminding us that publicity in the West about the plight of threatened
protesters can provide them with a measure of safety. For a recent
reminder, see 'Unliberated Women of Russia', *New Haven Advocate*, 19
November 1980, reporting statements by the recently-exiled Soviet feminist
leader, Tatyana Mamonova.
88. Valentin Turchin, *The Inertia of Fear and the Scientific Worldview*, trans.
from Russian by Guy Daniels (New York 1981) 289.
89. For example, Ivan Kovalev, son of the prominent civil rights veteran, the
biologist Sergei Kovalev.

Major Publications of
H. Gordon Skilling

1941 'Austrian Origins of National Socialism', *University of Toronto Quarterly*, 10, no. 4 (July 1941) 482–92.

1945 *Canadian Representation Abroad: From Agency to Embassy*, under the sponsorship of the Canadian Institute of International Affairs (Toronto, 1945) 359pp.
'Canada: Good Neighbour to the North', ch. 20, in T.C.T. McCormick (ed.), *Problems of the Post-War World* (New York, 1945).

1947 'The Rise of a Canadian Diplomatic Service', *Journal of Politics*, 9, no. 2 (May 1947) reprinted in W.H. Bennett (ed.), *Postwar Governments of the British Commonwealth* (Gainesville, Florida, 1947).

1949 'Revolutions in Prague', *International Journal*, 4, no. 2 (Spring 1949) 119–36.
'The Partition of the University of Prague', *Slavonic and East European Review*, 27, no. 69 (May 1949) 430–49.

1951 'Czechoslovakia – The Soviet Impact', *International Journal*, 6, no. 2 (Spring 1951) 109–17.
'People's Democracy, the Proletarian Dictatorship and the Czechoslovak Path to Socialism', *American Slavic and East European Review*, 10, no. 2 (April 1951) 100–16.
'"People's Democracy" in Soviet Theory', Part I, *Soviet Studies*, 3, no. 1 (July 1951) 16–33.
'"People's Democracy" in Soviet Theory', Part II, *Soviet Studies*, 3, no. 2 (October 1951) 131–49.

1952 'The Czechoslovak Constitutional System: The Soviet Impact', *Political Science Quarterly*, 67, no. 2 (June 1952) 198–224.

1955 'The Soviet Impact on the Czechoslovak Legal Revolution', *Soviet Studies*, 6, no. 4 (April 1955) 361–81.
'Czechoslovakia: Government in Communist Hands', *Journal of Politics*, 17, no. 3 (August 1955) 424–47.
'The Formation of a Communist Party in Czechoslovakia', *American Slavic and East European Review*, 14, no. 3 (October 1955) 346–58.

1959 'The Prague Overturn in 1948', *Canadian Slavonic Papers*, 4 (1959) 88–114.

1960 'The Czechoslovak Struggle for National Liberation in World War II', *Slavonic and East European Review*, 39, no. 92 (December 1960) 174–97.
'The Comintern and Czechoslovak Communism: 1921–1929', *American*

Slavic and East European Review, 19, no. 2 (April 1960) 234–47.

'Soviet and Communist Politics: A Comparative Approach', *Journal of Politics*, 22, no. 2 (May 1960) 300–13.

'The Break-up of the Czechoslovak Coalition, 1947–48', *Canadian Journal of Economics and Political Science*, 26, no. 3 (August 1960) 396–412.

1961 'Revolution and Continuity in Czechoslovakia, 1945–1946', *Journal of Central European Affairs*, 20, no. 4 (January 1961) 357–77.

'People's Democracy and the Socialist Revolution, A Case Study in Communist Scholarship', Part I, *Soviet Studies*, 12, no. 3 (January 1961) 241–62.

'People's Democracy and the Socialist Revolution, A Case Study in Communist Scholarship', Part II, *Soviet Studies*, 12, no. 4 (April 1961) 421–35.

'Scholarship and the Soviet Riddle', *International Journal*, 16, no. 3 (Summer 1961) 260–5.

'Gottwald and the Bolshevization of the Communist Party of Czechoslovakia, 1929–1939', *Slavic Review*, 20, no. 4 (December 1961) 641–55.

'Permanent or Uninterrupted Revolution; Lenin, Trotsky and their Successors on the Transition to Socialism', *Canadian Slavonic Papers*, 5 (1961) 3–30.

1962 'The Czechoslovak Constitution of 1960 and the Transition to Communism', *Journal of Politics*, 24, no. 1 (1962) 142–66.

1963 'In Search of Political Science in the USSR', *Canadian Journal of Economics and Political Science*, 29, no. 4 (November 1963) 519–29.

1964 'National Communism in Eastern Europe since the 22nd Congress', *Canadian Journal of Economics and Political Science*, 30, no. 3 (August 1964) 313–27.

'Communism in Eastern Europe: Personal Impressions, 1961–1962', *Canadian Slavonic Papers*, 6 (1964) 18–37.

Communism National and International: Eastern Europe After Stalin, published in association with the Canadian Institute of International Affairs (Toronto, 1964) ix, 168pp.

'Canadian Attitudes to Change and Conflict in the Soviet Bloc', in Edward McWhinney (ed.), *Law, Foreign Policy, and the East-West Detente* (Toronto, 1964) 83–100.

1965 'Soviet and American Politics: The Dialectic of Opposites', *Canadian Journal of Economics and Political Science*, 31, no. 2 (May 1965) 273–80.

'Czechoslovakia', in Adam Bromke (ed.), *Communist States at the Crossroads, Between Moscow and Peking* (New York, Washington and London, 1965) 87–105.

1966 'Communism and Czechoslovak Tradition', *Journal of International Affairs*, 20, no. 1 (1966) 118–37.

'Interest Groups and Communist Politics', *World Politics*, 18, no. 3 (April 1966) 435–51.

'Canada and Eastern Europe', *Canadian Slavonic Papers*, 8 (1966) 3–15, 46–52.

The Governments of Communist East Europe (New York, 1966) 256pp.

1967 'Eastern Europe and the West', in Adam Bromke and Philip E. Uren (eds), *The Communist States in the West* (New York, 1967) 35–53.

1968 'Background to the Study of Opposition in Communist East Europe', *Government and Opposition*, 3, no. 3 (Summer 1968) 294–324.

'Crisis and Change in Czechoslovakia', *International Journal*, 23, no. 2 (Summer 1968) 456–65.

'Czechoslovakia's Interrupted Revolution', *Canadian Slavonic Papers*, 10, no. 4 (1968) 409–29.

'The Party, Opposition, and Interest Groups in Communist Politics: Fifty Years of Continuity and Change', in Kurt London (ed.), *The Soviet Union, A Half-Century of Communism* (Baltimore, Md., 1968) 119–49.

1969 'The Dialectic of Czechoslovak History', *The Canadian Forum*, 49, no. 585 (October 1969) 155–7.

'Thaw and Freeze-up: Prague 1968', *International Journal*, 25, no. 1 (Winter 1969–70) 192–201.

1970 'The Fall of Novotný in Czechoslovakia', *Canadian Slavonic Papers*, 12, no. 3 (Fall 1970) 225–42.

'Group Conflict and Political Change', in Chalmers Johnson (ed.), *Change in Communist Systems* (Stanford, Calif., 1970) 215–34.

The Czech Renascence of the Nineteenth Century, edited with Peter Brock (Toronto, 1970) 345pp including 'The Politics of the Czech Eighties', 254–281.

'Leadership and Group Conflict in Czechoslovakia', in R. Barry Farrell (ed.), *Political Leadership in Eastern Europe and the Soviet Union* (Chicago, 1970) 276–93.

1971 *Interest Groups in Soviet Politics*, edited with Franklyn Griffiths (Princeton, 1971), 433pp including 'Groups in Soviet Politics: Some Hypotheses', 19–45; 'Group Conflict in Soviet Politics', 379–416.

1973 'Reform Aborted: Czechoslovakia in Retrospect', *International Journal*, 28, no. 3 (Summer 1973) 431–45.

'Opposition in Communist East Europe', in Robert A. Dahl (ed), *Regimes and Oppositions* (New Haven, Conn., 1973) 121–41.

'Czechoslovakia's Interrupted Revolution', in Robert A. Dahl (ed), *Regimes and Oppositions* (New Haven, Conn., 1973) 89–119.

1974 'The Fall of Novotny in Czechoslovakia', in Lenard J. Cohen and Jane P. Shapiro (eds), *Communist Systems in Comparative Perspective* (New York, 1974) 129–44.

'Pressure Groups' in der Sowjetunion (trans. E. Werfel), edited with Franklyn Griffiths (Vienna, 1974) 424pp.

1976 'Czechoslovakia and Helsinki', *Canadian Slavonic Papers*, 18, no. 3 (September 1976) 245–65.

Czechoslovakia's Interrupted Revolution (Princeton, N.J., 1976) 924pp.

1977 '"The Spring that Never Ends"', *International Journal*, 32 (Autumn 1977) 865–79.

'Stalinism and Czechoslovak Political Culture', in Robert C. Tucker (ed.), *Stalinism, Essays in Historical Interpretation* (New York, 1977) 257–82.

1978 'Czechoslovakia', in A. Bromke and D. Nowak (eds), *The Communist States in the Era of Detente 1971–1977* (Oakville, Ontario, 1978) 306pp.

'Socialism and Human Rights: Charter 77 and the Prague Spring', in Hannelore Horn, Alexander Schwarn and Thomas Weingartner (eds), *Sozialismus in Theorie und Praxis*, festschrift fur Richard Lowenthal (Berlin and New York, 1978) 195–215 also in *Canadian Slavonic Papers*, 20, no. 2 (June 1978) 157–75.

'Sixty-Eight in Historical Perspective', *International Journal*, 33, no. 4 (Autumn 1978) 678–701.

1979 '"From Soviet Studies to Comparative Politics: The Unfinished Revolution": A Comment', in *Soviet Studies*, 31, no. 3 (July 1979) 441–2.

1980 'Charter 77 and the Musical Underground', *Canadian Slavonic Papers*, 22 (March 1980) 1–14.

'Pluralism in Communist Societies: Straw Men and Red Herrings', *Studies in Comparative Communism*, 13, no. 1 (Spring 1980) 82–90.

'Czechoslovakia on Trial', *Queen's Quarterly* (Autumn 1980) 387–96.

1981 *Parallel Politics, Essays on Politics from Czech and Slovak Samizdat*, edited with V. Prečan, special issue, *International Journal of Politics*, 11, no. 1 (Spring 1981).

'CSCE in Madrid', *Problems of Communism* (July–August 1981) 1–16.

Charter 77 and Human Rights in Czechoslovakia (London, 1981) xv, 363pp.

1982 'Samizdat: A Return to the pre-Gutenberg Era?', *Transactions of Royal Society of Canada* (to be published).

Index

173